Uncovering
STUDENT THINKING
in
MATHEMATICS
Grades 6–12

To my precious grandson, Adam, my sweet pea and "most favoritest person,"
and to my grandchildren who have not yet joined us here on earth. May your questions
and answers guide your paths to great joy and contentment.

—Carolyn

To Corey: Thank you for listening and supporting and especially for making me smile.
To Grandad: Your commitment to the kids is very much appreciated!

—Cheryl

Uncovering
STUDENT THINKING
in
MATHEMATICS
Grades 6–12

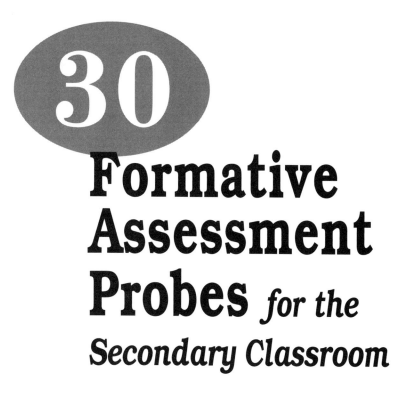

30

Formative Assessment Probes *for the* Secondary Classroom

CHERYL M. ROSE • CAROLYN B. ARLINE
Foreword by Johnny W. Lott

CORWIN PRESS
A SAGE Company

For information:

Corwin Press
A SAGE Company
2455 Teller Road
Thousand Oaks, California 91320
www.corwinpress.com

SAGE Ltd.
1 Oliver's Yard
55 City Road
London EC1Y 1SP
United Kingdom

SAGE India Pvt. Ltd.
B 1/I 1 Mohan Cooperative
     Industrial Area
Mathura Road, New Delhi 110 044
India

SAGE Asia-Pacific Pte. Ltd.
33 Pekin Street #02-01
Far East Square
Singapore 048763

Printed in the United States of America

Library of Congress Cataloging-in-Publication Data

Rose, Cheryl M.
Uncovering student thinking in mathematics, grades 6–12: 30 formative assessment probes for the secondary classroom /Cheryl M. Rose, Carolyn B. Arline.
        p. cm.
Includes bibliographical references and index.
ISBN 978-1-4129-6376-3 (cloth)
ISBN 978-1-4129-6377-0 (pbk.)
    1. Mathematical ability—Testing. 2. Mathematics—Study and teaching (Secondary)—Evaluation. 3. Mathematics—Study and teaching (Middle school)—Evaluation.
I. Arline, Carolyn. II. Title.

QA11.2.R6712 2009
510.71′2—dc22   2008017843

This book is printed on acid-free paper.

08   09   10   11   12   10   9   8   7   6   5   4   3   2   1

Acquisitions Editor:	Cathy Hernandez
Editorial Assistant:	Ena Rosen
Production Editor:	Libby Larson
Copy Editor:	Teresa Herlinger
Typesetter:	C&M Digitals (P) Ltd.
Proofreader:	Joyce Li
Indexer:	Sylvia Coates
Cover Designer:	Monique Hahn

Contents

Foreword

*U*ncovering Student Thinking in Mathematics, Grades 6–12: 30 Formative Assessment Probes by Cheryl Rose and Carolyn Arline is a valuable resource for teachers interested in determining how their students think and answer questions in their mathematics classes. The authors have researched many traditional questions and have taken the time and care to write additional items that can be used for both teachers' own personal formative assessment for how they have taught different topics in their classes and how individual students have understood those topics as well.

The book is organized so that readers know how the probes were built, the reason for their use with students, and what implications might be provided for both the classroom and the student as a result of their use. Much care has been taken by the authors to make this a reader-friendly set of materials.

Through the use of QUEST as defined below, the authors provide a complete implementation process with needed materials that teachers can use.

Questioning student understanding of a particular concept

Uncovering understanding and misunderstandings using a probe

Examining student work

Seeking links to cognitive research to drive next steps in instruction

Teaching implications based on findings and determining impact on learning by asking an additional question.

The probes can be used to differentiate instruction, assess a student's entry level to a topic, analyze trends in student thinking, and assess the effectiveness of instructional activities. Use of the probes as intended will take a teacher's time, but that time will be well spent for student learning.

As noted in one section, the use of the probes can help a teacher develop a "sense of a class" when a particular topic is being taught and learned. A teacher asking questions about the primary methods students use, those methods that produce correct responses, the generalizability of the methods, the most efficient of the methods, any outlier methods that could still be fruitful, and using the answers to change instructional strategies can only help the class and concept under consideration.

With a continued use of probes as those presented, teachers can truly assess whether students entering a class or approaching a concept have the needed prior knowledge necessary for learning the concept. Additionally the use of the probes early in the teaching cycle can show a teacher whether students already have an understanding of the concept they are about to study and if they do have, the alert teacher should be prepared to use very little class time re-teaching what is already prior knowledge for the students.

Of particular import for the teacher is the discussion of traditional questioning in the material. Often teachers allow students to answer questions and use those answers to decide how to move with a class or a concept. Frequently however, the decision may be based only on what is heard from a few students. The use of probes and the "think time" that is suggested with varied responses from students may help provide better information for teacher decision making. This formative use of questioning and probes aligns well with the high level of assessment indicators in the National Council of Supervisors of Mathematics (2008) *The Prime Leadership Framework: Principles and Indicators for Mathematics Education Leaders:* develop and implement "formative assessments that will optimize opportunities for every student to learn" and use "formative assessment processes to inform teacher practice and student learning" (p. 66).

Overall, Rose and Arline have provided a very useful set of materials for teachers in this book. If used as suggested, it should help make for a better student learning experience.

Johnny W. Lott
Professor of Education
Professor of Mathematics
Director, Center for Excellence in Teaching and Learning
University of Mississippi

Preface

OVERVIEW

With mandates from No Child Left Behind and other state-driven assessment initiatives, substantial amounts of educator time and energy are being spent on developing, implementing, scoring, and analyzing summative assessments of students' mathematical knowledge. Although the importance of summative assessment is recognized, findings point to formative assessment as an important strategy in improving student achievement in mathematics.

Formative assessment informs instruction through various methods and strategies, the purposes of which are to determine students' prior knowledge of a learning target and to use the information to drive instruction, moving each student toward understanding of the targeted concepts and procedures. Questioning, observation, and student self-assessment are examples of instructional strategies that educators can incorporate to gain insight into student understanding. These instructional strategies become formative assessment if the results are used to plan and implement learning activities designed specifically to address the specific needs of the students.

This book focuses on using diagnostic questions, called Mathematics Assessment Probes, to elicit prior understandings and commonly held misconceptions. This elicitation allows the educator to make sound instructional choices based on the specific needs of a particular group of students.

> Diagnostic assessment is as important to teaching as a physical exam is to prescribing an appropriate medical regimen. At the outset of any unit of study, certain students are likely to have already mastered some of the skills that the teacher is about to introduce, and others may already understand key concepts. Some students are likely to be deficient in prerequisite skills or harbor misconceptions. Armed with this diagnostic information, a teacher gains greater insight into what to teach. (McTighe & O'Connor, 2005)

The Mathematics Assessment Probes provided in this resource are tools for middle and high school teachers to gather these important insights.

AUDIENCE

The first collection of Mathematics Assessment Probes and the accompanying Teachers' Notes was designed for the busy K–12 classroom teacher who understands there is a growing body of research on students' learning difficulties and that thoughtful use of this research in developing and selecting diagnostic assessments promises to enhance the efficiency and effectiveness of mathematics instruction. Since the publication of the collection, *Uncovering Student Thinking in Mathematics: 25 Formative Assessment Probes* (Rose, Minton, & Arline, 2006), we have received continuous requests for additional probes. Both teachers and education leaders have communicated the need for a collection of research-based probes that focuses on a narrower grade span. Due to these requests, we set to work writing, piloting, and field testing a more extensive set of probes for middle and high school teachers.

BACKGROUND

The probes are designed to uncover student understandings and misunderstandings based on research findings, and have been piloted and field tested with teachers and students.

Because the probes are based on cognitive research, examples of such probes exist in multiple resources but not as a collection and not for the specific purpose of action research in the classroom. In addition, the questions are spread throughout various research materials and are not ready for classroom use. The probes in this book were developed using the process described in *Mathematics Curriculum Topic Study: Bridging the Gap Between Standards and Practice* (Keeley & Rose, 2007) and were originally piloted with the Maine teachers participating in the State Mathematics and Science Partnership Project: Mathematics: Access and Teaching in High School (MATHS). The use of the probes was expanded to include past participants in the other mathematics projects, including the National Science Foundation (NSF)-funded Northern New England Co-Mentoring Network, Maine Governor's Academy for Mathematics and Science Education Leadership, a State Mathematics and Science Partnership Project: Building Administrators' and Leaders' Abilities and the Numeracy Capacity of Educators (BALANCE), and various other mathematics professional development programs offered through the Maine Mathematics and Science Alliance. In addition, the probes were field tested nationally through a network of leaders involved with the Curriculum Topic Study Project.

ORGANIZATION

This book is organized to provide readers with the purpose, structure, and development of the Mathematics Assessment Probes, as well as to support the use of applicable research and instructional strategies in mathematics classrooms.

Chapter 1 provides in-depth information about the process and design of the Mathematics Assessment Probes along with the development of an action research structure we refer to as a QUEST cycle. Chapter 2 highlights instructional implications and images from practice to illuminate how easily and in how many varied ways the probes can be used in mathematics classrooms. Chapters 3–5 are the collections of probes categorized by content strands, within grade spans, with accompanying Teachers' Notes that provide the specific research and instructional strategies designed to directly address students' challenges with mathematics.

Acknowledgments

We would like to thank Page Keeley, our science colleague, who designed the process for developing diagnostic assessment probes and who tirelessly promotes the use of formative assessments, helping to disseminate our work in her travels.

A special thank you to Suzanne Archer, Preston Dean, Natalia Garroni, Elizabeth Hall, Renee Henry, Gloria Powers, Mary Jo Schwartz, Julie Scarboro-Silva, and Jean Stoney for foundational work on several of the diagnostic probes. They graciously allowed us to build on their thinking, collect field test data, and include the revised versions and teachers' notes in this volume. We would also like to acknowledge and thank Dr. Margaret Wyckoff for her continuous support and sharing of her mathematical knowledge. She was always willing to reflect and share in many ways during the process of writing this volume.

Thank you to the students and teachers involved in Mathematics: Access and Teaching in High School (MATHS): MSAD 9, MSAD 11, MSAD 34, MSAD 41, MSAD 56, Augusta School Department, Deer-Isle Stonington, and Old Town School Department. Thank you to Kittson Central School, Dr. Jenson, Mark Christenson, and Kyal Brandt in northwestern Minnesota. Their willingness to administer probes and collect student work is greatly appreciated. Thank you to Maureen Ryden and Julie Pastir who graciously shared their space, and the wonderful students of St. Vincent School.

We thank the many educators who field tested the probes and would especially like to acknowledge the contributions of the following educators for supplying ample student work, ideas for probes, or feedback for this project: Marie Bahlert, Sue Bisallon, Cynthia Blanchard, Vanessa Clarida, Katie Coleman, Fred Conlogue, Ray Danielson, Michelle Donovan, Christine Downing, Carla Fancy, Sally Foley, Shannon Gallant, Bonnie Gallagher, M. Guidry, Judith Graichen, Katrina Hall, Elizabeth Haynes, Amy Ketch, Gretchen Kimball, Beverly Koelbl, Kelly Littlefield, Karen Medeiros, Mike Moholland, Dennis Nardone, Michele Philbrick, Candace Resmini, Carol Jean Sawyer, Angela Smith, Valerie Spiller, Gail Weatherbee, Glen Widmer, and Johnette Winfrey.

In addition, several of our colleagues contributed to this work in many ways, including giving support, providing resources, examining the probes, and reviewing available research. Thank you to Francis Eberle, Leslie Minton, and especially to Meghan Southworth.

PUBLISHER'S ACKNOWLEDGMENTS

Corwin Press gratefully acknowledges the contributions of the following reviewers:

Lesa M. Covington Clarkston
Assistant Professor
University of Minnesota
Minneapolis, MN

Jason Cushner
Residential and Mathematics Instructor
Pine Ridge School
Williston, VT

JoAnn Hiatt
Mathematics Teacher
Olathe East High School
Olathe, KS

Amanda Mayeaux
Mathematics Teacher
Dutchtown Middle School
Geismar, LA

Lyneille Meza
Mathematics Teacher
Gayler High School
Denton, TX

Debra A. Scarpelli
Mathematics Teacher
Samuel Slater Junior High School
Pawtucket, RI

Zsuzsanna Toth-Laughland
Mathematics Teacher
Kennett High School
Conway, NH

About the Authors

Cheryl M. Rose is a project director for the Northeast and the Islands Regional Educational Laboratory (REL Northeast and Islands/REL-NEI) housed at the Education Development Center (EDC). Her work is primarily in the areas of leadership, mathematics professional development, and school reform. Before joining EDC, Rose was the senior program director for mathematics at the Maine Mathematics and Science Alliance (MMSA) where she served as the coprincipal investigator of the mathematics section of the National Science Foundation (NSF)-funded project, Curriculum Topic Study, and principal investigator and project director of two Title IIa State Mathematics and Science Partnership projects. Prior to working on these projects, Rose was the coprincipal investigator and project director for MMSA's NSF-funded Local Systemic Change Initiative, Broadening Educational Access to Mathematics in Maine (BEAMM), and she was a fellow in Cohort 4 of the National Academy for Science and Mathematics Education Leadership. Before joining MMSA in 2001, Rose was a high school and middle school mathematics educator for 10 years. Rose received her B.S. in secondary mathematics education from the University of Maine at Farmington and her M.Ed. in curriculum and instruction from City University in Seattle, Washington.

Carolyn B. Arline is a secondary mathematics educator and is currently working with the Kittson Central School District in northern Minnesota. Carolyn previously worked as a mathematics specialist at the Maine Mathematics and Science Alliance. She continues her work with MMSA as a consultant. Carolyn's work is primarily in the areas of mathematics professional development, learning communities, leadership, systematic school reform, assessment, and technology. She is a fellow of the second cohort group of the Governor's Academy for Science and Mathematics Educators, and was a mathematics mentor in the NSF-funded Northern New England Co-Mentoring Network. Prior to working at the MMSA, Carolyn taught high school mathematics and served as a mathematics department chair. She received her B.S. in secondary mathematics education from the University of Maine at Orono.

1

Mathematics Assessment Probes

To differentiate instruction effectively, teachers need diagnostic assessment strategies to gauge their students' prior knowledge and uncover their misunderstandings. By accurately identifying and addressing misunderstandings, teachers prevent their students from becoming frustrated and disenchanted with mathematics, which can reinforce the student preconception that "some people don't have the ability to do math." Diagnostic strategies also allow for instruction that builds on individual students' existing understandings while addressing their identified difficulties. The Mathematics Assessment Probes in this book allow teachers to target specific areas of difficulty as identified in research on student learning. Targeting specific areas of difficulty—for example, the transition from reasoning about whole numbers to understanding numbers that are expressed in relationship to other numbers (decimals and fractions)—focuses diagnostic assessment effectively (National Research Council, 2005, p. 310).

Mathematics Assessment Probes represent one approach to diagnostic assessment. They typically include a prompt or question and a series of responses. The probes specifically elicit prior understandings and commonly held misconceptions that may or may not have been uncovered during an instructional unit. This elicitation allows teachers to make instructional choices based on the specific needs of students. Examples of commonly held misconceptions elicited by a Mathematics Assessment Probe include ideas such as "multiplication makes bigger" and "the larger the denominator, the larger the fraction."

It is important to make the distinction between what we might call a silly mistake and a more fundamental one, which may be the product of a deeprooted misunderstanding. It is not uncommon for different students to display the same misunderstanding every year. Being aware of and eliciting common misunderstandings and drawing students' attention to them can be a valuable teaching technique (Griffin & Madgwick, 2005).

The process of diagnosing student understandings and misunderstandings and making instructional decisions based on that information is the key to increasing students' mathematical knowledge. To use the Mathematics Assessment Probes for this purpose, teachers need to

- Determine a question
- Use a probe to examine student understandings and misunderstandings
- Use links to cognitive research to drive next steps in instruction
- Implement the instructional unit or activity
- Determine the impact on learning by asking an additional question

The above process is described in detail in this chapter. The Teachers' Notes that accompany each of the Mathematics Assessment Probes in Chapters 3 through 5 include information on research findings and instructional implications relevant to the individual probe.

WHAT TYPES OF UNDERSTANDINGS AND MISUNDERSTANDINGS DOES A MATHEMATICS ASSESSMENT PROBE UNCOVER?

Developing understanding in mathematics is an important but difficult goal. Being aware of student difficulties and the sources of those difficulties, and designing instruction to diminish them, are important steps in achieving this goal (Yetkin, 2003). The Mathematics Assessment Probes are designed to uncover student understandings and misunderstandings; the results are used to inform instruction rather than make evaluative decisions. As shown in Figure 1.1, the understandings include both conceptual and procedural knowledge, and misunderstandings are classified as common errors or overgeneralizations. Each of these is described in more detail below.

Figure 1.1 Diagnostic Assessment Probes

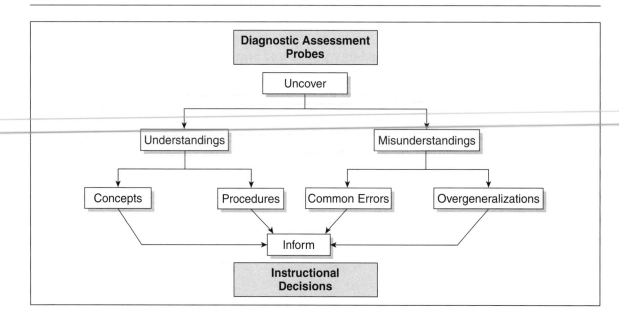

Understandings: Conceptual and Procedural Knowledge

Research has solidly established the importance of conceptual understanding in becoming proficient in a subject. When students understand mathematics, they are able to use their knowledge flexibly. They combine factual knowledge, procedural facility, and conceptual understanding in powerful ways. (National Council of Teachers of Mathematics [NCTM], 2000)

Conceptual Understanding

Students demonstrate conceptual understanding in mathematics when they

- Recognize, label, and generate examples and non-examples of concepts
- Use and interrelate models, diagrams, manipulatives, and so on
- Know and apply facts and definitions
- Compare, contrast, and integrate concepts and principles
- Recognize, interpret, and apply signs, symbols, and terms
- Interpret assumptions and relationships in mathematical settings

Procedural Knowledge

Students demonstrate procedural knowledge in mathematics when they

- Select and apply appropriate procedures
- Verify or justify a procedure using concrete models or symbolic methods
- Extend or modify procedures to deal with factors in problem settings
- Use numerical algorithms
- Read and produce graphs and tables
- Execute geometric constructions
- Perform noncomputational skills such as rounding and ordering

(U.S. Department of Education, 2003, Chap. 4)

The relationship between understanding concepts and being proficient with procedures is complex. The following description gives an example of how the Mathematics Assessment Probes elicit conceptual or procedural understanding. The "Value of the Digit" probe (see Figure 1.2) is designed to elicit whether students understand place value beyond being able to procedurally connect numbers to their appropriate places. Students who are able to correctly choose (B) there is a 2 in the ones place and (E) there is a 1 in the tenths place, but do not choose (C) there are 21.3 tenths and (H) there are 213 hundredths, are often lacking a conceptual understanding of place value.

The following student responses to the "Explain Your Reasoning" prompt are indicative of conceptual understanding of place value:

I know for a whole number like 253 the 2 means 200 and the 5 means 50 so for decimals it is similar but opposite because it is a part of a whole number. For the 2.13 the three is in the 100th place which means there is $^{213}/_{100}$.

Expanded, the number 2.13 is $2 + ^1/_{10} + ^3/_{100}$. How many 10th? Look at $2 + ^1/_{10}$ or .1 plus the extra $^3/_{100}$ or .03. How many 100th? Combine all three.

Figure 1.2   The Value of the Digit

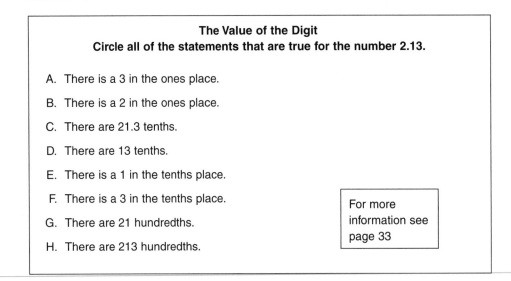

Misunderstandings: Common Errors and Overgeneralizations

In *Hispanic and Anglo Students' Misconceptions in Mathematics*, Jose Mestre summarizes cognitive research as follows: Students do not come to the classroom as "blank slates" (Resnick, 1983, quoted in Mestre, 1989). Instead, they come with theories constructed from their everyday experiences. They have actively constructed these theories, an activity crucial to all successful learning. Some of the theories that students use to make sense of the world are, however, incomplete half-truths (Mestre, 1989). They are misconceptions.

Misconceptions are a problem for two reasons. First, they interfere with learning when students use them to interpret new experiences. Second, students are emotionally and intellectually attached to their misconceptions because they have actively constructed them. Hence, students give up their misconceptions, which can have such a harmful effect on learning, only with great reluctance. For the purposes of this book, these misunderstandings or misconceptions will be categorized into common errors and overgeneralizations. Each of these categories of misunderstandings is described in more detail below.

Common Error Patterns

Common error patterns refer to systematic uses of inaccurate/inefficient procedures or strategies. Typically, this type of error pattern indicates nonunderstanding of an important math concept (University of Kansas, 2005). Examples of common error patterns include consistent misuse of a tool or steps of an algorithm, such as an inaccurate procedure for computing or the misreading of a measurement device. The following description gives an example of how the Mathematics Assessment Probes elicit common error patterns.

One of the ideas the "What's the Measure?" probe (see Figure 1.3) is designed to elicit is the understanding of zero point. "A significant minority of older children (e.g., fifth grade) respond to nonzero origins by simply reading off whatever number on a ruler aligns with the end of the object (Lehrer et al., 1998a)" (NCTM, 2003, p. 183). We have found many middle school students also make this same mistake.

The correct answers are A, C, D, and E. For students who incorrectly choose B and do not choose D and E, their error is typically based on the common error of not considering the beginning point on the ruler as it relates to the beginning of the object being measured.

Figure 1.3   What's the Measure?

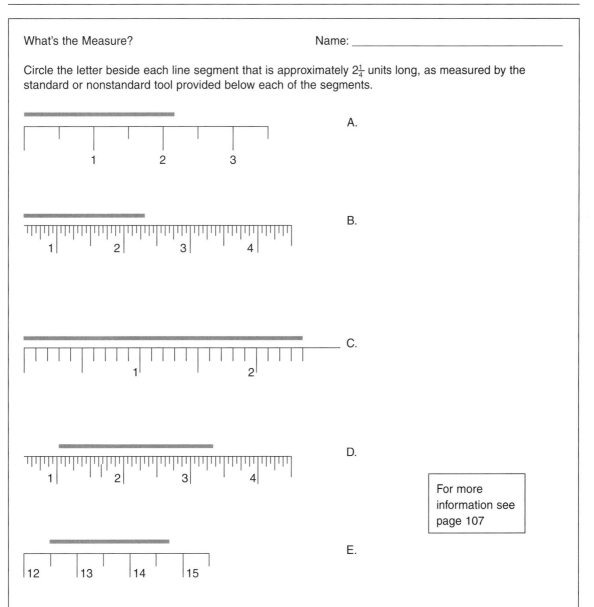

Overgeneralizations

Often, students learn an algorithm, rule, or shortcut and then extend this information to another context in an inappropriate way. These misunderstandings are often overgeneralizations from cases that students have seen in prior instruction (Griffin & Madgwick, 2005). To teach in a way that avoids creating any misconceptions is not possible, and we have to accept that students will make some incorrect generalizations that will remain hidden unless the teacher makes specific efforts to uncover them (Askew & Wiliam, 1995).

The following example illustrates how the Mathematics Assessment Probes can elicit overgeneralizations. The "Is It a Variable? Probe (see Figure 1.4) is designed to elicit the overgeneralization of the use of letters and symbols to represent variables. Students often overgeneralize from the general definition of a variable, a letter or symbol that represents a quantity, leading to identifying any letter or symbol used in a mathematical situation as a variable. Students who incorrectly choose B, C, and D often have overgeneralized in this way.

In addition to uncovering common misunderstandings, the Mathematics Assessment Probes also elicit uncommon misconceptions that may not be uncovered and could continue to cause difficulty in understanding a targeted concept. An example of this is highlighted in the following Image From Practice.

Figure 1.4   Is It a Variable?

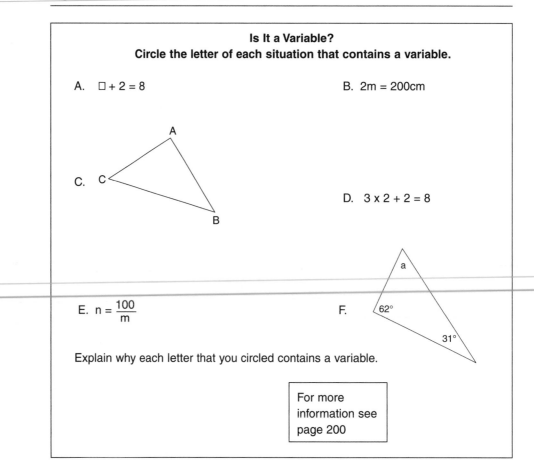

Is It a Variable?
Circle the letter of each situation that contains a variable.

A. $\square + 2 = 8$ B. 2m = 200cm

C. (triangle with vertices A, B, C)   D. 3 x 2 + 2 = 8

E. $n = \dfrac{100}{m}$ F. (triangle with angles a, 62°, 31°)

Explain why each letter that you circled contains a variable.

For more information see page 200

Image From Practice: Gumballs in a Jar

While reviewing student responses to Gumballs in a Jar [see Figure 1.6], I was intrigued by one particular student's response that didn't seem to fit any of the suggested typical misunderstandings. Having just spent time on using red and white chips to discover the rules of adding and subtracting integers, the student responded, "Jar B is better because if you take out zero pairs from Jar A [you leave] a chance of +1 and tak[ing] zero pairs from Jar B leav[es] a chance of +2." Although I was not expecting this misunderstanding, thinking about misconceptions as overgeneralized ideas helped me realize just how easy it is for students to make incorrect connections across processes and concepts.

HOW WERE THE MATHEMATICS ASSESSMENT PROBES DEVELOPED?

Developing an assessment probe is different from creating appropriate questions for summative quizzes, tests, or state and national exams. The probes in this book were developed using the process described in *Mathematics Curriculum Topic Study: Bridging the Gap Between Standards and Practice* (Keeley & Rose, 2007). The process is summarized as follows:

- Identify the topic you plan to teach and use national standards to examine concepts and specific ideas related to the topic. The national standards used to develop the probes for this book were NCTM's (2000) *Principles and Standards for School Mathematics* and the American Association for the Advancement of Science (AAAS)'s *Benchmarks for Science Literacy* (AAAS, 1993).

- Select the specific concepts or ideas you plan to address and identify the relevant research findings. The source for research findings include NCTM's *Research Companion to Principles and Standards for School Mathematics* (2003), Chapter 15 of AAAS's (1993) *Benchmarks for Science Literacy*, and additional supplemental articles related to a topic.

- Focus on a concept or a specific idea you plan to address with the probe, and identify the related research findings. Choose the type of probe format that lends itself to the situation (see more information on probe format following the Gumballs in a Jar example on p. 9). Develop the stem (the prompt), key (correct response), and distracters (incorrect responses derived from research findings) that match the developmental level of your students.

- Share your assessment probe(s) with colleagues for constructive feedback, pilot with students, and modify as needed.

Figure 1.5, which is taken from Keeley and Rose (2007), provides the list of concepts and specific ideas related to the probability of simple events.

The shaded information was used as the focus in the development of the probe, Gumballs in a Jar (see Figure 1.6). The probe is used to reveal common

Figure 1.5   Probability Example

Topic: Probability (Simple Events)

Concepts and Ideas	Research Findings
• Events can be described in terms of being more or less likely, impossible, or certain. (*BSL*, 3–5, p. 228)	**Understandings of Probability** (*Research Companion*, pp. 216–223)
• Probability is the measure of the likelihood of an event and can be represented by a number from 0 to 1. (*PSSM*, 3–5, p. 176)	• Lack of understanding of ratio leads to difficulties in understanding of chance.
	• Students tend to focus on absolute rather than relative size.
• Understand that 0 represents the probability of an impossible event and 1 represents the probability of a certain event. (PSSM, 3–5, p. 181)	• Although young children do not have a complete understanding of ratio, they have some intuitions of chance and randomness.
• Probabilities are ratios and can be expressed as fractions, percentages, or odds. (*BSL*, 6–8, p. 229)	• A continuum of probabilistic thinking includes subjective, transitional, informal quantitative, and numerical levels.
• Methods such as organized lists, tree diagrams, and area models are helpful in finding the number of possible outcomes. (*PSSM*, 6–8, pp. 254–255)	• Third grade (approx.) is an appropriate place to begin systematic instruction.
	• "Equiprobability" is the notion that all outcomes are equally likely, disregarding relative and absolute size.
• The theoretical probability of a simple event can be found using the ratio of # favorable outcome/total possible outcomes. (*BSL*, 6–8, p. 229)	• The outcome approach is defined as the misconception of predicting the outcome of an experiment rather than what is likely to occur. Typical responses to questions are "anything can happen."
• The probability of an outcome can be tested with simple experiments and simulations. (*PSSM*, 6–8, pp. 254–255)	• Intuitive reasoning may lead to incorrect responses. Categories include representativeness and availability.
• The relative frequency (experimental probability) can be computed using data generated from an experiment or simulation. (*PSSM*, 6–8, pp. 254–255)	• Wording of task may influence reasoning.
	• NAEP results show fourth and eighth graders have difficulty with tasks involving probability as a ratio of "m chances out of n" but not with "1 chance out of n."
• The experimental and theoretical probability of an event should be compared with discrepancies between predictions and outcomes from a large and representative sample taken seriously. (*PSSM*, 6–8, pp. 254–255)	• Increased understanding of sample space stems from multiple opportunities to determine and discuss possible outcomes and predict and test using simple experiments.
	Uncertainty (*BSL*, Chap. 15, p. 353)
	• Upper elementary students can give correct examples for certain, possible, and impossible events, but have difficulties calculating the probability of independent and dependent events.
	• Upper elementary students create "part to part" rather than "part to whole" relationships.

NOTES: BSL = *Benchmarks for Science Literacy;* PSSM = *Principles and Standards for School Mathematics.*

Figure 1.6   Gumballs

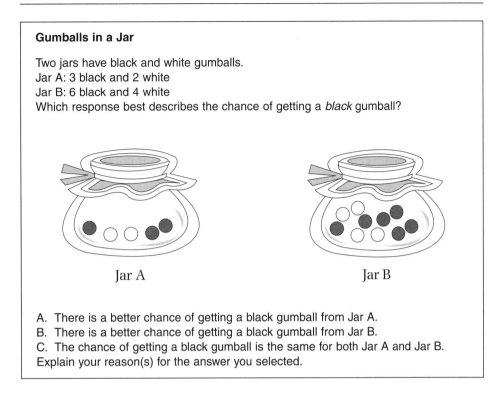

Gumballs in a Jar

Two jars have black and white gumballs.
Jar A: 3 black and 2 white
Jar B: 6 black and 4 white
Which response best describes the chance of getting a *black* gumball?

Jar A   Jar B

A. There is a better chance of getting a black gumball from Jar A.
B. There is a better chance of getting a black gumball from Jar B.
C. The chance of getting a black gumball is the same for both Jar A and Jar B.
Explain your reason(s) for the answer you selected.

errors regarding probability, such as focusing on absolute size, or a lack of conceptual understanding of probability as a prediction of what is likely to happen. There is the same chance you will pick a black gumball out of each jar. Jar A has a probability of $^3/_5$, and Jar B has a probability of $^6/_{10} = ^3/_5$. There are a variety of trends in correct thinking related to this probe, some of which are doubling, ratios, and percents. Some students might correctly choose answer C but use incorrect reasoning such as "you can't know for sure since anything can happen," an explanation that indicates a lack of conceptual understanding of probability. Other students may demonstrate partial understanding with responses such as "each jar has more black than white." Some students reason there are fewer white gumballs in Jar A compared to Jar B and therefore there is a better chance of picking a black gumball from Jar A.

Others observe that Jar B has more black gumballs compared to Jar A and therefore reason that there is a better chance of picking a black gumball. In both cases, students are focusing on absolute size instead of relative size in comparing the likelihood of events. Students sometimes choose Distracter A due to an error in counting or calculation.

Additional probes can be written using the same list of concepts and specific ideas related to the probability of simple events. For example, by focusing on the statement from the research, "NAEP results show fourth and eighth graders have difficulty with tasks involving probability as a ratio of 'm chances out of n' but not with '1 chance out of n'" a probe using an example of each can diagnose if students are demonstrating this difficulty.

WHAT IS THE STRUCTURE OF A MATHEMATICS ASSESSMENT PROBE?

The probes are designed to include two tiers, one for elicitation of common understandings and misunderstandings and the other for the elaboration of individual student thinking. Each of the tiers is described in more detail below.

Tier 1: Elicitation

Since the elicitation tier is designed to uncover common understandings and misunderstandings, a structured format using stems, correct answers, and distracters is used to narrow ideas found in the related research. The formats typically fall into one of six categories.

Selected Response

One stem, one correct answer, and several distracters (see Figure 1.7)

Figure 1.7   What's Your Estimate?

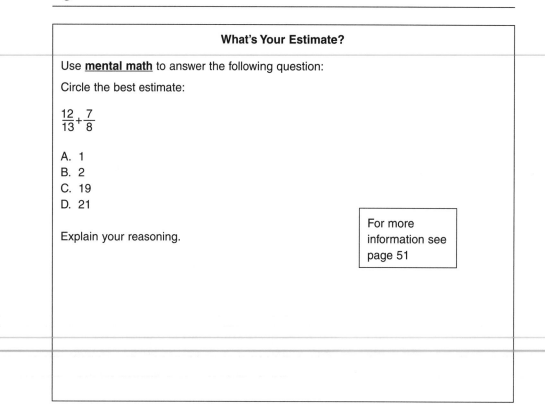

What's Your Estimate?

Use **mental math** to answer the following question:

Circle the best estimate:

$$\frac{12}{13} + \frac{7}{8}$$

A. 1
B. 2
C. 19
D. 21

Explain your reasoning.

For more information see page 51

Multiple Selections Response

- Two or more sets of problems, each with one stem, one correct answer, and one or more distracters (see Figure 1.8)

Figure 1.8 Expressions: Equal or Not Equal?

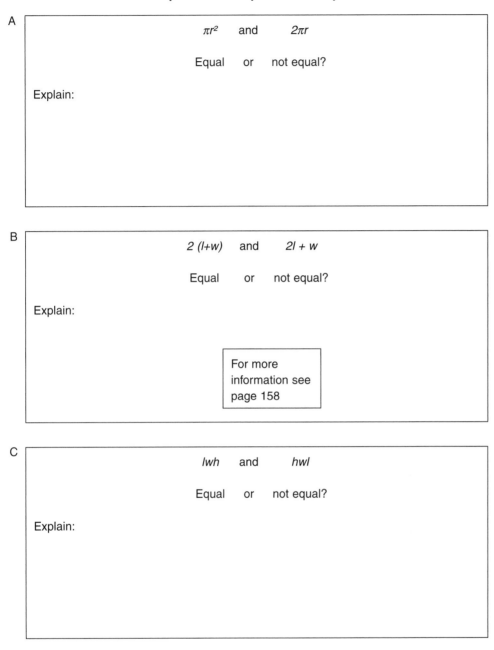

Expressions: Equal or Not Equal?

A

πr^2 and $2\pi r$

Equal   or   not equal?

Explain:

B

$2(l+w)$ and $2l + w$

Equal   or   not equal?

Explain:

For more information see page 158

C

lwh and hwl

Equal   or   not equal?

Explain:

Opposing Views/Answers

- Two or more statements are provided and students are asked to choose the statement they agree with (see Figure 1.9). This format is adapted from *Concept Cartoons in Education*, created by Stuart Naylor and Brenda Keogh (2000) for probing student ideas in science.

Figure 1.9 Are Area and Perimeter Related?

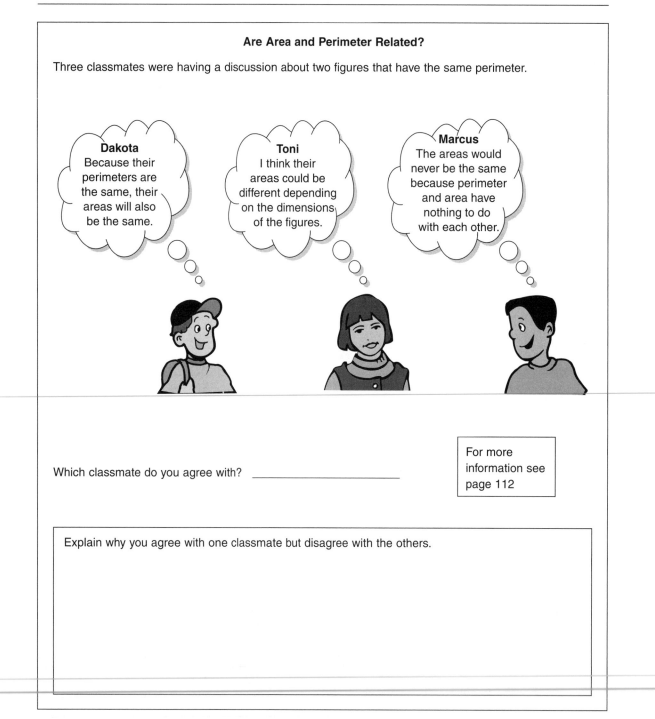

Examples and Non-Examples List

- Several examples and non-examples are given, and students are asked to check only the examples based on a given statement (see Figure 1.10).

Justified List

- Two or more separate problems or statements with each answer choice needing to be justified (see Figure 1.11).

Figure 1.10   Is It True?

Is It True?

If m = 5, circle all of the statements below that are true for the expression 3m.

A. 3m = 35

B. 3m = 8

C. 3m = 3 + 5

D. 3m = 3 meters

E. 3m = 15

F. 3m = 3 times 5

G. 3m means the slope is $^3/_5$

H. 3m = 3 miles

For more
information see
page 180

Explain your reasoning for each circled statement.

Figure 1.11   What Do You *Mean?*

What Do You *Mean*?

Each statement below can be preceded by one of the following statements:

The mean is always . . .

The mean is sometimes . . .

The mean is never . . .

For more
information see
page 136

Read each statement and indicate **A** (always), **S** (sometimes), or **N** (never):

Statement	Justify Response
1. ☐ the value obtained by dividing the sum of a set of data points by the number of data points in the set.	
2. ☐ equal to the value of the term in the middle.	
3. ☐ equivalent to the value of the mode.	
4. ☐ changed when the same amount is added to each of the data points.	
5. ☐ affected when a 0 is added as one of the data points.	
6. ☐ one of the data points in the original set.	

Strategy Elicitation

- A problem is stated with multiple solution strategies given. Students provide an explanation regarding making sense of each strategy. (see Figure 1.12).

Figure 1.12   What's Your Addition Strategy? Decimals

Sam, Julie, Pete, and Lisa each added the numbers 11.5 + 2.7.

Sam's Method: "I broke the 2.7 apart." 11.5 + 2.7 11.5 + 2 = 13.5 13.5 + .5 = 14 14 + .2 = 14.2	**Does each of the methods make sense mathematically? Why or why not?**
Pete's Method: "I rounded up, then subtracted the extra." 11.5 + 2.7 11.5 + 3 = 14.5 14.5 − .3 = 14.2	 For more information see page 82
Julie's Method: "I added the numbers in the columns." $\overset{1}{1}1.5$ 2.7 ————— 14.2	

Tier 2: Elaboration

The second tier of each of the probes is designed for individual elaboration of the reasoning used to respond to the question asked in the first tier. Mathematics teachers gain a wealth of information by delving into the thinking behind students' answers, not just when answers are wrong but also when they are correct (Burns, 2005). Although the Tier 1 answers and distracters are designed around common understandings and misunderstandings, the elaboration tier allows educators to look more deeply at student thinking. Often a student chooses a specific response, correct or incorrect, for an atypical reason. Also, there are many different ways to approach a problem correctly; therefore, the elaboration tier allows educators to look for trends in thinking and in methods used.

WHAT ADDITIONAL INFORMATION IS PROVIDED WITH EACH MATHEMATICS ASSESSMENT PROBE?

In *Designing Professional Development for Teachers of Science and Mathematics,* Loucks-Horsley, Love, Stiles, Mundry, and Hewson (2003) describe action research as an effective professional development strategy. To use the probes in this manner, it is important to consider the complete implementation process.

We refer to an action research *quest* as working through the full cycle of

- Questioning student understanding of a particular concept
- Uncovering understandings and misunderstandings using a probe
- Examining student work
- Seeking links to cognitive research to drive next steps in instruction
- Teaching implications based on findings and determining impact on learning by asking an additional question

The Teachers' Notes, included with each probe, have been designed around the action research QUEST cycle, and each set of notes includes relevant information for each component of the cycle (see Figure 1.13). These components are described in detail below.

Figure 1.13   QUEST Cycle

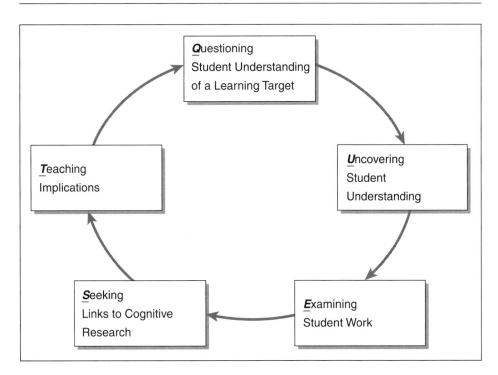

Q*uestioning student understanding of a particular concept.* This component helps to focus a teacher on what a particular probe elicits and to provide information on grade-appropriate knowledge. Figure 1.14 shows an example question from the Mathematics Assessment Probe, What's the Capacity?

Figure 1.14   Questioning Student Understanding of a Particular Concept

---

Example Question: *What's the Capacity?*

Question: *Do students recognize how a change in the dimensions affects the volume of a figure?*

Grade Level:

6–8	9–12

Grade span bars are provided to indicate the developmentally appropriate level of mathematics as aligned to the NCTM standards and cognitive research. The dark gray band represents the grade levels where the mathematics required of the probe is aligned to the standards, and the lighter gray band shows where field-testing has indicated students still have difficulties.

*U*ncovering *understanding by giving the Mathematics Assessment Probe to students.* Figure 1.15 shows an example, Uncovering Understanding, from the Mathematics Assessment Probe, What's the Capacity?

Figure 1.15   Uncovering Understandings

Example: *What's the Capacity?*

*U*ncover Understandings Using the Following Mathematics Assessment Probe:
What's the Capacity? (Content Standard: Geometry and Measurement)

---

*E*xamining *student work.* This section includes information about the stem, answer(s), and distracters as related to the research on cognitive learning. Example student responses are given for a selected number of elicited understandings and misunderstandings. The categories, conceptual/procedural and common errors/overgeneralizations are used where appropriate and are written in italics. Figure 1.16 shows an example, Examining Student Work, from the Mathematics Assessment Probe, What's the Capacity?

*S*eeking *links to cognitive research.* This section provides additional information about research that teachers can use for further study of the topic. Figure 1.17 shows an example from the Mathematics Assessment Probe, What's the Capacity?

Figure 1.16   Examining Student Work

Example: *What's the Capacity?*

*E*xamining Student Work

The distracters may reveal *common misunderstandings* regarding geometric measurement such as a lack of *conceptual understanding* of how a change in the size of the base and height impacts the volume of a figure, or the *overgeneralization* about the size or shape of the cylinder.

- *The correct answer is A:* Figure A with an approximate volume of 93 cubic units has a greater volume than Figure B with an approximate volume of 88 cubic units). **(See Student Responses 1, 2, and 3)**

- *Distracter B:* Students answering B often are incorrectly applying the intuitive rule of More A - More B (Stavy and Tirosh, 2000): overgeneralizing that taller figures have greater volume. **(See Student Responses 4 and 5)**

- *Distracter C:* Students overgeneralize about the equivalent portion of the figure's net as shown in the diagram and so do not incorporate the size of the base. They often are incorrectly applying the intuitive rule of Same A - Same B (Stavy and Tirosh, 2000): since the initial 8.5 × 11 rectangle is the same, the volume must be equivalent. **(See Student Responses 6 and 7)**

Figure 1.17   Seeking Links to Cognitive Research

Example: *What's the Capacity?*

*S*eeking Links to Cognitive Research

Findings suggest that, as with area and length measure, students' models of spatial structure influence their conceptions of an object's volume measure. (NCTM, 2003, p. 186)

The intuitive rule, Same A–Same B, is activated in comparison tasks in which two objects are equal in a certain quantity and differ in another quantity. . . . When students start to conserve the area of two sheets of paper, they will also argue that the volumes of the two cylinders are equal. Our data show . . . a very small percentage of the students in the upper grades [6–9] correctly argued about the cylinder with the greater volume. "There is no evidence of a decrease with age in students' incorrect judgments about conservation of volume." (Stavy & Tirosh, 2000, pp. 51–52)

Teaching implications. Being aware of student difficulties and their sources is important, but designing instruction is most important to help diminish those difficulties. Although some ideas are included, the authors strongly encourage educators to use the Curriculum Topic Study (CTS) process to search for additional teaching implications. Each set of Teachers' Notes includes the related CTS Guide for further study, additional references, and a "teacher sound bite" from a field-tester of the probe. Figure 1.18 shows an example from the Mathematics Assessment Probe, What's the Capacity?

Figure 1.18 Teaching Implications

Example: *What's the Capacity?*

In order to support a deeper understanding for students in regard to geometric measurement, the following are ideas and questions to consider in conjunction with the research.

Focus Through Instruction

- Students should be provided opportunities to experiment with volumes of objects using concrete objects.
- Students need experience composing and decomposing two- and three-dimensional shapes.
- Composing and decomposing shapes should be used as a method of finding volumes for various three-dimensional objects.
- Students should develop formulas through inquiry and investigation.
- Students with prior knowledge about the relationship between perimeter and area (see the "Are Area and Perimeter Related?" probe) are better able to understand the relationship of surface area and volume.

Questions to Consider . . . *when working with students as they grapple with the ideas of surface area and volume*

- Do the students understand how the dimensions of the base and the height of an object impact its volume?
- Over time, are students able to use properties and formulas to justify their answers and check their assumptions?

Teacher Sound Bite

Students easily jumped to conclusions based on a visual assumption, and it was difficult to convince them otherwise. Prior to using this probe, I was not explicit in helping students [connect their] understanding that two or more figures can have the same perimeter but different areas to new ideas concerning surface area and volume.

Additional References for Research and Teaching Implications:

NCTM (2000), *Principles and Standards for School Mathematics,*. pp. 243–245.

NCTM (2003), *Research Companion to Principles and Standards for School Mathematics,* p. 186.

Stepans et al. (2005), *Teaching for K–12 Mathematical Understanding Using the Conceptual Change Model,* pp. 103+.

Van de Walle (2007), *Elementary and Middle School Mathematics,* pp. 387–388.

> **Curriculum Topic Study**
>
> *What's the Capacity?*
> Related CTS Guide:
> Volume

Following the Teachers' Notes and sample student responses, adaptations, or variations of the Mathematics Assessment Probe are provided for some of the probes. Variations of the probe provide a different structure (selected response, multiple selections, opposing views, examples/non-examples, justified list, and strategy harvest) for the question within the same grade span. An adaptation to the probe is similar in content to the original, but the level of mathematics changes for use with a different grade span. In addition to the Teachers' Notes, a Note Template is included in Resource A. The Note Template provides a structured approach to working through a probe quest. The components of the template are described in Figure 1.19.

Figure 1.19   Note Template

---

*Q*uestion to Answer

*U*ncover Understandings Using the Following Mathematics Assessment Probe

Adaptations made to the probe:

*E*xamine student thinking:

*S*eek Additional Research Findings

   Source:

   Findings:

   Source:

   Findings:

   Source:

   Findings:

*T*eaching implications

   Source:

   Findings:

   Source:

   Findings:

   Source:

   Findings:

Summary of instructional implications/Plan of Action:

Results of Instruction:

WHAT MATHEMATICS ASSESSMENT PROBES ARE INCLUDED IN THE BOOK?

Many of the samples included in this book fall under numeric operations, symbolic representation, and geometric measurement because the cognitive research is abundant in these areas. The book also includes multiple examples for the following additional content standards: Numbers and Operations, Algebra, Data Analysis, Probability, Geometry, and Measurement. Figure 1.20 provides an "at a glance" look of the grade span and content of the probes included in Chapters 3 through 5. Grade-span bars are provided to indicate the developmentally appropriate level of mathematics as aligned to NCTM Standards as well as the cognitive research.

An important note to high school teachers: Many of the mathematics expectations in the Grades 6–8 span of the NCTM Standards are being introduced to some students for the first time in high school mathematics courses.

Figure 1.20   Grade Span and Content of the Probes

Grade Span Bar Key

▨	Target for Instruction Depending on Local Standards
▨	Prerequisite Concept/Field Testing Indicates Student Difficulty

Number and Operation Probes		Grade Span Bars	
Question	Probe	Grade 6–8	Grades 9–12
Can students choose all correct values of various digits of a given decimal?	What is the Value of the Digit? p. 33		
Do students correctly choose the various meanings of a/b?	What Is the Meaning of $\frac{2}{3}$? p. 39		
Are students able to choose equivalent forms of a fraction?	Is It Equivalent? p. 45		
Can students use estimation to choose the closest benchmark to an addition problem involving fractions?	What's Your Estimate? p. 51		
Do students understand there are multiple methods of estimating the sum of three 3-digit numbers?	Is It an Estimate? p. 56		
Do students use the "canceling of zeros" shortcut appropriately?	Is It Simplified? p. 61		
Are students able to locate 1 million on a number line labeled from 0 to 1 billion?	Where Is One Million? p. 66		
Do students understand how various integer exponents affect the value of the numerical expression?	How Low Can You Go? p. 71		
When adding, can students apply and understand a variety of different strategies?	What's Your Addition Strategy? p. 76		
When subtracting, can students apply and understand a variety of different strategies?	What's Your Subtraction Strategy? p. 84		
When multiplying, can students apply and understand a variety of different strategies?	What's Your Multiplication Strategy? p. 92		
When dividing, can students apply and understand a variety of different strategies?	What's Your Division Strategy? p. 99		

Measurement, Geometry, and Data Probes			
Question	**Probe**	**Grade 6–8**	**Grades 9–12**
Are students able to choose the correct measure of a line given a change in the interval?	What's the Measure? p. 107		
Do students understand that figures can have the same perimeter but different areas?	Are Area and Perimeter Related? p. 112		
Do students recognize how a change in the dimensions affects the area of a figure?	What's the Area? p. 117		
Do students recognize how a change in the dimensions affects the volume of a figure?	What's the Capacity? p. 122		
Do students recognize dilations (reduction or contraction and enlargement or magnification) as types of transformation?	Is It Transformed? p. 126		
Are students able to identify needed information in determining whether two figures are similar?	Are They Similar? p. 131		
Do students understand mean and how it is affected by changes to a data set?	What Do You *Mean?* p. 136		
Are students able to move beyond point-by-point graph interpretation?	Name of the Graph? p. 145		
Can students identify correct graphical construction and accurate use of interval scale?	Graph Construction p. 151		
Algebra Probes			
Question	**Probe**	**Grade 6–8**	**Grades 9–12**
Are students able to identify equivalent expressions in the form of familiar formulas?	Equal or Not Equal? p. 158		
Do students misuse "key words" when writing expressions?	Is It the Same as a + b? p. 165		
Do students correctly apply knowledge of equality and relationships among quantities?	M & N's? p. 170		
Do students understand how to evaluate an expression of the form "ax"?	What's the Substitute? p. 175		
Do students understand the operation implied by concatenation of literal symbols and numbers?	Is It True? p. 180		
Do students understand appropriate methods and notations when solving for an unknown?	Solving Equations p. 187		
Are students able to identify various representations of an inequality?	Correct Representation of the Inequality? p. 194		
Are students able to identify when a literal symbol is being used as a variable?	Is It a Variable? p. 200		
Do students correctly use the distributive law when multiplying algebraic binomials?	Binomial Expansion? p. 207		
Do students recognize the characteristics of the graph of a quadratic function?	Is It Quadratic? p. 213		

2

Instructional Implications

An important first step for making classroom assessment work is to understand the difference between assessment and evaluation. Some people use the terms assessment and evaluation interchangeably, but they have different meanings. When we assess, we are gathering information about student learning that informs our teaching and helps students learn more. We may teach differently, based on what we find as we assess. When we evaluate, we decide whether or not students have learned what they needed to learn and how well they have learned it. (Davies, 2000, p. 1)

Mathematics Assessment Probes represent one approach to diagnostic assessment. They can be used for formative assessment purposes if the information about students' understandings and misunderstandings is used to focus instruction. Purposes for using the Mathematics Assessment Probes included in this chapter are

- Differentiating instruction
- Assessing point of entry
- Analyzing trends in thinking
- Giving student interviews
- Promoting student-to-student dialogue
- Allowing for individual think time
- Developing vocabulary
- Improving students' process skills
- Assessing effectiveness of instructional activities
- Moving beyond the individual classroom

Each of the contexts is briefly described below, and in some cases, images from practice are used to highlight strategies within the contexts. The images from practice provide a window into the classroom of a teacher who uses the Mathematics Assessment Probes in the classroom.

DIFFERENTIATING INSTRUCTION

> Diagnostic assessments provide information to assist teacher planning and guide differentiated instruction. (McTighe & O'Connor, 2005, p. 11)

Differentiation is an organized yet flexible way of proactively adjusting teaching and learning to meet students where they are and to help all students meet maximum growth as learners (Tomlinson, 1999). Differentiation looks dissimilar across classrooms as educators incorporate different strategies, including varying the size of the numbers within a problem set, reducing the number of assigned problems, or allowing the use of tools. The important consideration in differentiating instruction is to allow all students access to an "excellent and equitable mathematics program that provides solid support for their learning and is responsive to their prior knowledge, intellectual strengths, and personal interests" (NCTM, 2000, p. 13).

The following Image From Practice highlights how a teacher used the information from a probe to plan instruction so that all students could learn the same concept even if some required various methods of intervention along the way.

Image From Practice: What's the Measure?

After giving the What's the Measure? probe, I organized the students into three groups. The first group consisted of the students who chose lines A, B, and C, as these lines include those ending near the 2¼ unit mark regardless of the starting point and exclude those that did not end near 2¼ units. These students do not consider the starting point when measuring length. I needed to provide these students with experiences to help them understand that any point on the ruler can serve as the starting point and build an understanding of measurement as counting lengths rather than as simply an endpoint number. I had these students work on an activity using various broken rulers to measure segments. The second group of students correctly chose A, D, and E, but also included choice C using the incorrect reasoning that the fourth "tick mark" would indicate ¼, although the unit is partitioned into tenths (excluded from this group were the two students who explained their choice of E by including in their explanation the measure of 2.4 and stating that this was approximate to ¼), and/or the students excluded choice A, which was only partitioned into halves. These students need more experience with the partitioning of units and the relationship of these parts to a fourth of the unit. I had this group work on an activity that required them to create their own rulers with varying numbers of partitions and then use their rulers to measure the length of objects. The third group, consisting of students who answered and explained the choices correctly, was provided with an extension activity on precision and accuracy.

ASSESSING POINT OF ENTRY

While teachers may fully grasp the importance of working with students' prior conceptions, they need to know the typical conceptions of students with respect to the topic about to be taught. (National Research Council [NRC], 2005, p. 20)

Assessing prior knowledge is a key first step in using assessment to inform teaching. Often, assumptions are made about what students do or do not know. Assumptions about lack of readiness may be based on teachers' experiences with students' lack of understanding in previous years. Assumptions that students are ready are often based on the fact that the students have studied the materials before (Stepans, Schmidt, Welsh, Reins, & Saigo, 2005). Because of these assumptions, the mathematics concepts of an instructional unit are sometimes beyond students' readiness. Just as prevalent is wasting valuable classroom time by incorporating activities below the instructional level of the students. The Mathematics Assessment Probes can be given prior to a specific unit of investigation to gauge the starting point and allow teachers to make decisions based on evidence rather than assumption.

ANALYZING TRENDS IN STUDENT THINKING

Compiling an inventory for a set of papers can provide a sense of the class's progress and thus inform decisions about how to differentiate instruction. (Burns, 2005, p. 29)

In her recent article, "Looking at How Students Reason," Marilyn Burns (2005) describes a process for taking a classroom inventory:

After asking a class of 27 fifth graders to circle the larger fraction— $2/3$ or $3/4$—and explain their reasoning, I reviewed their papers and listed the strategies they used. Their strategies included drawing pictures (either circles or rectangles); changing to fractions with common denominators ($8/12$ and $9/12$); seeing which fraction was closer to 1 ($2/3$ is $1/3$ away, but $3/4$ is only $1/4$ away); and relating the fractions to money ($2/3$ of $1.00 is about 66 cents, whereas $3/4$ of $1.00 is 75 cents). Four of the students were unable to compare the two fractions correctly. I now had direction for future lessons that would provide interventions for the struggling students and give all the students opportunities to learn different strategies from one another. (p. 29)

Developing this "sense of the class" allows for instructional decision making. The probes can be used for this purpose by categorizing student responses and asking the following questions:

- What are the primary methods students used for solving this problem?
- How often do the primary methods result in the correct response?

- Which of the methods is generalizable?
- What student methods are considered outliers?
- Which of the primary methods are more efficient?
- Based on the sense of the class, what instructional strategies are effective for this particular learning target?

The last question is an important one because "students' preconceptions must be addressed explicitly in order for them to change their existing understanding and beliefs. If students' initial ideas are ignored, the understanding that they develop can be very different from what the teacher intends" (Stepans et al., 2005, p. 35).

GIVING STUDENT INTERVIEWS

Interviewing provides the opportunity to talk with students—that is, to hear their explanations and to pose follow-up questions that probe the rationale behind their beliefs. (Stepans et al., 2005, p. 36)

Giving student interviews is an important and useful strategy for several purposes. The main purpose for interviewing a student is to probe that student's mathematical thinking. By interviewing a variety of students in a class, [teachers] can get a better sense of the range of thinking in that class. Interviewing takes time, but the potential payoff is great for helping make sense of students' responses to questions. (Bright & Joyner, 2004, p. 184)

The following Image From Practice highlights how a teacher used the probe What's the Interval? as a tool to "interview" students.

Image From Practice: What's the Interval?

I created a card for each example and non-example of the probe so individual students could sort the cards into two piles. As students were working independently on revisions to a portfolio task, I asked them one at a time to sort the cards into two piles: one showing correct graph constructions and the other showing those with errors. Since the students were already familiar with "think-alouds," I encouraged them to talk about the graph and their choice of placement in the example or non-example pile. The "think aloud" process minimized the number of questions I needed to ask, but some additional probing was necessary. Using and analyzing data are integral parts of our curriculum, but students always seem to have difficulty constructing appropriate graphs. By focusing first on identifying possible misunderstandings about intervals, I was able to pinpoint a few areas to address, such as keeping the same interval on both the positive and negative half of the same axis. By addressing these specific areas first, future class discussions about deciding on an appropriate range for each of the axes, given the data, can stay focused on that particular concept.

PROMOTING STUDENT-TO-STUDENT DIALOGUE

A focus on student thinking requires classroom norms that encourage the expression of ideas (tentative and certain, partially and fully informed, as well as risk taking). It requires that mistakes be viewed not as revelations of inadequacy, but as helpful contributions in the search for understanding. (NRC, 2005, p. 20)

The Mathematics Assessment Probes can be used as conversation starters for class discussions. These conversation starters can promote both conflict and collaboration as students work to validate answers and refine their thinking based on their peers' justifications.

The following Image From Practice highlights how a teacher used the probe What Is the Area? to address a misunderstanding typical of students at a prior grade span.

Image From Practice: What Is the Area?

Before moving into a unit on volume, I wanted to elicit student understanding of concepts of area and perimeter. I gave my students the What Is the Area? probe with the same information copied on both the front and back of the paper. After giving students time to complete the elicitation tier, I asked them to put the letter of their response on a sticky note. While students worked on the elaboration tier of the probe I collected the sticky notes and quickly created a bar graph with them as a visual display of the individual responses. After students finished with the elaboration of their thought process, I led a class discussion, with students justifying their choice by describing their reasoning.

Without stating the correct answer, I closed the activity by asking students to turn over the handout to the "fresh" What Is the Area? probe and to re-answer the question, taking into consideration the preceding discussion. Each time I use the Post-it Bar Chart process, I enjoy comparing the before and after responses and looking for changes in how students choose to explain their choice. More often than not, even with a correct first answer, student responses after the class discussion are more precise and mathematically justified.

This process allows students to practice *metacognition*, thinking about one's own thinking. When asked to redo the problem based on the discussion that followed individual process time, students are forced to think about their original ideas and how they may or may not have changed.

DEVELOPING VOCABULARY

Mathematics and science textbooks are often filled with unfamiliar, abstract terminology. Merely asking students to look up terms in a dictionary and memorize their definitions doesn't help learners develop an adequate understanding of these new concepts. (Barton, Heidema, & Jordan, 2002, p. 24)

There is a difference between learning a definition and understanding a concept. Revisited from Chapter 1, conceptual understanding is exhibited when students

- Recognize, label, and generate examples and non-examples of concepts
- Use and interrelate models, diagrams, manipulatives, and so on
- Know and apply facts and definitions
- Compare, contrast, and integrate concepts and principles
- Recognize, interpret, and apply signs, symbols, and terms
- Interpret assumptions and relationships in mathematical settings

---

(U.S. Department of Education, 2003, Chap. 4)

The examples and non-examples format of some of the Mathematics Assessment Probes provide an important tool for assessing and building conceptual knowledge by eliciting this prior knowledge from students. Small-group and whole-class discussions focused on choices lead students to justify their categorization. The following Image From Practice highlights how a teacher used the probe Is It a Variable? to enhance students' understanding of the concept of a variable.

Image From Practice: Is It a Variable?

My eleventh-grade Algebra II students seem to be able to work procedurally manipulating variables to solve equations but lack conceptual understanding of basic algebraic ideas. I found incorporating the probes in a building vocabulary activity using the Frayer model (Frayer, Frederick, & Klausmeier, 1969), a graphic organizer that is often used with students for concept and vocabulary development, to be helpful for students. The four-square model prompts students to think more deeply about and describe the meaning of a word, symbol, or concept by defining the term, describing its essential characteristics and uses, and providing examples and non-examples of the idea. Before listing characteristics/uses and a definition of a variable, the students individually complete the Is It a Variable? probe and then participate in a class discussion on the examples of situations containing a variable. After coming to an agreement on examples, the students work in groups to categorize the examples into the various uses of variables. Each group contributes one category to the class list, rotating around the groups until all generated categories are organized on the board. To summarize, groups are then asked to generate a definition of a variable that incorporates the listed categories.

ALLOWING FOR INDIVIDUAL THINK TIME

> A problem with traditional questioning is that the teacher gets to hear only one student's thinking. (Leahy, Lyon, Thompson, & Wiliam, 2005, p. 22)

Eliciting student ideas using a Mathematics Assessment Probe allows for individual students to express their initial thinking—the first phase of eliciting student thinking—without the interference of other students' thought processes. Although student conversation about the learning target addressed in the probe is important, the conversation does not necessarily need to occur by having students discuss the probe. Often, the student conversation takes place during activities specifically chosen to meet the needs of the students, based on evidence of understanding uncovered by the probe. The following excerpt from the article, "Classroom Assessment: Minute by Minute, Day by Day" (Leahy et al., 2005) provides additional ideas for allowing for individual think time. The strategies described below can be incorporated while using a Mathematics Assessment Probe.

> Teachers can also use questions to check on student understanding before continuing the lesson. We call this a "hinge point" in the lesson because the lesson can go in different directions, depending on student responses. By explicitly integrating these hinge points into instruction, teachers can make their teaching more responsive to their students' needs in real time. However, no matter how good the hinge-point question, the traditional model of classroom questioning presents two additional problems. The first is lack of engagement. If the classroom rule dictates that students raise their hands to answer questions, then students can disengage from the classroom by keeping their hands down.
>
> The second problem with traditional questioning is that the teacher gets to hear only one student's thinking. To gauge the understanding of the whole class, the teacher needs to get responses from all the students in real time. One way to do this is to have all students write their answers on individual dry-erase boards, which they hold up at the teacher's request. The teacher can then scan responses for novel solutions as well as misconceptions.
>
> Another approach is to give each student a set of four cards labeled A, B, C, and D, and ask the question in multiple-choice format. If the question is well designed, the teacher can quickly judge the different levels of understanding in the class. If all students answer correctly, the teacher can move on. If no one answers correctly, the teacher might choose to reteach the concept. If some students answer correctly and some answer incorrectly, the teacher can use that knowledge to engineer a whole-class discussion on the concept or match up the students for peer teaching. Hinge-point questions provide a window into students' thinking and, at the same time, give the teacher some ideas about how to take the students' learning forward. (p. 22)

IMPROVING STUDENTS' PROCESSING SKILLS

Examining and discussing both exemplary and problematic pieces of mathematics writing can be beneficial at all levels. (NCTM, 2000, p. 62)

Although the primary purpose of a Mathematics Assessment Probe is to elicit understandings, partial understandings, and misunderstandings, a secondary benefit is the improvement of students' written communication skills. After instruction and discussion of the underlying mathematics, individual student responses to a probe can be critiqued for clarity, correct information, and coherency.

The following Image From Practice highlights how a teacher used the probe What Do You *Mean?* to improve students' methods of justification.

Image From Practice: What Do You *Mean?*

Many of my high school students can calculate the mean but do not have a conceptual understanding of the concept. Since I am building on ideas of measure to include measures of spread, I use the What Do You Mean? *probe to enhance their understanding of the concept of the mean. In addition to teaching about the concept, the probe also builds students' awareness of the justification needed for an always, sometimes, and never response. As the discussion progresses, students begin to provide examples and counterexamples and realize that if they can provide one of each, then the answer has to be "sometimes." They also become aware that creating a list of examples is not enough to claim "always."*

ASSESSING EFFECTIVENESS OF INSTRUCTIONAL ACTIVITIES

In planning individual lessons, teachers should strive to organize the mathematics so that fundamental ideas form an integrated whole. (NCTM, 2000, p. 15)

Using probes in a pre- and post-assessment format allows for evaluation of curriculum and instruction. When implementing a new or revised set of activities, evaluating their impact on student learning is an important component of analyzing the effectiveness of the activities and making further revisions. In using Mathematics Assessment Probes for this purpose, it is important to consider the conceptual understanding or mathematical "big ideas" that are addressed within the activities.

The following Image From Practice highlights how a teacher used the probe What's Your Addition Strategy? Fractions before and after implementing an instructional unit to assess an increase in students' fluency with multiple strategies.

Image From Practice:
What's Your Addition Strategy? Fractions

Since learning about probes from the school's mathematics specialist, I have replaced unit pretests with probes aligned to key concepts within the unit. Since our curriculum encourages student-invented algorithms and multiple strategies for operations with fractions, I used the What's Your Addition Strategy? probe to get a sense of the various strategies students were introduced to in prior grades. I was curious to see if students would be able to use this prior knowledge and extend the strategy for use with fractions so I gave the fraction variation prior to beginning instruction. I noticed some strategies, such as doubling/halving, seemed to be more intuitive than the others and that most students commented they did not know the common denominator strategy. As we moved through the unit, the students created a strategy bank, labeling various examples by the mathematics strategy used to solve the problem. At the end of the unit, I again gave the students the probe. As they finished, I gave each of them back their original responses to have them reflect on changes in their own thinking.

MOVING BEYOND
THE INDIVIDUAL CLASSROOM

The engine of improvement, growth, and renewal in a professional learning community is collective inquiry. The people in such a school are relentless in questioning the status quo, seeking new methods, testing those methods, and then reflecting on the results. (DuFour & Eaker, 1998)

Another important opportunity provided by using the probes is that of examining student work with other educators.

The most important aspect of this strategy is that teachers have access to, and then develop for themselves the ability to understand, the content students are struggling with and ways that they, the teachers, can help. Pedagogical content knowledge—that special province of excellent teachers—is absolutely necessary for teachers to maximize their learning as they examine and discuss what students demonstrate they know and do not know. (Loucks-Horsley et al., 2003, p. 183)

By providing a link to Curriculum Topic Study (Keeley & Rose, 2007) as well as to resources with additional research and instructional implications specific to the ideas of the probe, Mathematics Assessment Probes provide a means for a collaborative approach to examining student thinking and planning for improving instruction.

The following Image From Practice highlights how a teacher uses probes to address typical student misunderstandings with other mathematics teachers in the district.

Image From Practice: Professional Learning Communities

Our school schedule allows for a common hour of subject department meeting time once every 2 weeks. As department chair, I struggle with finding meaningful activities that shift the group from the discussion of school and classroom logistics to a focus on student learning. We now use 30 minutes of each bimonthly meeting to look at student work, generate possible solutions and next steps, and review a new set of teacher notes in preparation for giving students the next probe. The focus on using diagnostic tasks for the purpose of formative assessment changes the conversation about students' mathematical understanding in ways that collaboratively scoring student work doesn't lend itself to. Our discussions now center on what students conceptually and procedurally understand, further questions to ask, and instructional implications. Unlike our common assessments, we give the probes to students in various courses and at various grade levels, allowing all teachers to participate in the activity. These cross-course conversations are helping to create a more coherent program for our students, since many of our instructional implications include an agreement among the teachers on use of vocabulary and establishing common knowledge of what it means to have conceptual understanding.

SUMMARY

In *How Students Learn: Mathematics in the Classroom*, the National Research Council (2005) describes a use of assessment as follows:

> Assessments are a central feature of both a learner-centered and a knowledge-centered classroom. They permit the teacher to grasp students' preconceptions, which is critical to working with and building on those notions. (p. 16)

The purposes this chapter described for using Mathematics Assessment Probes represent the multiple ways the probes can support educators in "engaging students' preconceptions and building on existing knowledge" as well as developing an "assessment-centered classroom environment" (NRC, 2005).

3

Number and Operations Assessment Probes

Grade Span Bar Key

	Target for Instruction Depending on Local Standards
	Prerequisite Concept/Field Testing Indicates Student Difficulty

Number and Operation Probes		Grade Span Bars	
Question	**Probe**	**Grade 6–8**	**Grades 9–12**
Can students choose all correct values of various digits of a given decimal?	What Is the Value of the Digit? p. 33		
Do students correctly choose the various meanings of a/b?	What Is the Meaning of 2/3? p. 39		
Are students able to choose equivalent forms of a fraction?	Is It Equivalent? p. 45		
Can students use estimation to choose the closest benchmark to an addition problem involving fractions?	What's Your Estimate? p. 51		
Do students understand there are multiple methods of estimating the sum of three 3-digit numbers?	Is It an Estimate? p. 56		
Do students use the "canceling of zeros" shortcut appropriately?	Is It Simplified? p. 61		
Are students able to locate 1 million on a number line labeled from 0 to 1 billion?	Where Is One Million? p. 66		
Do students understand how various integer exponents affect the value of the numerical expression?	How Low Can You Go? p. 71		
When adding, can students apply and understand a variety of different strategies?	What's Your Addition Strategy? p. 76		
When subtracting, can students apply and understand a variety of different strategies?	What's Your Subtraction Strategy? p. 84		
When multiplying, can students apply and understand a variety of different strategies?	What's Your Multiplication Strategy? p. 92		
When dividing, can students apply and understand a variety of different strategies?	What's Your Division Strategy? p. 99		

WHAT IS THE VALUE OF THE DIGIT?

Circle all of the statements that are true for the number 2.13.

Explain your choices:

A. There is a 3 in the ones place.

B. There is a 2 in the ones place.

C. There are 21.3 tenths.

D. There are 13 tenths.

E. There is a 1 in the tenths place.

F. There is a 3 in the tenths place.

G. There are 21 hundredths.

H. There are 213 hundredths.

TEACHERS' NOTES:
WHAT IS THE VALUE OF THE DIGIT?

Grade Level for "What Is the Value of the Digit?"

6–8	9–12

Questioning for Student Understanding

Can students choose all correct values of various digits of a given decimal?

Uncovering Understandings

What Is the Value of the Digit? (Content Standard: Number and Operations)
Variation: *What Is the Value of the Digit?* Card Sort

Examining Student Work

The distracters may reveal lack of *procedural* and *conceptual understanding* of the place value positions in the base-ten number system as well as *conceptual understanding* of the value of individual digits in relationship to the represented number.

- *The correct answers are B, C, E, and H.* Students who choose B and E understand they can name the value of the place of digits within a number. By choosing C and H, these students also demonstrate a conceptual understanding of the relationship between the value of the places and the number represented by the specific combination of digits. **(See Student Responses 1 and 2)**

   Many students can accurately identify B and E but exclude choices C and H. These students demonstrate a procedural understanding of naming digits in specific places but lack conceptual understanding of the value of the digits in relationship to the represented number. **(See Student Response 3)**

- *Distracters A and F.* Students who choose A or F are demonstrating a *common error* related to the place value of the digits in a decimal. These students *overgeneralize* from their work with whole numbers by thinking the ones place is always the left-most number, or since the tens place is second from the left of the decimal point, the tenths place must be second from the right of the decimal point. **(See Student Response 4)**

- *Distracters D and G.* Students who choose D and/or G demonstrate the *common error* of considering only the numbers to the left of the identified place. This typically is related to a lack of conceptual understanding of the relationship of each digit to size of the number. **(See Student Response 5)**

Seeking Links to Cognitive Research

Elementary and middle school students may have limited ability with place value. Sowder (1992) reports that middle school students are able to identify the place values of the digits that appear in a number, but they cannot use the knowledge confidently in context.

> Upper elementary- and middle-school students often do not understand that decimal fractions represent concrete objects that can be measured by units, tenths of units, hundredths of units, and so on (Hiebert, 1992). (AAAS, 1993, p. 350)

> Other students have little understanding of the value represented by each of the digits of a decimal number or know the value of the number is the sum of the value of its digits. (AAAS, 1993, p. 350)

> Student errors suggest students interpret and treat multi-digit numbers as single-digit numbers placed adjacent to each other, rather than using place-value meanings for the digits in different positions. (Fuson, 1992, quoted in AAAS, 1993, p. 358)

> Students' understanding and ability to reason will grow as they represent fractions and decimals with physical materials and on number lines and as they learn to generate equivalent representations of fractions and decimals. By the middle grades, students should understand that numbers can be represented in various ways, so they see that $\frac{1}{4}$, 25%, and 0.25 are all different names for the same number. Students' knowledge about, and use of, decimals in the base-ten system should be very secure before high school. (NCTM, 2000, p. 33)

> Research has confirmed that a solid conceptual grounding in decimal numbers is difficult for students to achieve (Hiebert et al., 1991). The similarities between the symbol systems for decimals and whole numbers lead to a number of misconceptions and error types (Resnick et al., 1989). Grasping the proportional nature of decimals is particularly challenging. (NRC, 2005, p. 332)

> In their struggle to find meaning with decimal place value, students display a variety of difficulties, including language difficulties. They may say "tens" for "tenths" and "hundreds" for "hundredths" (Resnick et al., 1989). (NCTM, 1993b, p. 140)

Teaching Implications

To support a deeper understanding for students in secondary grades in regard to number and operations, the following are ideas and questions to consider in conjunction with the research.

Focus Through Instruction

- The foundation of students' work with decimal numbers must be an understanding of whole numbers and place value. In Grades 3–5, students should have learned to think of decimal numbers as a natural extension of the base-ten place-value system to represent quantities less than 1 or between two whole numbers. In Grades 6–8, they should also understand decimals as fractions whose denominators are powers of 10. The absence of a solid conceptual foundation can greatly hinder students.
- Representing numbers with various physical materials should be a major part of mathematics instruction in the elementary and middle grades.
- The study of rational numbers in the middle grades should build on students' encounters with fractions, decimals, and percentages in lower grades and in everyday life. For example, students can use fractions and decimals to report measurements, to compare survey responses from samples of unequal size, to express probabilities, to indicate scale factors for similarity, and to represent constant rate of change in a problem or slope in a graph of a linear function.
- Students can develop a deep understanding of rational numbers through experiences with a variety of models, such as fraction strips, number lines, 10×10 grids, area models, and objects. These models offer students concrete representations of abstract ideas and support students' meaningful use of representations and their flexible movement among them.
- A metacognitive approach to instruction helps students monitor their understanding and take control of their own learning. The complexity of rational numbers—the different meanings and representations, the challenges of comparing quantities across the very different representations, the unstated unit—means that students must be actively engaged in sensemaking.
- Use of the terminology "tenth-parts" and "hundredth-parts" can help students connect language and concepts. It might be helpful for students to think of decimal fractions as the composition of tenths, hundredths, and so on. For example, 0.374 could be described as 3 tenths plus 7 hundredths plus 4 thousandths. It is recommended that teachers be careful to use, and require students to use, meaningful language and avoid the use of the word "point" when referring to decimals.

Questions to Consider . . . *when working with students as they grapple with the idea of place value*

- Do students understand the role of the decimal point and the relationship among the digits in the ones, tenths, and hundredths place?
- Are students able to move beyond just naming digits in various places to the value of the digit in relationship to the number?
- Are students able to show various concrete representations of the number (e.g., using base-ten blocks or other visual representations)?

Teacher Sound Bite

"By far the most common response from my four classes of seventh-grade students was B and E. Although I was happy to see students accurately labeling the positions, I was disappointed with the lack of application of this knowledge to number of tenths or hundredths signified by the given number. I had to step back to whole numbers, giving students the experience of representing a number such as 137 in multiple ways first, with concrete materials and then using expanded notation. Students were then able to apply these techniques to decimals."

Additional References for Research and Teaching Implications

AAAS (1993), *Benchmarks for Science Literacy*, pp. 350 and 358–359.
NCTM (1993b), *Research Ideas for the Classroom: Middle Grades Mathematics*, pp. 137–156.
NCTM (2000), *Principles and Standards for School Mathematics*, pp. 32–36 and 214–221.
NCTM (2002), *Lessons Learned From Research*, pp. 143–150.
NRC (2005), *How Students Learn Mathematics in the Classroom*, pp. 309–343.

Curriculum Topic Study

What Is the Value of the Digit?

Related CTS Guide:
Place Value, p. 130

STUDENT RESPONSES TO "WHAT IS THE VALUE OF THE DIGIT?" PROBE

Sample Responses: B, C, E, and H

Student 1: For B and E, I learned the place value names and wrote them under each number in 2.13. For C and H, I looked at the place value name and moved the decimal to the number after the place it told me to and then checked the number.

Student 2: First I just used place value names and found only B and E to be correct. Then for C, since there is a 2 in the ones and a one in the tenths, it means 21 tenths because the ones column is 10 times the amount of the tenths column. The hundredth place means a tenth of a tenth so the three represent .3 tenths. I continued to use this idea to check for correct numbers and the other one was H.

Sample Response: B and E

Student 3: There is a 2 in the ones place, a 1 in the tenths place, and a 3 in the hundredths place. I went through each of the possible answers and found the ones that were correct.

Sample Response: Inclusion of A or F

Student 4: F because the three is in the second place in the decimal part of the number.

Sample Response: Inclusion of D and/or G

Student 5: D is chosen because in 2.13 there are 13 tenths. I just looked at the numbers after the decimal.

VARIATION: WHAT IS THE VALUE OF THE DIGIT? CARD SORT

Directions: Precut a set of cards for each student. Ask students to sort the cards into two piles.

Pile 1: Statements that are true for the number 2.13

Pile 2: Statements that are not true for the number 2.13

A. There is a 3 in the ones place.	B. There is a 2 in the ones place.
C. There are 21.3 tenths.	D. There are 13 tenths.
E. There is a 1 in the tenths place.	F. There is a 3 in the tenths place.
G. There are 21 hundredths.	H. There are 213 hundredths.

WHAT IS THE MEANING OF $^2/_3$?

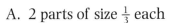

Probe
2

**For each statement, decide if it shows
a correct meaning of $^2/_3$.**

A. 2 parts of size $\frac{1}{3}$ each   Explain choice:

yes or no

B. 3 parts of size $\frac{1}{2}$ each   Explain choice:

yes or no

C. 3 divided by 2   Explain choice:

yes or no

D. 2 divided by 3   Explain choice:

yes or no

E. 2 compared to 3   Explain choice:

yes or no

F. 3 compared to 2   Explain choice:

yes or no

TEACHERS' NOTES:
WHAT IS THE MEANING OF ²/₃

Grade Level for "What is the Meaning of ²/₃?" Probe

6–8	9–12

*Q*uestioning for Student Understanding

Do students correctly choose the various meanings of a/b?

*U*ncovering Understandings

What Is the Meaning of ²/₃? (Content Standard: Number and Operation)
Variation: *What Is the Meaning of ²/₃?* Card Sort

*E*xamining Student Work

The distracters may reveal *common errors* in students' *conceptual under-standing* of fraction and the different meanings that a/b can have. Errors occur when students only think of a/b as part of a whole. They may have difficulty recognizing that a/b can also represent division or a ratio (which is a comparison of two numbers).

- *The correct answers are A, D, and E.* These responses demonstrate an understanding of the various meanings of a/b. Students who choose all three recognize that a/b can represent a part–whole relationship, a quotient or indicated division, and a ratio.
- *Students who answered only one or two of A, D, or E.* Students who choose only one or two of the three correct responses may lack an understanding of one of the meanings of a/b. For instance, they may not choose D because they fail to recognize that a/b can mean "a divided by b." **(See Student Responses 1 and 2)**
- *Students who answer B, C, or F.* Students who choose any or all of these may understand one or more of the meanings of a/b, but may fail to recognize that the numerator and denominator denote different parts of the relationship and cannot be interchanged.

*S*eeking Links to Cognitive Research

People—adults, students, even teachers—find the rational number system to be very difficult (Carpenter et al., 1980). This number system requires that students reformulate their concept of number in a major way. They must go beyond whole-number ideas, in which a number expresses a fixed quantity, to understand numbers that are expressed in relationship to other numbers. (NRC, 2005, p. 310)

Many students understand "a/b" as denoting a part–whole relationship, for example, that "$3/7$" means "three out of seven" (Brown, 1993). This understanding is unproblematic until they attempt to interpret "$7/3$." Students often will think, if not say aloud, "$7/3$ sort of doesn't make any sense. You can't have 7 out of 3" (Mack, 1993, p. 91; 1995). (NCTM, 2003, p. 95)

Kieren (1980) identified four basic ways in which rational numbers can be interpreted. The four, which he terms *subconstructs*, are as a measure, a quotient or indicated division, a ratio, and an operator. These four subconstructs have similar mathematical properties, but they have been shown to elicit different responses from students. Kieren recommended that all four subconstructs be present in a well-designed mathematics curriculum. (NCTM, 1993b, p. 120)

Students often have difficulty in recognizing that a/b can mean "a divided by b." One researcher reported that many children thought the answers to 3 divided by 4 and 4 divided by 3 were the same, while several children thought one of the answers was zero (Kerslake, 1986). But when these children were presented with the task of sharing three cakes with four people, almost all of the children were able to solve it correctly, with some children even connecting the fraction ¾ to the result. (NCTM, 1993b, p. 120)

One study found that the use of manipulative materials (including circular and rectangular pieces, colored chips, paper folding, number lines, and Cuisenaire rods) as well as pictures, symbols, and words was of vital importance in developing students' understanding of fraction concepts and operations (Behr et al., 1983). (NCTM, 1993b, p. 121)

By the end of 8th grade, students should know that the expression *a/b* can mean different things: *a* parts of size *1/b* each, *a* divided by *b*, or *a* compared to *b*. (AAAS, 1993, p. 213)

*T*eaching Implications

To support a deeper understanding for students in secondary grades in regard to number and operations, the following are ideas and questions to consider in conjunction with the research.

Focus Through Instruction

- Initially teach a concept using one subconstruct of fractions, such as part–whole. Once the concept is learned, introduce students to the same fraction in another subconstruct (e.g., as a ratio), having the students compare what is different and what is the same.
- Use manipulatives, real-world materials, verbal expression, and written expression (symbols) for each fraction concept taught, being careful not

to introduce symbols until students are familiar with the concepts and related vocabulary.

- Introduce a concept using one material, such as fraction circles. Once the concept is learned, students should examine the same concept with a different manipulative, such as colored chips, having the students compare what was different and what was the same.

Questions to Consider . . . *when working with students as they grapple with the various meanings of a/b*

- Are students able to move beyond whole-number ideas, in which a number expresses a fixed quantity, to understand that a fraction expresses a relationship between two numbers?
- Do students understand that a fraction can have different meanings? Or do they only see fractions as representing a part of a fixed whole (like a circle)?
- Do students demonstrate an understanding of what the parts of a fraction mean?

Teacher Sound Bite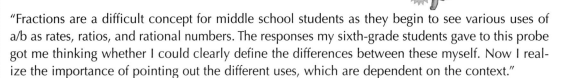

"Fractions are a difficult concept for middle school students as they begin to see various uses of a/b as rates, ratios, and rational numbers. The responses my sixth-grade students gave to this probe got me thinking whether I could clearly define the differences between these myself. Now I realize the importance of pointing out the different uses, which are dependent on the context."

Additional References for Research and Teaching Implications

Curriculum Topic Study
What Is the Meaning of ²⁄₃?
Related CTS Guides: Ratio and Proportion, p. 132; Rational Numbers, p. 133

AAAS (1993), *Benchmarks for Science Literacy*, pp. 213, 350, 358–359.

NCTM (1993b), *Research Ideas for the Classroom: Middle Grades Mathematics*, pp. 118–134.

NCTM (2000), *Principles and Standards for School Mathematics*, pp. 32–33.

NCTM (2003), *A Research Companion to Principles and Standards for School Mathematics*, pp. 95–110.

NRC (2005), *How Students Learn Mathematics in the Classroom*, pp. 309–343.

STUDENT RESPONSES TO "WHAT IS THE MEANING OF ²/₃?"

Sample Response: Yes to A and B only

Student 1: Fractions mean a part of something that's been divided up, like a circle or a pan of brownies. A and B both show that ²/₃ is part of something that's been divided up into either halves or thirds. It's the same thing.

Sample Response: Yes to A and E only

Student 2: All the other choices are wrong. B and F are messed up because the numbers are switched around. C and D don't work because of the division. There is no division sign in ²/₃.

VARIATION: **WHAT IS THE MEANING OF ²/₃? CARD SORT**

Directions: Precut a set of cards for each student. Ask students to sort the cards into two piles.

Pile 1: Correct statements

Pile 2: Incorrect statements

A. 2 parts of size $\frac{1}{3}$ each	B. 3 parts of size $\frac{1}{2}$ each
C. 3 divided by 2	D. 2 divided by 3
E. 2 compared to 3	F. 3 compared to 2

IS IT EQUIVALENT?

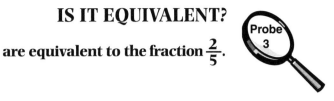

Circle all of the values below that are equivalent to the fraction $\frac{2}{5}$. Explain your choices.

A. $\frac{6}{15}$

B. 0.4

C. 25%

D. $\frac{12}{15}$

E. 2.5

F. $\frac{7}{10}$

G. 40%

H. 0.2

I. $\frac{20}{50}$

TEACHERS' NOTES: IS IT EQUIVALENT?

Grade Level for "Is It Equivalent?" Probe

6–8	9–12

*Q*uestioning for Student Understanding

Are students able to choose equivalent forms of a fraction?

*U*ncovering Understandings

Is It Equivalent? (Content Standard: Number and Operations)
Variation: *Is It Equivalent? Card Sort*

*E*xamine Student Work

The distracters may reveal *common misunderstandings* regarding fraction, decimal, and percentage conversions.

- *The correct answers are A, B, G, and I.* Students who include each of the correct responses are able to find equivalent fractions and understand the relationship between fractions, decimals, and percentages. **(See Student Responses 1 and 2)**
- *Distracter C.* Students who include C are simply converting $^2/_5$ by removing the fraction bar. **(See Student Response 3)**
- *Distracter D.* Students who include D often notice that 12 is divisible by 2 and 15 is divisible by 5, but fail to apply a common divisor when simplifying. **(See Student Response 4)**
- *Distracter E.* Students who include E divide 5 by 2 or replace the fraction bar with a decimal point. **(See Student Responses 5 and 6)**
- *Distracter F.* Students who include F typically are comparing fractions by using the difference between the denominator and the numerator. **(See Student Response 7)**
- *Distracter H.* Students include H for a wide variety of reasons, from miscalculations to disregarding the numerator. **(See Student Response 8)**

*S*eeking Links to Cognitive Research

Upper elementary- and middle-school students may exhibit limited understanding of the meaning of fractional number (Kieren, 1992). For example, many 7th graders do not recognize that $5^1/_4$ is the same as $5 + ^1/_4$ (Kouba et al., 1988). In addition, elementary-school students may have difficulties perceiving a fraction as a single quantity (Sowder, 1988), but rather see it as a pair of whole numbers. An intuitive basis for developing the concept of fractional number is provided by partitioning (Kieren, 1992) and by seeing fractions as multiples of basic units—for example, ¾ is ¼ and ¼ and ¼ rather than 3 of 4 parts (Behr et al., 1983). (AAAS, 1993, p. 350)

Of all the ways in which rational numbers can be interpreted and used, the most basic is the simplest—rational numbers are numbers. The fact is so fundamental that [it] is easily overlooked. A rational number like ¾ is a single entity just as the number 5 is a single entity. Each rational number holds a unique place (or is a unique length) on the number line. Further, the way common fractions are written (e.g., ¾) does not help students see a rational number as a distinct number. Research has verified what many teachers have observed, that students continue to use properties they learned from operating with whole numbers even though many whole-number properties do not apply to rational numbers. With common fractions, for example, students may reason that $^1/_8$ is larger than $^1/_7$ because 8 is larger than 7. Or they may believe that $^3/_4$ equals $^4/_5$ because in both fractions, the difference between numerator and denominator is 1. (NRC, 2001, p. 235)

Lower middle-school students may have difficulties understanding the relationship between fractions and decimal numbers (Markovits & Sowder, 1991). They may think that fractions and decimals can occur together in a single expression, like 0.5 + ½, or they might believe that they must not change from one representation to the other (from ½ to 0.5 and back) within a given problem. Instruction that focuses on the meaning of fractions and decimals forms a basis on which to build a good understanding of the relationship between fractions and decimals. Instruction that merely shows how to translate between the two forms does not provide a conceptual base for understanding the relationship (Markovits & Sowder, 1991). (AAAS, 1993, p. 359)

Kieren (1980) identified four basic ways in which rational numbers can be interpreted. The four, which he terms *subconstructs*, are as a measure, a quotient or indicated division, a ratio, and an operator. The measure subconstruct involves measuring the area of a region by partitioning it and covering it with appropriately sized units (e.g., when ¾ of a circle is shaded). The quotient subconstruct refers to using rational numbers as solutions to a division situation. For example, a $^2/_8$ is the result of 2 objects shared by 3 people. A rational number is a ratio. For example, the fraction ¼ can describe the ratio of one can of orange juice concentrate to four cans of water. A rational number also can be an operator or a mapping. For example, a ¼ operator describes the relationship of filling packages of four cookies each; there are one-fourth as many packages as cookies. (NCTM, 1993b, p. 120)

Teaching Implications

To support a deeper understanding for students in secondary grades in regards to number and operations the following are ideas and questions to consider in conjunction with the research.

Focus Through Instruction

- Teachers should use a variety of models and representations such as fraction strips, number lines, grid paper, area models (rectangles and circles), and symbolic representations.
- By solving problems in contexts, students can consider how best to model a situation.
- Since the symbolic representations of rational numbers have meaning, connections between fractions and decimals and fractions and percentages should be explicit. Decimals, fractional base-ten equivalents making use of place value, and percentages are fractional relationships based on one hundred parts to a whole.
- Instruction should be built on students' intuitive ideas about sharing, partitioning, and measuring.
- A solid conceptual understanding of rational numbers is important for students to be able to compare, convert, and operate with fractions and decimals.

Questions to Consider . . . *when working with students as they grapple with the concepts of a fraction*

- Are students able to represent fractions in a variety of ways, including use of area and linear models, as parts of sets, and symbolically?
- Do students understand the relationship between fractions, decimals, and percentages?
- Do students understand that the numerator and denominator of a fraction are related by multiplication and division rather than addition and subtraction?

Teacher Sound Bite

"I was pleasantly surprised at the variety of models and reasoning students used to consider equivalence. By using a think-pair-share method, the students had a lively debate, and I now have a better grasp on what my students know, what they have been exposed to, and what they need more instruction on."

Additional References for
Research and Teaching Implications

AAAS (1993), *Benchmarks for Science Literacy*, pp. 350, 358–359.

NCTM (1993b), *Research Ideas for the Classroom: Middle Grades Mathematics*, pp. 118–134.

NRC (2001), *Adding It Up: Helping Children Learn Mathematics*, p. 235.

Curriculum Topic Study

Is It Equivalent?

Related CTS Guide:
Fractions, Decimals, and
Percentages, p. 122

STUDENT RESPONSES
TO "IS IT EQUIVALENT?"

Sample Responses: A, B, G, and J

Student 1: A is right since 2 * 3 = 6 and 5 * 3 = 15 so $\frac{2}{5}$ is the same as $\frac{6}{15}$.

2 divided by 5 is .4 (think like 5 into 20 is 4) so B is right. .4 is 40% so G is right.

Student 2: For decimals you need out of 10 and for percents out of 100 so change $\frac{2}{5}$ to $\frac{4}{10}$ and that gives you the only decimal. Change $\frac{2}{5}$ to $\frac{40}{100}$ and that gives you the only percent. For the other fraction answer you have to reduce to see if you get $\frac{2}{5}$.

Sample Response: C

Student 3: 2/5 is the same as 25%, the / means %.

Sample Response: D

Student 4: 12 can be reduced to 2 and 15 can be reduced to 5.

Sample Responses: E

Student 5: 2.5 is the same as 2/5 since you divide bottom by top.

Student 6: Used a pizza and divided into 5 parts and colored two so $\frac{2}{5}$ is 2.5.

Sample Response: F

Student 7: 2/5 and 7/10 are both $\frac{1}{3}$ so they are the same.

Sample Response: H

Student 8: 2/5 is 20 so I circled everything with a 20 and I know .2 is the same as .20.

VARIATION: IS IT EQUIVALENT? CARD SORT

Directions: Precut a set of cards for each student. Ask students to sort the cards into two piles.

Pile 1: Values that are equivalent to ²/₅

Pile 2: Values that are not equivalent to ²/₅

A. $\dfrac{6}{15}$	B. 0.4
C. 25%	D. $\dfrac{12}{15}$
E. 2.5	F. $\dfrac{7}{10}$
G. 40%	H. 0.2
I. $\dfrac{20}{50}$	

WHAT'S YOUR ESTIMATE?

Use <u>mental math</u> to answer the following question:

Circle the best estimate:

$$\frac{12}{13} + \frac{7}{8}$$

A. 1

B. 2

C. 19

D. 21

Explain your reasoning:

TEACHERS' NOTES: WHAT'S YOUR ESTIMATE?

Grade Level for "What's Your Estimate?" Probe

6–8	9–12

Questioning for Student Understanding

Can students use estimation to choose the closest benchmark to an addition problem involving fractions?

Uncovering Understandings

What's Your Estimate? (Content Standard: Number and Operations)

Examine Student Work

The distracters may reveal *common misunderstandings* regarding fractions such as lack of *conceptual* understanding of the size of a fraction and common errors related to inaccurate use of procedures when adding fractions.

- *The correct answer is B.* Students who choose B indicate the size of both of the fractions as being close to 1, resulting in an estimated sum of 2. **(See Student Responses 1 and 2)**
- *Distracter A.* Students who choose A typically add the numerators, then the denominators, and use the result of $^{19}/_{21}$ to determine their choice of an estimate. **(See Student Responses 3 and 4)**
- *Distracter C.* Students who choose C typically add the numerators, 12 and 7, disregarding the denominators altogether. **(See Student Response 5)**
- *Distracter D.* Students who choose D typically add the denominators, 13 and 8, disregarding the numerators altogether. **(See Student Responses 6 and 7)**

Seeking Links to Cognitive Research

Making judgments about answers is as much a part of computation as the calculation itself. Students need to develop estimation skills and the habit of checking answers against reality. (AAAS, 1993, p. 288)

In Grades 3 through 5, students can learn to compare fractions to familiar benchmarks such as $^{1}/_{2}$. And, as their number sense develops, students should be able to reason about numbers by, for instance, explaining that $^{1}/_{2} + ^{3}/_{8}$ must be less than 1 because each addend is less than or equal to $^{1}/_{2}$. (NCTM, 2000, p. 33)

By Grades 6–8, students should become fluent in computing with rational numbers in fraction and decimal form. When asked to estimate $^{12}/_{13} + {}^{7}/_{8}$, only 24% of thirteen-year-old students in a national assessment said the answer was close to 2 (Carpenter et al., 1981). Most said it was close to 1, 19, or 21, all of which reflect common computational errors in adding fractions and suggest a lack of understanding of the operation being carried out. (NCTM, 2000, p. 35)

Fewer than one-third of the thirteen-year-old U.S. students tested in the National Assessment of Educational Progress (NAEP) in 1988 correctly chose the largest number from $^{3}/_{4}$, $^{9}/_{16}$, $^{5}/_{8}$, and $^{2}/_{3}$ (Kouba, Carpenter, & Swafford, 1989). (NCTM, 2000, p. 216)

Elementary- and middle-school students make several errors when they operate on decimals and fractions (Benander & Clement, 1985; Kouba et al., 1988; Peck & Jencks, 1981; Wearne & Hiebert, 1988). These errors are due in part to the fact that students lack essential concepts about decimals and fractions and have memorized procedures that they apply incorrectly. (AAAS, 1993, pp. 358–359)

Upper elementary- and middle-school students taught traditionally cannot compare fractions successfully (Sowder, 1988). Students' difficulties here indicate they do not perceive a fraction as a single quantity. Instead, they treat the numerator and denominator separately as a pair of whole numbers. (AAAS, 1993, p. 359)

*T*eaching Implications

To support a deeper understanding for students in secondary grades in regards to number and operations the following are ideas and questions to consider in conjunction with the research.

Focus Through Instruction

- Visual images of fractions as fraction strips should help many students think flexibly in comparing fractions. Students may also be helped by thinking about the relative locations of fractions on a number line.
- Teachers can help students add and subtract fractions correctly by helping them develop meanings for numerator and denominator, and equivalence, and by encouraging them to use benchmarks and estimation.
- In the lower grades, students should have had experiences in comparing fractions between 0 and 1 in relation to such benchmarks as 0, ¼, ½, ¾, and 1. In the middle grades, students should extend this experience to tasks in which they order and compare fractions, which many students find difficult.
- Repeated experience with computations in meaningful contexts will foster the higher-level skill of judging when computations can most appropriately be made in one's head or on paper.

- Make sure that students have lots of practice estimating—this happens if estimation is routinely treated as a standard part of problem solving.
- When students are frequently called upon to explain how they intend to calculate an answer before carrying it out, they find that making step-by-step estimations is not hard. They also gain confidence in their ability to figure out ahead of time approximately what the answer will be—bigger than this and smaller than that.
- Students should have experiences that help them learn to choose among mental computation, paper-and-pencil strategies, estimation, and calculator use. The particular context, the questions, and the numbers involved all play roles in those choices.

Questions to Consider . . . *when working with students as they grapple with concepts related to fractions*

- Can students accurately judge the size of fractions in relation to common benchmarks such as $1/3$, $1/4$, $1/2$, $3/4$, and so on?
- Can students use various models to represent fractions, including fraction strips, area models, and sets of objects?
- Can students explain how the size of the numerator and denominator of a fraction helps determine its size?
- Do students understand they need common denominators when adding fractions?

Teacher Sound Bite

"I expected my eighth graders to have no problem solving this correctly but was surprised when about $1/3$ of them answered incorrectly. I followed up by giving these students three sets of two fractions to add, and the majority of these students applied the correct procedure, finding common denominators, creating equivalent fractions, and adding the numerators. They seemed to know the process for adding fractions but didn't have a concept of the size of many of the fractions in order to make accurate estimates even after finding the answer to the problem."

Additional References for Research and Teaching Implications

Curriculum Topic Study
What's Your Estimate?
Related CTS Guide: Fractions, p. 121

AAAS (1990), *Science for All Americans*, pp. 187–191.

AAAS (1993), *Benchmarks for Science Literacy*, pp. 288–291, 358–359.

AAAS (2001), *Atlas of Science Literacy*, p. 119.

NCTM (2000), *Principles and Standards for School Mathematics*, pp. 32–36, 214–221.

NCTM (2003), *A Research Companion to Principles and Standards for School Mathematics*, pp. 95–110.

STUDENT RESPONSES
TO "WHAT'S YOUR ESTIMATE?"

Sample Responses: B

Student 1: $^{12}/_{13}$ is almost 1 and $^{7}/_{8}$ is almost 1 so the answer is 2.

Student 2: Each is 1 part off from being a whole.

Sample Responses: A

Student 3: If you added them diagonally and divided it, it would equal 1.

Student 4: $^{12}/_{13} + ^{19}/_{21} = ^{19}/_{21}$ and $^{19}/_{21}$ is close to 1.

Sample Response: C

Student 5: $^{12}/_{13} + ^{19}/_{21} = ^{19}/_{21}$ and the top number is 19.

Sample Responses: D

Student 6: Because when you add them together the denominator is 21.

Student 7: Because D is the largest answer and it has to be the largest.

IS IT AN ESTIMATE?

Circle each example that shows a method of estimating $456 + 234 + 353$.

In each box, explain why you did or did not circle the example.

(1) Add the numbers
$$456$$
$$234$$
$$+ 353$$
$$400 + 200 + 300 = 900$$
$$50 + 30 + 50 = 130$$
$$6 + 4 + 3 = 13$$

<u>*Estimate = 1043*</u>

(2) Add the numbers
$456 + 234 + 353 = 1043$
Round the answer.

<u>*Estimate = 1000*</u>

(3) Round each to nearest
hundred: $500 + 200 + 400$
Add the numbers
$500 + 200 + 400 = 1100$

<u>*Estimate = 1100*</u>

(4) Use benchmarks of 25.
$450 + 225 + 350$
$400 + 300 + 200 + 125 = 1025$

<u>*Estimate = 1025*</u>

TEACHERS' NOTES: IS IT AN ESTIMATE?

Grade Level for "Is It an Estimate?" Probe

6–8	9–12

*Q*uestioning for Student Understanding

Do students understand there are multiple methods of estimating the sum of three 3-digit numbers?

*U*ncovering Understandings

Is It an Estimate? (Content Standard: Number and Operations)

*E*xamining Student Work

Student answers may reveal lack of conceptual understanding regarding methods of estimation. Responses may reveal a common *misunderstanding* that there is only one correct way to estimate and common *procedural errors* such as estimation is rounding an answer to a computation problem.

- *Method 1:* Students who choose this method view estimation as solving a problem or solving a problem in an alternative way. **(See Student Responses 1 and 2)**
- *Method 2:* Students who choose this method as an example view estimation and rounding as the same procedure. **(See Student Responses 3 and 4)**
- *Method 3:* Student who choose this method are demonstrating an understanding of estimation but may not realize that how precise an estimate is needed depends on the context of the situation. This partial understanding can be indicated by responses such as "this is an estimate but not as good as rounding to the nearest 10's." **(See Student Responses 5 and 6)**
- *Method 4:* Students who choose this method along with #3 are demonstrating an understanding of estimation. Those who do not are often associating estimation only with rounding to the nearest 10 or 100. **(See Student Responses 7 and 8)**

*S*eeking Links to Cognitive Research

In Grades 3–5, all students should develop and use strategies to estimate the results of whole-number computations and to judge the reasonableness of such results. (NCTM, 2000, p. 148)

Middle school and even high school students may have limited understanding about the nature and purpose of estimation. They often think it is inferior to exact computation and equate it with guessing (Sowder, 1992b), so that they do not believe estimation is useful (Sowder & Wheeler, 1989). (AAAS, 1993, p. 350)

Researchers attempting to identify and characterize the computational processes used by good estimators found three key processes. The first was called reformulation and referred to changing the numbers to other numbers that were easier to manage mentally. A second process was called translation and referred to changing the structure of the problem so that the operations could be more easily carried out mentally. The third process used was compensation where adjustments were made both during and after estimating. (NCTM, 1993b, pp. 43–44)

Good estimators have a good grasp of basic facts, place value, and arithmetic operations; are skilled at mental computation; [and] are self-confident, tolerant of error, and flexible in their use of strategies. (NCTM, 1993b, p. 44)

Estimation serves as an important companion to computation. However, being able to compute exact answers does not automatically lead to an ability to estimate or judge the reasonableness of answers, as Reys and Yang (1998) found in their work with sixth and eighth graders. (NCTM, 2000, pp. 155–156)

*T*eaching Implications

To support a deeper understanding for students in secondary grades in regard to number and operations, the following are ideas and questions to consider in conjunction with the research.

Focus Through Instruction

- Estimation skills can be learned, but only if teachers make sure that students have lots of practice. This happens if estimation is routinely treated as a standard part of problem solving.
- When students are frequently called upon to explain how they intend to calculate an answer before carrying it out, they find that making step-by-step estimations is not hard and contributes to thinking through the problem at hand.
- Instructional attention and frequent modeling by the teacher can help students develop a range of computational estimation strategies including flexible rounding, the use of benchmarks, and front-end strategies.
- As with exact computation, sharing estimation strategies allows students access to others' thinking and provides many opportunities for rich class discussions.

- For students to become really skilled at estimation, it has to be incorporated into their regular instruction over several years.
- Teachers must demonstrate the value of estimation and, paradoxically, help students become more tolerant of error. It is difficult to become skilled at a process one does not understand or believe is useful.

Questions to Consider . . . *when working with students as they grapple with the process of estimation*

- Are students using various methods of estimating to check reasonableness of computation results?
- Do students view estimation as more than just guessing?
- Do students understand when to overestimate versus underestimate?
- Do students have number sense regarding types of numbers they are estimating with?

Teacher Sound Bite

"I never really stopped to think about how students may view estimation. About one month before giving the probe, we were working with repeating decimals requiring students to round their answers. During our class discussion on the methods in the probe, a student brought out the fact that in some cases we do round after getting an answer, referring back to the repeating decimal lesson. I had groups of students brainstorm the difference between the two situations. The probe definitely helped me think about how I teach estimation and how I can change my instruction so that the students can take more ownership in developing various strategies."

Additional References for Research and Teaching Implications

AAAS (1989), *Science for All Americans*, pp. 190–191.
AAAS (1993), *Benchmarks for Science Literacy*, pp. 288–299 and 350.
NCTM (1993b), *Research Ideas for the Classroom: Middle Grades Mathematics*, pp. 41–46.
NCTM (2000), *Principles and Standards for School Mathematics*, pp. 32–36.

Curriculum Topic Study
Is It an Estimate?
Related CTS Guides: Estimation, p. 195

STUDENT RESPONSES TO "IS IT AN ESTIMATE?"

Sample Responses: Method 1

Student 1: All this shows is adding all the numbers. The estimate is supposed to be close but not exact.

Student 2: Since sometimes an estimate ends up being the correct number, I think you can say this is an estimate.

Sample Responses: Method 2

Student 3: This is how I like to estimate cuz then you no it is right [sic].

Student 4: Rounding is estimating.

Sample Responses: Method 3

Student 5: [Method] 3 is the most common way to estimate and gives you a good answer.

Student 6: That's ok but sometimes you have to round to tens not hundreds.

Sample Responses: Method 4

Student 7: The answer 1025 is close to 1043 so it's a good way.

Student 8: I was taught rounding but think this works too because it just uses easier numbers that are close to the real numbers.

IS IT SIMPLIFIED?

Circle the examples showing an appropriate use of the shortcut of "canceling digits" to simplify a fraction.

(A)

$$\frac{5\cancel{0}}{7\cancel{0}} = \frac{5}{7}$$

(B)

$$\frac{5\cancel{0}1}{7\cancel{0}2} = \frac{51}{72}$$

(C)

$$\frac{4\cancel{2}}{7\cancel{2}} = \frac{4}{7}$$

(D)

$$\frac{52\cancel{0}}{7\cancel{0}5} = \frac{52}{75}$$

(E)

$$\frac{7\cancel{5}}{1\cancel{5}0} = \frac{7}{10}$$

(F)

$$\frac{1\cancel{00}}{70\cancel{00}} = \frac{1}{70}$$

How did you decide which one(s) to circle?

TEACHERS' NOTES: IS IT SIMPLIFIED?

Grade Level for "Is It Simplified" Probe

6–8	9–12

*Q*uestioning for Student Understanding

Do students use the "canceling of zeros" shortcut appropriately?

*U*ncovering Understandings

Is It Simplified? (Content Standard: Number and Operations)
Possible adaptations/variations to the probe: *Is It Simplified? Canceling Algebraic Symbols*

*E*xamining Student Work

The distracters may reveal lack of *conceptual understanding* of the use of the common shortcut of "canceling" the zeros to simplify a fraction. Often, student lack of understanding of rational numbers hinders the ability to justify by comparing in cases of incorrect canceling of digits.

- *The correct answers are A and F.* Students who choose only A and F are correctly applying the canceling zeros rule as a specific case by showing understanding of dividing the numerator and denominator by a common factor, which in these special cases are a multiple of 10. **(See Student Response 1)**
- *Distracter B.* Students who choose B tend to view zero as "only" a place holder, and although they often recognize the need for the zeros to be in the same position in both numbers, there is a lack of understanding of the need for the numbers to also be multiples of 10. **(See Student Response 2)**
- *Distracter C.* Students who choose C *overgeneralize* the rule from zeros to include other digits, showing lack of conceptual understanding of why the rule is a special case for use with multiples of 10. **(See Student Response 3)**
- *Distracter D.* Students who choose D *overgeneralize* the rule to situations where both the numerator and denominator contain a zero, regardless of the place in which the zero is located. Typically, these students are incorrectly applying a procedure with no attempt at justifying by comparing the resulting fraction to the original **(See Student Response 4)**
- *Distracter E.* Students who choose E *overgeneralize* the rule to situations where both the numerator and denominator contain the digit, regardless of the place in which the digit is located. Typically, these students are incorrectly applying a procedure, paying no attention to making sense of the results. **(See Student Response 5)**

Seeking Links to Cognitive Research

Researchers reported that "children are going through the motions of operations with fractions, but they have not been exposed to the kinds of experiences that could provide them with necessary understandings" (Peck & Jencks, 1981). (NCTM, 1993b, p. 130)

The role of zero as a placeholder in the symbolic representation of number is frequently documented as problematic for children learning to read and write numbers in conventional formats. (Wheeler & Feghali, 1983, p. 147)

Care must be taken in sequencing the development of the number names and the number symbols to allow an appreciation of the lack of particular units and the use of zero to signify that there is "none of that place" (Booker et al., 1997). (Anthony & Walshaw, 2004, pp. 38, 41)

Teaching Implications

To support a deeper understanding for students in secondary grades in regard to number and operations, the following are ideas and questions to consider in conjunction with the research.

Focus Through Instruction

- Provide instruction that is concrete and process oriented rather than abstract and procedure oriented.
- Help students generalize the symbolic algorithm from their experiences with manipulatives.
- True/false number sentences provide an ideal context in which children can begin to articulate mathematical properties involving operations with zero. Exploration of such statements as $^{50}/_{70} = {}^5/_7$ and $^{502}/_{702} = {}^{52}/_{72}$ gives students opportunities to articulate and examine these ideas.
- Encourage students to simplify by watching for common factors in the numerator and denominator equal to 1. For example, $^{42}/_{72} = (2 \times 3 \times 7)/(2 \times 2 \times 2 \times 3 \times 3)$. One factor of 2×3 in both the numerator and denominator equals 1 and so can be canceled. This technique will be particularly useful in later algebraic work with factoring.

Questions to Consider . . . *when working with students as they grapple with ideas related to the concept of fraction*

- Do students understand simplifying as dividing by a common factor?
- Are students able to compare fractions?
- Are students developing their own generalized rules based on conceptual understanding and pattern recognition?
- Are students able to justify appropriate use of the generated rule?
- When giving explanations such as canceling the zeros or moving the decimal point, can students answer "when and why does that procedure result in a correct solution"?

Teacher Sound Bite

"I have always taught shortcuts in my math classes and am careful to explain the mathematics behind the process. Year after year, I have students who forget the shortcut completely or make a mistake somewhere in the step-by-step process. Talking with other math teachers about student solutions to this probe has helped me consider the importance of students developing their own idea of a shortcut based on a lot of experience. I now try to recognize when a student is ready for a simpler procedural approach and encourage him or her to explore whether the process will work for all cases. Not all students are ready for shortcuts at the same time, and it is my job to figure out how to move all students toward the abstract without just teaching the procedure to the whole class."

Additional References for
Research and Teaching Implications

Curriculum Topic Study

Is It Simplified?

Related CTS Guide:
Fractions, p. 121

Anthony, G. J., & Walshaw, M. A. (2004), Zero: A "None" Number? *Teaching Children Mathematics, 11*(1), pp. 38–42.
Bay Area Mathematics Task Force (1999), *A Mathematics Source Book for Elementary and Middle School Teachers*, pp. 59–70.
NCTM (1993b), *Research Ideas for the Classroom: Middle Grades Mathematics*, pp. 118–134.

STUDENT RESPONSES
TO "IS IT SIMPLIFIED?"

Sample Response: A and F

Student 1: I chose A and F because in Example A, both numbers were divided by 10 and in F, both numbers were divided by 100. I know this because the zeros always have to be to the far right of the number and this only works for zeros, not other numbers.

Sample Responses: Inclusion of B

Student 2: B is one because zeros are like placeholders meaning there are no tens in either number. It makes sense since 501 is 1 more than 500 and 702 is 2 more than 700. Also 51 is 1 more than 50 and 72 is 2 more than 70.

Sample Response: Inclusion of C

Student 3: C is true because I checked it by $72 - 42 = 30$ and $7 - 3 = 4$. $^{42}/_{72}$ is 10 times more than $^{4}/_{7}$.

Sample Response: Inclusion of D

Student 4: D is appropriate cuz both numbers have a zero that can be eliminated.

Sample Response: Inclusion of D

Student 4: All of them are right since I can get rid of any of the numbers that have the same numbers in the top and bottom.

IS IT SIMPLIFIED? ALGEBRAIC VARIATION

Probe 6a

Circle the examples showing an appropriate use of "canceling digits" to simplify an expression.

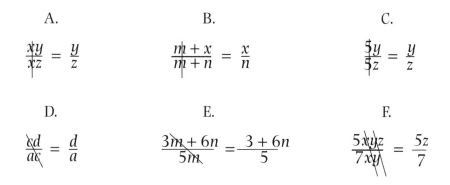

A.

$$\frac{\cancel{x}y}{\cancel{x}z} = \frac{y}{z}$$

B.

$$\frac{\cancel{m} + x}{\cancel{m} + n} = \frac{x}{n}$$

C.

$$\frac{\cancel{5}y}{\cancel{5}z} = \frac{y}{z}$$

D.

$$\frac{\cancel{c}d}{a\cancel{c}} = \frac{d}{a}$$

E.

$$\frac{3\cancel{m} + 6n}{5\cancel{m}} = \frac{3 + 6n}{5}$$

F.

$$\frac{5\cancel{xy}z}{7\cancel{xy}} = \frac{5z}{7}$$

How did you decide which one(s) to circle?

WHERE IS ONE MILLION?

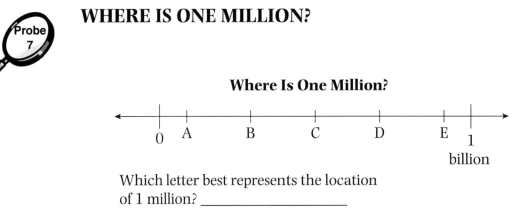

Where Is One Million?

Which letter best represents the location
of 1 million? _____

Why did you choose this location?

TEACHERS' NOTES: WHERE IS ONE MILLION?

Grade Level for "Where Is One Million?"

6–8	9–12

Questioning for Student Understanding

Are students able to locate 1 million on a number line labeled from 0 to 1 billion?

Uncovering Understandings

Where Is One Million? (Content Standard: Number and Operations)
Possible adaptations/variations to the probe: *Where Is 10,000?*

Examining Student Work

The distracters may reveal *common misunderstandings* regarding large numbers such as a lack of *conceptual understanding* of the magnitude of 1 million in relationship to 1 billion and the lack of ability to transfer understanding of the relationship of the numbers to placement on a number line.

- *The correct answer is A.* One million is $1/1000$ of a billion, which on the number line represented on the probe is very close to 0. **(See Student Responses 1 and 2)**
- *Distracter B.* Students who choose B typically understand that 1 million would be less than halfway across the number line, but lack the *conceptual understanding* to incorrectly choose A instead of B. **(See Student Responses 3 and 4)**
- *Distracter C.* Students who choose C exhibit the *common error* that 1 million is "halfway" to 1 billion. Often, students understand that 1 million is not half of a billion but do not transfer this understanding to the placement of numbers on a number line. **(See Student Responses 5 and 6)**
- *Distracter D.* Students who choose D lack *conceptual understanding* of the magnitude of number and the idea of scale on a number line. These students typically begin to label each of the intervals, with no concern for the lack of equivalent intervals. **(See Student Responses 7 and 8)**
- *Distracter E.* Students who choose D lack *conceptual understanding* of the magnitude of number and the idea of scale on a number line. These students typically label each of the intervals as a power of 10 (i.e., A is 10, B is 100, C is 10,000, D is 100,000) with no concern for the lack of equivalent intervals. **(See Student Responses 9 and 10)**

Seeking Links to Cognitive Research

The range of numbers that people can grasp increases with age. It has been argued that people really can't comprehend a range of more than about 1,000 to 1 at any one moment. A million becomes meaningful, as a thousand thousands, once a thousand becomes comprehensible. (AAAS, 1993, p. 276)

By the end of the 12th grade, students should be able to recall immediately the relations among 10, 100, 1000, 1 million, and 1 billion. (AAAS, 1993, p. 291)

In Grades 9–12, all students should develop a deeper understanding of very large and very small numbers and of various representations of them. (NCTM, 2000, p. 290)

Numbers acquire meaning for students when they recognize that each number refers to a particular quantity, and when they realize that numbers provide a means of describing quantity more precisely than is possible using everyday language. To help children construct this understanding, it is crucial to introduce numbers to children in the context of quantity representations that will give these numbers meaning. (NRC, 2005, p. 280)

Teaching Implications

To support a deeper understanding for students in secondary grades in regards to number and operations the following are ideas and questions to consider in conjunction with the research.

Focus Through Instruction

- Students should become increasingly facile in dealing with very large and very small numbers. Such numbers occur frequently in the sciences and economics. For example, as citizens, students will need to grasp the difference between $1 billion, the cost of a moderate-sized government project, and $1 trillion, a significant part of the national budget.
- A number line in the classroom can be transformed with the use of a brightly colored rope that stretches the length of the room. Originally an approach to help young children order numbers from 1 to 10, this "living number line" can be adapted for middle and high school students. The scope of the activity can be expanded to include exploration of very large numbers. Students are eventually able to see, stretched out in front of them, the relationships between numbers such as 1 million and 1 billion.
- Activities should expose children to the ways in which large numbers are represented and talked about in developed societies.
- Activities should provide visual and spatial analogs of number representations that students can actively explore in a hands-on fashion.

Questions to Consider . . . *when working with students as they grapple with the magnitude of numbers*

- Do students consider the relationship between the numbers and accurately transfer this to placement on the number line?
- Are students able to accurately place numbers given a nonzero starting point?
- Are student correctly able to label a number line?

Teacher Sound Bite

"Only a few of my students answered correctly with appropriate explanations. Some of the students felt that they must label each of the letters on the number line with a power of 10 and put a million somewhere chronologically. Others were thrown off by the spacing of the letters, and some had reasons that made no sense at all. The next day I asked the students to tell me how many millions are in 1 billion, and the majority of students could answer this correctly. I was surprised that while most of them know this, they could not apply it when using the probe. Although students might learn that a billion is one thousand times larger than a million, that concept is meaningless without somehow making the magnitude of these numbers more real to them."

Additional References for Research and Teaching Implications

AAAS (1993), *Benchmarks for Science Literacy*, pp. 276–279.

Bay, J. (2001), Developing Number Sense on the Number Line, *Mathematics Teaching in the Middle School*, 6(8), pp. 448–451.

NCTM (2000), *Principles and Standards for School Mathematics*, pp. 290–291.

NRC (2005), *How Students Learn: Mathematics in the Classroom*, pp. 279–283.

Curriculum Topic Study
Where Is One Million?
Related CTS Guide: Large and Small Numbers, p. 124

STUDENT RESPONSES TO "WHERE IS ONE MILLION?"

Sample Responses: A

Student 1: C is half of a billion, 1,000,000,000/2 is 500 million.

B is half of 500 million, 500 million/2 is 250 million.

A is the closet choice to one million.

Student 2: I chose A considering there are one thousand millions in one billion. It has to be close to 0 since the line is pretty short.

Sample Responses: B

Student 3: I thought that it wasn't C, D, or E, so it had to be A or B. I chose B.

Student 4: Because it wouldn't be towards the beginning or the end.

Sample Responses: C

Student 5: Because it is half and 1 million is half of 1 billion.

Student 6: If you start at zero and go up by 500,000, you should end up at around letter C for 1 million.

Sample Responses: D

Student 7: 1 million has 6 zeros and 1 billion has 9, $6/9 = 2/3$ and D is closest to $2/3$ way.

Student 8: Because it is close to the billions place and you could count by 10, 100, 1000, 10000 . . .

Sample Responses: E

Student 9: 1 million is close to 1 billion.

Student 10: I labeled the number line 100, 1000, 10000, 1000000 until I got to 1 million.

HOW LOW CAN YOU GO?

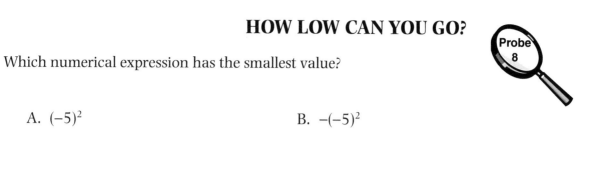

Which numerical expression has the smallest value?

A. $(-5)^2$

B. $-(-5)^2$

C. 5^2

D. 5^{-2}

Explain your answer:

TEACHERS' NOTES: HOW LOW CAN YOU GO?

Grade Level for "How Low Can You Go?" Probe

6–8	9–12

Questioning for Student Understanding

Do students understand how various integers and exponents affect the value of the numerical expression?

Uncovering Understandings

How Low Can You Go? (Content Standard: Number and Operations)
Variation: *How Low Can You Go?*

Examining Student Work

The distracters may reveal *common errors* in student understanding of the meaning and effects of arithmetic operations with integers and exponents.

- *The correct answer is B.* Some students may see the two negative signs and interpret the value as being positive because "two negatives make a positive" when multiplying and dividing.
- *Distracter A.* Students who answer A may see the negative sign and automatically think the value will be negative.
- *Distracter D.* Students who answer D may see the negative exponent and think it makes the value "really, really negative." Or, they may correctly apply the negative exponent as repeated division but think that $^1/_{15}$ is less than -25.
- *Distracter C.* Although this distracter is not usually chosen, including the example as part of the probe allows for a more complete discussion of exponents and large/small numbers.

Seeking Links to Cognitive Research

Few research studies have addressed the difficulties experienced by students in operating with negative numbers. Some studies have emphasized the importance of introducing negative numbers to younger students and have illustrated the value of the "zero-pairs" approach using such models as positive and negative chips (Duncan & Saunders, 1980). Kohn (1978), however, questions the introduction of integers by means of thermometers, countdowns, and number lines because none of these models aids in the teaching of operations involving integers. (NCTM, 1993b, p. 194)

Human and Murray (1987) conducted a teaching experiment focusing on the thermometer model with several classes of seventh graders. They found that the students generally chose not to think about the thermometer in calculating the answers to questions such as $^-8 - 3$. They responded on the basis of operations with whole numbers (e.g., "8 − 3 is 5 and you add a minus to the answer because of the minus before the 8"). Errors such as this, however, were not reported in studies using variations of positive and negative chips as models. (NCTM, 1993b, p. 194)

Students may confuse exponentiation with multiplication facts when working with simpler exponential expressions. For example, they may intuitively think that $10^2 = 20$ or $5^2 = 10$. (Bay Area Mathematics Task Force, 1999, p. 117)

Another misconception about negative exponents comes up frequently in the discussion of exponents. Students may think that $x^{-n} = -x^n$. (Bay Area Mathematics Task Force, 1999, p. 120)

Teaching Implications

To support a deeper understanding for students in secondary grades in regard to number and operations, the following are ideas and questions to consider in conjunction with research.

Focus Through Instruction

- In Grades 6–8, all students should develop meaning for integers and represent and compare quantities with them. In lower grades, students may have connected negative integers in appropriate ways to informal knowledge derived from everyday experiences, such as below-zero winter temperatures or lost yards on football plays. In the middle grades, students should extend these initial understandings of integers.
- From earlier work with whole numbers, students should be familiar with the inverse relationship between the operation pairs of addition–subtraction and multiplication–division. In the middle grades, they should also add another pair to their repertoire of inverse operations—squaring and taking square roots.
- Work with positive exponents as students develop the concept of exponents as a notational device for repeated multiplication of the same base.
- Explore operations with negative exponents through examples. Students should see that the definition of exponents and established rules for multiplication and division are maintained when working with both positive and negative exponents. Being that $x^4 * x^{-1} = x^3$, it follows that x^{-1} must represent division by x, or multiplication by $1/x$.

Questions to Consider . . . *when working with students as they grapple with the meaning and effects of arithmetic operations involving integers and exponents*

- Do students understand that positive exponents are a notational device for repeated multiplication?
- Do students understand the role of the parenthesis symbols in order of operations?

- Do students overgeneralize the fact that the product of two negative numbers is positive to mean that "two negatives always makes a positive"?
- Do students understand that a negative exponent is a notational device representing repeated division by the base?
- Do students recognize that positive rational numbers less than 1 are still greater than negative numbers whose absolute value is greater than 1?

Teacher Sound Bite

"Prior to using this probe with my eighth-grade students, I was pretty confident they understood the rules for operations with negative numbers and both positive and negative exponents. After examining student work, it was clear that some of them still had some problematic misconceptions. I wonder whether I may have moved on to operations too quickly before they had developed a solid understanding of the concepts, and I had to really stop to consider ways to make this concept more concrete for students."

Additional References for
Research and Teaching Implications

Curriculum Topic Study
How Low Can You Go?
Related CTS Guides: Integers, p. 123; Exponents, p. 118

NCTM (1993b), *Research Ideas for the Classroom: Middle Grades Mathematics*, p. 194.

NCTM (2000), *Principles and Standards for School Mathematics*, pp. 214–221.

Bay Area Mathematics Task Force (1999), *A Mathematics Source Book for Elementary and Middle School Teachers*, pp. 109–120.

STUDENT RESPONSES
TO "HOW LOW CAN YOU GO?"

Sample Response: B

Student 1: –25 is the smallest since A and C are both 25 and I know a negative power means a fraction but the number stays positive. A negative is still smaller than the fraction since the fraction is between 0 and 1.

Sample Response: A

Student 2: I chose A because it's the only one that will be negative. B won't be negative because the two negatives make it positive. In C, the negative sign isn't in front of the 5 so it won't matter.

Sample Response: D

Student 3: Exponents make things get bigger really fast. I figured a negative exponent must make things get small really fast so that one would be the smallest.

VARIATION: HOW LOW CAN YOU GO?

Which numerical expression has the **smallest** value?

Problem Set	Circle Choice	Explain Choice
1. A. $(-5)^2$ B. -5^2	A B	
2. A. $(-5)^2$ B. 5^{-2}	A B	
3. A. $-(-5)^2$ B. -5^{-2}	A B	

WHAT'S YOUR ADDITION STRATEGY?

Sam, Julie, Pete, and Lisa each added the numbers **234** and **456**. <u>Circle</u> the method that most closely matches how you would solve the problem.

Sam's Method

$$
\begin{array}{r}
^{1} \\
\text{A.} \quad 234 \\
+456 \\
\hline
690
\end{array}
$$

Do the other three methods make sense mathematically? Why or why not?

Julie's Method

$$
\begin{array}{r}
\text{B.} \quad 234 \\
+456 \\
\hline
600 \\
80 \\
10 \\
\hline
690
\end{array}
$$

Pete's Method

$$
\begin{array}{l}
\text{D.} \quad 234 + 456 \\
\phantom{\text{D.}} \quad +6 \quad -6 \\[4pt]
\phantom{\text{D.}} \quad 240 + 450 \\[4pt]
\phantom{\text{D.}} \qquad = 690
\end{array}
$$

Lisa's Method

$$
\begin{array}{l}
\text{C.} \quad 456 + 234 \\[4pt]
456 + 200 = 656 \\
656 + 30 = 686 \\
686 + 4 = 690
\end{array}
$$

TEACHERS' NOTES:
WHAT'S YOUR ADDITION STRATEGY?

Grade Level for "What's Your Addition Strategy?" Probe

6–8	9–12

*Q*uestioning for Student Understanding

When adding, can students apply and understand a variety of different strategies?

*U*ncovering Understandings

What's Your Addition Strategy? (Content Standard: Number and Operations)

Note: Prior to giving students the probe, ask them to individually solve the indicated problem (from either the Whole Number, Decimal, or Fraction Variation).

Possible adaptations/variations to the probe: *What's Your Addition Strategies? Decimals* and *What's Your Addition Strategies? Fractions*

*E*xamining Student Work

Student answers may reveal *misunderstandings* regarding methods of addition including lack of *conceptual understanding* of properties of numbers. Responses also may reveal a common misconception that there is only one correct algorithm for each operation.

- **Sam's Method:** This method is usually recognized by middle and high school students, although in some situations students may not have been introduced to this standard U.S. algorithm. Those who have no experience with the method may show lack of procedural understanding of the algorithm and typically indicate the method "does not make sense since 1 + 234 + 456 is 691 not 690." Often students who do recognize the algorithm do not demonstrate place value understanding. **(See Student Responses 1 and 2)**
- **Julie's Method:** This method is recognized by students who have experience with multiple algorithms as well as those who were taught only the traditional algorithm. These latter students often apply variations of using an expanded notation form of the numbers. **(See Student Response 3)**
- **Pete's Method:** This strategy is the least recognized by middle-level students in terms of generalizing a method of adding and subtracting like amounts from the numbers to keep a constant total. **(See Student Responses 4 and 5)**

- **Lisa's Method:** This is a strategy of holding the first number constant and breaking the addend into place-value parts and adding on one part at a time. Students who have experience adding on an open number line are typically able to mathematically explain this method of addition. **(See Student Response 6)**

Seeking Links to Cognitive Research

Student errors when operating on whole numbers suggest students interpret and treat multi-digit numbers as single-digit numbers placed adjacent to each other, rather than using place-value meanings for digits in different positions. (AAAS, 1993, p. 358)

The written place-value system is a very efficient system that lets people write very large numbers. Yet it is very abstract and can be misleading: The digits in every place look the same. To understand the meaning of the digits in the various places, children need experience with some kind of *size-quantity supports* (e.g., objects or drawings) that show tens to be collections of 10 ones and show hundreds to be simultaneously 10 tens and 100 ones, and so on. (NCTM, 2003, p. 78)

Students can use roughly three classes of effective methods for multidigit addition and subtraction, although some methods are mixtures. *Counting list methods* are extensions of the single-digit counting methods. Children initially may count large numbers by ones, but these unitary methods are highly inaccurate and are not effective. All children need to be helped as rapidly as possible to develop prerequisites for methods using tens. These methods generalize readily to counting on or up by hundreds but become unwieldy for larger numbers. In *decomposing methods*, children decompose numbers so that they can add or subtract the like units (e.g., add tens to tens, ones to ones, hundreds to hundreds, etc.). These methods generalize easily to very large numbers. *Recomposing methods* are like the make-a-ten or doubles methods. The solver changes both numbers by giving some amount of one number to another number (i.e., in adding) or by changing both numbers equivalently to maintain the same difference (i.e., in subtracting). (NCTM, 2003, p. 79)

When students merely memorize procedures, they may fail to understand the deeper ideas that could make it easier to remember—and apply—what they learn. When subtracting, for example, many children subtract the smaller number from the larger in each column, no matter where it is. (NRC, 2002, p. 13)

By the end of the 3–5 grade band, students should be computing fluently with whole numbers. Computational fluency refers to having efficient and accurate methods for computing. Students exhibit computational fluency when they demonstrate flexibility in the computational methods they choose, understand and can explain these methods, and produce accurate answers efficiently. The computational methods that a student uses should be based on mathematical ideas that the student understands well, including the structure of the base-ten number system. (NCTM, 2000, p. 152)

Computation skills should be regarded as tools that further understanding, not as a substitute for understanding. (Paulos, 1991, p. 53)

When students merely memorize procedures, they may fail to understand the deeper ideas that could make it easier to remember—and apply—what they learn. . . . Understanding makes it easier to learn skills, while learning procedures can strengthen and develop mathematical understanding. (NRC, 2002, p. 13)

Study results indicate that almost all children can and do invent strategies and that this process of invention (especially when it comes *before* learning standard algorithms) may have multiple advantages. (NCTM, 2002, p. 93)

*T*eaching Implications

To support a deeper understanding for students in secondary grades in regard to number and operations, the following are ideas and questions to consider in conjunction with the research.

Focus Through Instruction

- Focusing on understanding multidigit addition and subtraction methods results in much higher levels of correct multidigit methods and produces children who can explain how they got their answers using quantity language.
- Students need some kind of visual quantity support to learn meanings of hundreds, tens, and ones, and these meanings should be related to the oral and written numerical methods developed in the classroom.
- Number lines and hundreds grids support counting-list methods the most effectively. However, they do not generalize easily to numbers greater than 100.
- Decomposition methods are facilitated by supports that enable children to physically add and subtract the different quantity units (e.g., base-ten blocks).
- If students believe that for each kind of math situation or problem there can be several correct methods, their engagement in strategy development is kept alive.
- When children solve multidigit addition and subtraction problems, two types of problem-solving strategies are commonly used: invented strategies and standard algorithms. Invented strategies naturally develop over

time as abstractions of children's strategies that are based on tens materials. Standard algorithms, in contrast, are not invented by children but have evolved over centuries for efficient, accurate calculation. Although this approach simplifies calculations, the procedures can be executed rotely without understanding, and significant ideas can be hidden.

- In addition to providing computational tools, algorithms can be important tools in their own right. They can be analyzed and compared, helping students understand the nature and properties of operation, place-value concepts for numbers, and characteristics of good algorithms.

Questions to Consider . . . *when working with students as they develop or interpret a variety of algorithms*

- When exploring or inventing algorithms, do students consider the generalizability of the method?
- Are students able to decompose and recompose the type of number they are operating with?
- Can students explain why the strategy results in the correct answer?
- When analyzing a strategy or learning a new method, do students focus on properties of numbers and the underlying mathematics rather than just memorizing a step-by-step procedure?
- Do students use a variety of estimation strategies to check the reasonableness of the results?

Teacher Sound Bite

"I struggle to know what methods students bring with them each year when transitioning from the K–5 program to the middle school program. These strategy probes help me consider my students' level of comfort with a variety of methods and whether they have more than just a mechanical understanding. The challenge then lies in how to move student thinking of these whole-number strategies when computing with fractions and decimals."

Additional References for Research and Teaching Implications

Curriculum Topic Study

What's Your Addition Strategy?

Related CTS Guides: Addition and Subtraction, p. 111

McREL (2002), *EDThoughts: What We Know About Mathematics Teaching and Learning,* pp. 82–83.

NCTM (2000), *Principles and Standards for School Mathematics,* p. 152.

NCTM (2002), *Lessons Learned From Research,* pp. 93–100.

NCTM (2003), *Research Companion to Principles and Standards for School Mathematics,* pp. 68–84.

NRC (2002), *Helping Children Learn Mathematics,* pp. 11–13.

NRC (2005), *How Students Learn Mathematics in the Classroom,* pp. 223–231.

Paulos (1991), *Beyond Numeracy,* pp. 52–55.

STUDENT RESPONSES TO "WHAT'S YOUR ADDITION STRATEGY?"

Sample Responses: Sam's Method

Student 1: Sam's method makes sense cuz it is the regular way to add. First add 6 and 4, put down the 0 and carry the 1, then add 1 and 3 and 5 to get 9, put down the 9 and there is nothing to carry. Finally add 2 and 4 and put down 6. Done.

Student 2: Sam's method makes no sense if the little 1 is in the problem too. I asked my teacher but she said to do what I think so I kept the 1 and got 691 not 690.

Sample Response: Julie's Method

Student 3: Julie's method is just a long way of thinking about 200 + 200 + 30 + 50 + 4 + 6.

Sample Responses: Pete's Method

Student 4: I think this works but I am not sure why. It does get you to 690 though.

Student 5: This doesn't make sense because it isn't asking them to add 6, it is asking them to add 456.

Sample Response: Lisa's Method

Student 6: This works because by breaking the second number into easy numbers like 100s, 10s, and 1s it is real quick to add each of the numbers to the beginning number. It doesn't matter which one adds first so she could have added like 456 + 4 then + 30 then the 200 . . . it still works just fine.

VARIATION: WHAT'S YOUR ADDITION STRATEGY? DECIMALS

Sam, Pete, and Julie each added the numbers **11.5** and **2.7.**

	Does each of the methods make sense mathematically? Why or why not?
Sam's Method: "I broke the 2.7 apart." 11.5 + 2.7 11.5 + 2 = 13.5 13.5 + .5 = 14 14 + .2 = 14.2	
Pete's Method: "I rounded up, then subtracted the extra." 11.5 + 2.7 11.5 + 3 = 14.5 14.5 − .3 = 14.2	
Julie's Method: "I added the numbers in the columns." $\overset{\scriptstyle 1}{1}1.5$ <u> 2.7</u> 14.2	

VARIATION: WHAT'S YOUR ADDITION STRATEGY? FRACTIONS

Sam, Julie, and Pete each added the numbers $\frac{3}{4}$ and $\frac{3}{8}$.

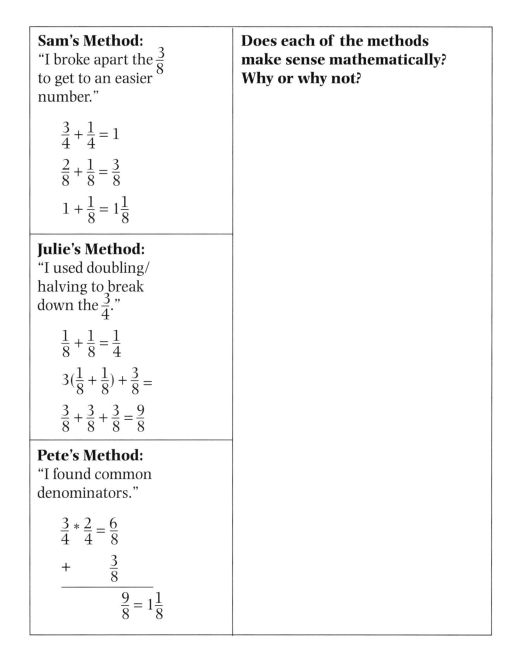

Sam's Method:
"I broke apart the $\frac{3}{8}$ to get to an easier number."

$$\frac{3}{4} + \frac{1}{4} = 1$$

$$\frac{2}{8} + \frac{1}{8} = \frac{3}{8}$$

$$1 + \frac{1}{8} = 1\frac{1}{8}$$

Julie's Method:
"I used doubling/halving to break down the $\frac{3}{4}$."

$$\frac{1}{8} + \frac{1}{8} = \frac{1}{4}$$

$$3\left(\frac{1}{8} + \frac{1}{8}\right) + \frac{3}{8} =$$

$$\frac{3}{8} + \frac{3}{8} + \frac{3}{8} = \frac{9}{8}$$

Pete's Method:
"I found common denominators."

$$\frac{3}{4} * \frac{2}{4} = \frac{6}{8}$$

$$+ \qquad \frac{3}{8}$$

$$\overline{\qquad \frac{9}{8} = 1\frac{1}{8}}$$

Does each of the methods make sense mathematically? Why or why not?

WHAT'S YOUR SUBTRACTION STRATEGY?

Sam, Lisa, Pete, and Julie each subtracted **284 from 672.** Circle the method that most closely matches how you would solve the problem.

Sam's Method (A) $\begin{array}{r} 672 \\ -284 \\ \hline +400 \\ -10 \\ -2 \\ \hline 388 \end{array}$	**Do the other three methods make sense mathematically? Why or why not?**
Lisa's Method (B) $672 - 284$ $672 - 200 = 472$ $472 - 80 = 392$ $392 - 4 = 388$	
Pete's Method (D) $672 - 284$ $\quad \downarrow {+6} \quad \downarrow {+6}$ $678 - 290$ $\quad \downarrow {+10} \quad \downarrow {+10}$ $688 - 300$ $= 388$	
Julie's Method (C) $\begin{array}{r} {}^{5}{}^{1}6 \\ \cancel{6}\cancel{7}{}^{1}2 \\ -28\,4 \\ \hline 38\,8 \end{array}$	

TEACHERS' NOTES:
WHAT'S YOUR SUBTRACTION STRATEGY?

Grade Level for "What's Your Subtraction Strategy?" Probe

6–8	9–12

*Q*uestioning for Student Understanding

When subtracting, can students apply and understand a variety of different strategies?

*U*ncovering Understandings

What's Your Subtraction Strategy? (Content Standard: Number and Operation)
Note: Prior to giving students the probe, ask them to individually solve the indicated problem (from either the Whole Number, Decimal, or Fraction Variation).

Possible adaptations/variations to the probe: *What's Your Subtraction Strategy? Decimals; What's Your Subtraction Strategy? Fractions*

*E*xamining Student Work

Student answers may reveal *misunderstandings* regarding methods of subtracting including lack of *conceptual understanding* of properties of numbers. Responses also may reveal a common misconception that there is only one correct algorithm for each operation.

- **Sam's Method:** This method of subtracting by the place and then adding the results is common in many elementary mathematics programs. Students who have only experienced a standard algorithm are typically confused because of the use of negative numbers. These students often refer to the incorrect idea that "you can never subtract a bigger number from a smaller number." **(See Student Responses 1 and 2)**
- **Lisa's Method:** This strategy consists of holding the minuend constant and breaking the subtrahend into place-value parts and subtracting on one part at a time. Students who have experience subtracting on an open number line are typically able to mathematically explain this method of subtraction. **(See Student Responses 3 and 4)**
- **Pete's Method:** This strategy is the least recognized by middle-level students in terms of generalizing a method of adding or subtracting like amounts from the numbers to keep the difference between the numbers constant. The subtracting can be done mentally once the subtrahend is a multiple of 100. **(See Student Response 5)**
- **Julie's Method:** This method is usually recognized by middle and high school students, although in some situations students may not have

been introduced to the standard U.S. algorithm. Those who have no experience with the algorithm indicate lack of understanding of the notation but can typically relate the method to regrouping with manipulatives. Those students who recognize the algorithm often do not demonstrate place-value understanding. **(See Student Responses 6 and 7)**

Seeking Links to Cognitive Research

Student errors when operating on whole numbers suggest students interpret and treat multi-digit numbers as single-digit numbers placed adjacent to each other, rather than using place-value meanings for digits in different positions. (AAAS, 1993, p. 358)

The written place-value system is a very efficient system that lets people write very large numbers. Yet it is very abstract and can be misleading: The digits in every place look the same. To understand the meaning of the digits in the various places, children need experience with some kind of *size-quantity supports* (e.g., objects or drawings) that show tens to be collections of 10 ones and show hundreds to be simultaneously 10 tens and 100 ones, and so on. (NCTM, 2003, p. 78)

Students can use roughly three classes of effective methods for multidigit addition and subtraction, although some methods are mixtures. *Counting-list methods* are extensions of the single-digit counting methods. Children initially may count large numbers by ones, but these unitary methods are highly inaccurate and are not effective. All children need to be helped as rapidly as possible to develop prerequisites for methods using tens. These methods generalize readily to counting on or up by hundreds but become unwieldy for larger numbers. In *decomposing methods*, children decompose numbers so that they can add or subtract the like units (e.g., add tens to tens, ones to ones, hundreds to hundreds, etc.). These methods generalize easily to very large numbers. *Recomposing methods* are like the make-a-ten or doubles methods. The solver changes both numbers by giving some amount of one number to another number (i.e., in adding) or by changing both numbers equivalently to maintain the same difference (i.e., in subtracting). (NCTM, 2003, p. 79)

When students merely memorize procedures, the may fail to understand the deeper ideas. When subtracting, for example, many children subtract the smaller number from the larger in each column, no matter where it is. (NRC, 2002, p. 13)

By the end of the 3–5 grade band, students should be computing fluently with whole numbers. Computational fluency refers to having efficient and accurate methods for computing. Students exhibit computational fluency when they demonstrate flexibility in the computational methods they choose, understand and can explain these methods, and produce accurate answers efficiently. The computational methods that a student uses should be based on mathematical ideas that the student understands well, including the structure of the base-ten number system. (NCTM, 2000, p. 152)

Computation skills should be regarded as tools that further understanding, not as a substitute for understanding. (Paulos, 1991, p. 53)

When students merely memorize procedures, they may fail to understand the deeper ideas that could make it easier to remember—and apply—what they learn. Understanding makes it easier to learn skills, while learning procedures can strengthen and develop mathematical understanding. (NRC, 2002, p. 13)

Study results indicate that almost all children can and do invent strategies and that this process of invention (especially when it comes *before* learning standard algorithms) may have multiple advantages. (NCTM, 2002, p. 93)

*T*eaching Implications

To support a deeper understanding for students in secondary grades in regard to number and operations, the following are ideas and questions to consider in conjunction with the research.

Focus Through Instruction

- Focusing on understanding multidigit addition and subtraction methods results in much higher levels of correct multidigit methods and produces children who can explain how they got their answers using quantity language.
- Students need some kind of visual quantity support to learn meanings of hundreds, tens, and ones, and these meanings should be related to the oral and written numerical methods developed in the classroom.
- Number lines and hundreds grids support counting-list methods the most effectively. However, they do not generalize easily to numbers greater than 100.
- Decomposition methods are facilitated by supports that enable children to physically add and subtract the different quantity units (e.g., base-ten blocks).
- If students believe that for each kind of math situation or problem there can be several correct methods, their engagement in strategy development is kept alive.
- When children solve multidigit addition and subtraction problems, two types of problem-solving strategies are commonly used: invented strategies and standard algorithms. Invented strategies naturally develop over time as abstractions of children's strategies that are based on tens

materials. Standard algorithms, in contrast, are not invented by children but have evolved over centuries for efficient, accurate calculation. Although this approach simplifies calculations, the procedures can be executed rotely without understanding, and significant ideas can be hidden.

- In addition to providing computational tools, algorithms can be important tools in their own right. They can be analyzed and compared, helping students understand the nature and properties of operation, place-value concepts for numbers, and characteristics of good algorithms.

Questions to Consider . . . *when working with students as they develop or interpret a variety of algorithms*

- Do students understand the different meanings of subtraction?
- When exploring or inventing algorithms, do students consider the generalizability of the method?
- Are students able to decompose and recompose the type of number they are operating with?
- Can students explain why the strategy results in the correct answer?
- When analyzing a strategy or learning a new method, do students focus on properties of numbers and the underlying mathematics rather than just memorizing a step-by-step procedure?
- Do students use a variety of estimation strategies to check the reasonableness of the results?

Teacher Sound Bite

"In the past I have stopped to teach my sixth-grade students how to subtract by regrouping. This was frustrating as it took away time from the math I was supposed to be teaching. After learning about the alternative methods and meanings of subtraction being taught in our elementary programs, I realized I needed to change my approach. I like to give the whole-number strategy probes at the beginning of the year to see how my students approach operations with whole numbers. This year I gave the decimal and fraction probe once at the beginning of each of those units and once at the end. I was surprised that students weren't able to easily transfer a strategy to a different type of number. We had to really work on this throughout the unit."

Additional References for Research and Teaching Implications

Curriculum Topic Study
What's Your Subtraction Strategy?
Related CTS Guides: Addition and Subtraction, p. 111

McREL (2002), *EDThoughts: What We Know About Mathematics Teaching and Learning*, pp. 82–83.

NCTM (2000), *Principles and Standards for School Mathematics*, p. 152.

NCTM (2002), *Lessons Learned From Research*, pp. 93–100.

NCTM (2003), *Research Companion to Principles and Standards for School Mathematics*, pp. 68–84.

NRC (2002), *Helping Children Learn Mathematics*, pp. 11–13.

NRC (2005), *How Students Learn Mathematics in the Classroom*, pp. 223–231.

Paulos (1991), *Beyond Numeracy*, pp. 52–55.

STUDENT RESPONSES TO "WHAT'S YOUR SUBTRACTION STRATEGY?"

Sample Responses: Sam's Method

Student 1: Sam's method does make sense to me because 600 – 400 is 400, 70 – 80 is short by 10 and 2 – 4 is short by 2. You have 400 but have to give up the 12 of it since you were short. 400 – 12 is 388.

Student 2: Sorry Sam, you got 388 but I think it must have been a good guess. Maybe Julie can explain how you need to borrow from the 7 in order to do this right.

Sample Responses: Lisa's Method

Student 3: This is fine to do since subtracting 200 then 80 then 4 is the same as just subtracting 284.

Student 4: I can follow this method since it comes out right, but I am not sure why anyone would want to subtract this way.

Sample Response: Pete's Method

Student 5: I think you are supposed to add and subtract [do the opposite]. I've never seen someone add to both numbers to subtract.

Sample Responses: Julie's Method

Student 6: This is just normal so of course it makes sense. Borrow 1 from the 7 and put it in front of the 2 to make 12. 12 – 4 is 8. Now it's tricky, take 1 from the 6 and put it in front if the new 6 to make 16. 16 – 8 is 8. 5 – 2 is 3.

Student 7: Julie regrouped her numbers to make it easier.

Probe
10a

VARIATION: WHAT'S YOUR SUBTRACTION STRATEGY? DECIMALS

Sam, Pete, and Julie each subtracted the number 7.3 from 11.5.

	Does each of the methods make sense mathematically? Why or why not?
Sam's Method: "I counted up from the 7.3." $7.3 + 3 = 10.3$ $10.3 + 1 = 11.3$ $11.3 + .2 = 11.5$ $3 + 1 + .2 = 4.2$ $11.5 - 7.3 = 4.2$	
Pete's Method: "I rounded up, then added back the extra." $11.5 - 7.3 =$ $11.5 - 7.5 = 4$ $4 + .2 = 4.2$ $11.5 - 7.3 = 4.2$	
Julie's Method: "I subtracted the numbers in the columns." $\overset{1}{11}.5$ $\underline{7.3}$ 4.2	

VARIATION: WHAT'S YOUR SUBTRACTION STRATEGY? FRACTIONS

Sam, Pete, and Julie each subtracted the numbers $5\frac{2}{5} - 3\frac{4}{5}$.

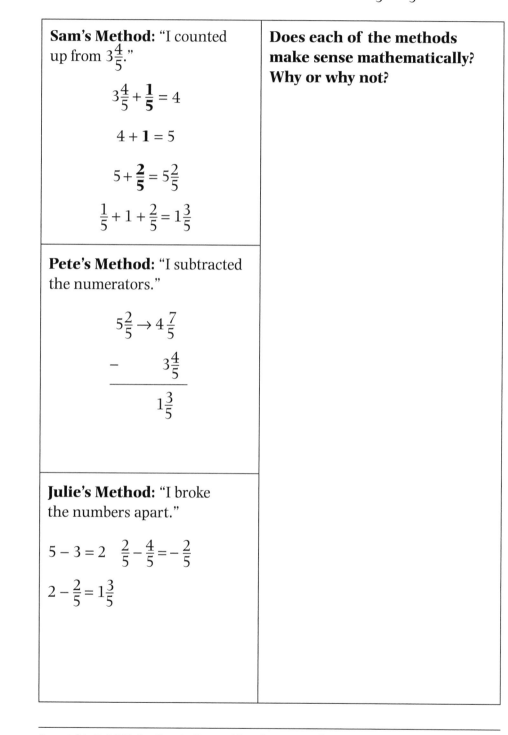

	Does each of the methods make sense mathematically? Why or why not?
Sam's Method: "I counted up from $3\frac{4}{5}$." $3\frac{4}{5} + \frac{1}{5} = 4$ $4 + 1 = 5$ $5 + \frac{2}{5} = 5\frac{2}{5}$ $\frac{1}{5} + 1 + \frac{2}{5} = 1\frac{3}{5}$	
Pete's Method: "I subtracted the numerators." $5\frac{2}{5} \rightarrow 4\frac{7}{5}$ $- \qquad 3\frac{4}{5}$ $\rule{3cm}{0.4pt}$ $1\frac{3}{5}$	
Julie's Method: "I broke the numbers apart." $5 - 3 = 2 \quad \frac{2}{5} - \frac{4}{5} = -\frac{2}{5}$ $2 - \frac{2}{5} = 1\frac{3}{5}$	

WHAT'S YOUR MULTIPLICATION STRATEGY?

Brianna, Jacob, Philip, and Ashlie each multiplied the numbers **18** and **17**. <u>Circle</u> the method that most closely matches how you would solve the problem.

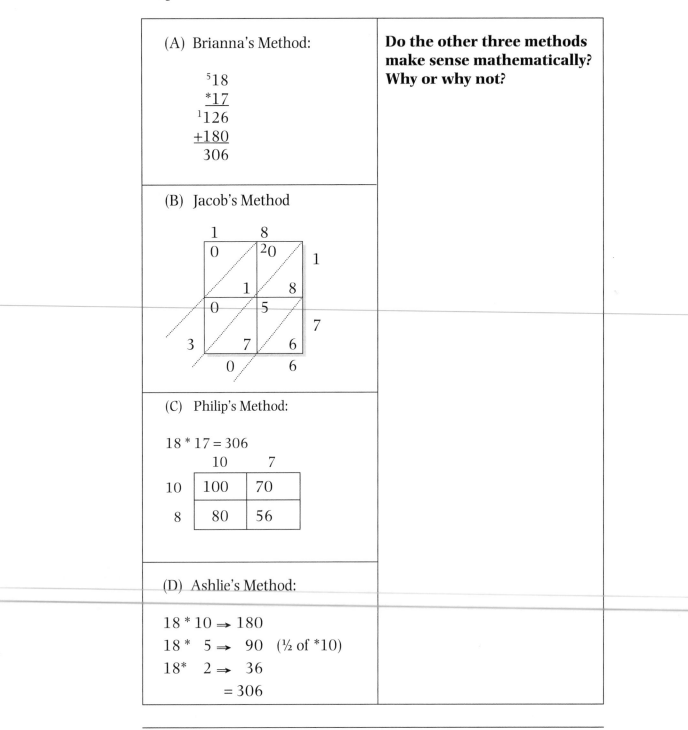

(A) Brianna's Method:	**Do the other three methods make sense mathematically? Why or why not?**
$^{5}18$ $*\underline{17}$ $^{1}126$ $+\underline{180}$ 306	

(B) Jacob's Method

(C) Philip's Method:

$18 * 17 = 306$

	10	7
10	100	70
8	80	56

(D) Ashlie's Method:

$18 * 10 \Rightarrow 180$

$18 * 5 \Rightarrow 90 \quad (\text{½ of } *10)$

$18 * 2 \Rightarrow 36$

$ = 306$

TEACHERS' NOTES: WHAT'S YOUR MULTIPLICATION STRATEGY?

Grade Level for "What's Your Multiplication Strategy?" Probe

6–8	9–12

*Q*uestioning for Student Understanding

When multiplying, can students apply and understand a variety of different strategies?

*U*ncovering Understandings

What's Your Multiplication Strategy? (Content Standard: Number and Operations)

Note: Prior to giving students the probe, ask them to individually solve the indicated problem (from either the Whole Number or Decimal Version).

Possible adaptations/variations to the probe: *What's Your Multiplication Strategy? Decimals*

*E*xamining Student Work

Student answers may reveal *misunderstandings* regarding methods of multiplication including lack of *conceptual understanding* of properties of numbers. Responses also may reveal a common misconception that there is only one correct algorithm for each operation.

- **Brianna's Method:** As the typical U.S. standard algorithm, this method is labeled as making sense by most students. Although familiar with the method, most students give a procedural explanation of the steps using incorrect place-value language. Those students who have not been introduced to the algorithm have great difficulty trying to interpret the steps. **(See Student Response 1)**
- **Jacob's Method:** The lattice method, which has been around for centuries, is a process taught in some of the K–5 elementary mathematics programs. In the chart, partial products are laid out in place-value diagonals. Students who successfully use this method may lack concepts of place value, seeing the numbers as single digits. **(See Student Response 2)**
- **Philip's Method:** This method breaks the numbers into place-value parts, resulting in partial products that are then added together. Students who understand this method are often better able to apply this knowledge to the multiplication of polynomials. **(See Student Responses 3 and 4)**

- **Ashlie's Method:** The method of keeping one factor whole while breaking up the other into several addends relies on known facts such as working with multiples of ten and doubling/halving. **(See Student Responses 5 and 6)**

Seeking Links to Cognitive Research

Student errors suggest students interpret and treat multi-digit numbers as single-digit numbers placed adjacent to each other, rather than using place-value meanings for the digits in different positions. (AAAS, 1993, p. 358)

Research has confirmed that a solid conceptual grounding in decimal numbers is difficult for students to achieve (Hiebert et al., 1991). The similarities between the symbol systems for decimals and whole numbers lead to a number of misconceptions and error types (Resnick et al., 1989). Grasping the proportional nature of decimals is particularly challenging. (NRC, 2005, p. 332)

Whatever algorithms are taught should be taught meaningfully. Instruction should stress estimation, number sense, and skill in selecting the tool to perform a given calculation. When procedures are only memorized, the rules for various operations often become confused. (NCTM, 1993b, pp. 112–113)

Researchers have reported a preliminary learning progression of multi-digit methods in which teachers fostered students' invention of algorithms. These methods moved from (a) direct modeling with objects or drawings, to (b) written methods involving repeatedly adding and/or doubling, to (c) partitioning methods. (NCTM, 2003, p. 84)

The multiplication algorithm currently most prevalent is a complex method that is not easy to understand or to carry out. It demands high levels of skill in multiplying a multi-digit number by a single-digit number within an embedded format in which multiplying and adding alternate. The meaning and scaffolding of sub-steps [have] been sacrificed, using aligning methods that keep the steps organized by correct place value without requiring any understanding of what is actually happening with the ones, tens, and hundreds. (NCTM, 2003, p. 85)

Researchers and experienced teachers alike have found that when students are encouraged to develop, record, explain, and critique one another's strategies for solving computational problems, a number of important kinds of learning can occur. For students to become fluent in arithmetic computation, they must have efficient and accurate methods that are supported by an understanding of numbers and operations. (NCTM, 2000, p. 35)

*T*eaching Implications

To support a deeper understanding for students in secondary grades in regard to number and operations, the following are ideas and questions to consider in conjunction with the research.

Focus Through Instruction

- Students should learn multiplication and division as necessary skills, using paper and pencil and calculators. Some of the practice needed to master these skills can be carried out using context-free numbers. But if students are to learn about the meaning of numbers and to use them properly, much of what they do must be based on solving problems in which the answers matter and the numbers are used for measured quantities.
- Memorization of algorithms by drill is not matched by learning when to use them. When numbers are used without units or attention to significance, students receive little, if any, help in learning how to judge how good their answers are.
- Because students typically range substantially in their rate of learning multiplication facts, many of them have not achieved full fluency by the time their class is discussing multidigit multiplication and division. An advisable tactic is to give such students a multiplication table that they can use to check their multiplications as they go. This aid will permit them to keep up with the class and learn an algorithm. Furthermore, each verification of, or search for, a product in the table creates another learning trial for basic multiplication.
- Regardless of the particular method used, students should be able to explain their method; understand that many methods exist; and see the usefulness of methods that are efficient, accurate, and general.
- Calculators should be available at appropriate times as computational tools, particularly when many or cumbersome computations are needed to solve problems. However, when teachers are working with students on developing computational algorithms, the calculator should be set aside to allow this focus.

Questions to Consider . . . *when working with students as they develop or interpret a variety of algorithms*

- Do student understand the multiple meanings and representations of multiplication?
- When exploring or inventing algorithms, do students consider the generalizability of the method?
- Are students able to decompose and recompose the type of number they are operating with?
- Can students explain why the strategy results in the correct answer?
- When analyzing a strategy or learning a new method, do students focus on properties of numbers and the underlying mathematics rather than just memorizing a step-by-step procedure?
- Do students use a variety of estimation strategies to check the reasonableness of the results?

Teacher Sound Bite

"When students first came to my class drawing charts and asking for blank lattice sheets, I told anybody and everyone how foolish and inefficient this method was and the rest of the sixth-grade teachers had the same concerns. After reviewing student responses to this probe at a fifth and sixth cross-team meeting, many of us left the meeting with new insight. The fifth-grade teachers vowed to help students understand why the lattice method works, and the sixth-grade teachers had a deeper appreciation of the meaning of efficiency and number sense. I still grow frustrated with some of the inefficient methods students use but do not think every alternative method is automatically deemed inefficient."

Additional References for Research and Teaching Implications

Curriculum Topic Study
What's Your Multiplication Strategy?
Related CTS Guides: Multiplication and Division, p. 125

AAAS (1993), *Benchmarks for Science Literacy*, pp. 350 and 358.

Bay Area Mathematics Task Force (1999), *A Mathematics Source Book for Elementary and Middle School Teachers*, pp. 71–79.

NCTM (1993b), *Research Ideas for the Classroom: Middle Grades Mathematics*, pp. 99–115 and 137–158.

NCTM (2000), *Principles and Standards for School Mathematics*, pp. 32–36.

NCTM (2003), *A Research Companion to Principles and Standards for School Mathematics*, pp. 84–91 and 114–120.

NRC (2001), *Adding It Up: Helping Children Learn Mathematics*, pp. 231–241.

NRC (2002), *Helping Children Learn Mathematics*, pp. 11–13.

NRC (2005), *How Students Learn Mathematics in the Classroom*, pp. 309–349.

Paulos (1991), *Beyond Numeracy*, pp. 52–55.

STUDENT RESPONSES TO "WHAT'S YOUR MULTIPLICATION STRATEGY?"

Sample Response: Brianna's Method

Student 1: This is correct because all the multiplying is correct and they remembered to add the zero before doing 1 times 8.

Sample Response: Jacob's Method

Student 2: It is right—it makes sense because it is much easier and is more like adding than multiplying because you always know where the numbers go.

Sample Responses: Philip's Method

Student 3: The work is right but it doesn't make sense to take all that time to draw out the boxes.

Student 4: This is the way I first learned so it makes sense but now I do it like Brianna cause I don't need to use chart paper no more.

Sample Responses: Ashlie's Method

Student 5: I know you can use this break down method with addition but I am not sure about multiplication.

Student 6: Not sure but I don't think your supposed to take the #'s apart.

VARIATION: WHAT'S YOUR MULTIPLICATION STRATEGY? DECIMALS

Sam, Julie, and Lisa each multiplied the numbers 8.4 * 2.7.

Sam's Method: "I multiplied by the .7, then by the 2."	**Does each of the methods make sense mathematically? Why or why not?**
$\overset{2}{8.4}$ $\underline{*\ 2.7}$ 588 $\underline{1680}$ 22.68	

Julie's Method: "I set up a chart."
 	
    8   4
  ┌──┬──┐
2 │1 │0 │ 2
  │ 6│ 8│
  ├──┼──┤
  │5 │2 │ 7
2 │ 6│ 8│
  └──┴──┘
    6 8	

Lisa's Method: "I broke apart the numbers." 8.4 * 2.7 8 * 2 = 16 8 * .7 = 5.6 2 * .4 = .8 .4 * .7 = .28 16 + 5.6 + .8 + .28 = 22.68	

WHAT'S YOUR DIVISION STRATEGY?

Makayla, Tommy, Scott, and Allison each divided the number **876** by the number **12**. <u>Circle</u> the method that most closely matches how you would solve the problem.

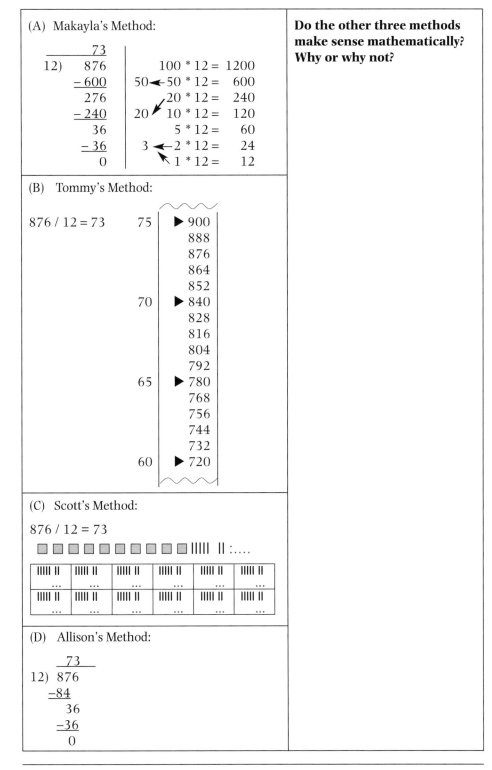

Do the other three methods make sense mathematically? Why or why not?

TEACHERS' NOTES:
WHAT'S YOUR DIVISION STRATEGY?

Grade Level for "What's Your Division Strategy?" Probe

6–8	9–12

*Q*uestioning for Student Understanding

When dividing, can students apply and understand a variety of different strategies?

*U*ncovering Understandings

What's Your Division Strategy? (Content Standard: Number and Operations)
Note: Prior to giving students the probe, ask them to individually solve the indicated problem (from either the Whole Number or Decimal Version).
Possible adaptations/variations to the probe: *What's Your Division Strategy? Decimals*

*E*xamine Student Work

Student answers may reveal *misunderstandings* regarding methods of division including lack of *conceptual understanding* of properties of numbers. Responses also may reveal a common misconception that there is only one correct algorithm for each operation.

- **Makayla's Method:** Often referred to as partial quotients, this method relies on repeated subtraction of known parts. **(See Student Responses 1 and 2)**
- **Tommy's Method:** This method involves starting with a known multiple of 10 that is close to the dividend, then counting on by the divisor. Students who rely heavily on addition when multiplying are able to divide more accurately using this method. **(See Student Response 3)**
- **Scott's Method:** This equal-share method indicates a conceptual understanding of division but can easily become cumbersome with larger numbers. **(See Student Response 4)**
- **Allison's Method:** As the typical U.S. standard algorithm, this method is labeled as making sense by most students. Although familiar with the method, most students give a procedural explanation of the steps using incorrect place-value language. Those students who have not been introduced to the algorithm have great difficulty trying to interpret the steps. **(See Student Response 5)**

Seeking Links to Cognitive Research

The usual U.S. division algorithm has two aspects that create difficulties for students. First, it requires them to determine exactly the maximum copies of the divisor that they can take from the dividend. Second, it creates no sense of the size of the answers that students are writing; in fact, they are always multiplying by single digits. Thus, students have difficulty gaining experience with estimating the correct order of magnitude of answers in division. (NCTM, 2003, pp. 85–86)

Student errors suggest students interpret and treat multi-digit numbers as single-digit numbers placed adjacent to each other, rather than using place-value meanings for the digits in different positions. (AAAS, 1993, p. 358)

An example of disconnection in proficiency is students' tendency to compute with written symbols in a mechanical way without considering what the symbols mean. A survey of students' performance showed that the most common error for the addition problem $4 + .3 = ?$ is .7, which is given by 68% of sixth graders and 51% of fifth and seventh graders (Hiebert and Wearne, 1986). The errors show that many students have learned rules for manipulating symbols without understanding what those symbols mean or why the rules work. (NRC, 2001, p. 234)

Whatever algorithms are taught should be taught meaningfully. Instruction should stress estimation, number sense, and skill in selecting the tool to perform a given calculation. When procedures are only memorized, the rules for various operations often become confused. (NCTM, 1993b, pp. 112–113)

Researchers have reported a preliminary learning progression of multi-digit methods in which teachers fostered students' invention of algorithms. These methods moved from (a) direct modeling with objects or drawings, to (b) written methods involving repeatedly adding and/or doubling, to (c) partitioning methods. (NCTM, 2003, p. 84)

Researchers and experienced teachers alike have found that when students are encouraged to develop, record, explain, and critique one another's strategies for solving computational problems, a number of important kinds of learning can occur. For students to become fluent in arithmetic computation, they must have efficient and accurate methods that are supported by an understanding of numbers and operations. (NCTM, 2000, p. 35)

Teaching Implications

To support a deeper understanding for students in secondary grades in regard to number and operations, the following are ideas and questions to consider in conjunction with the research.

Focus Through Instruction

- Students should learn multiplication and division as necessary skills, using paper and pencil and calculators. Some of the practice needed to master these skills can be carried out using context-free numbers. But if students are to learn about the meaning of numbers and to use them properly, much of what they do must be based on solving problems in which the answers matter and the numbers are used for measured quantities.
- Memorization of algorithms by drill is not matched by learning when to use them. When numbers are used without units or attention to significance, students receive little, if any, help in learning how to judge how good their answers are.
- Adding, subtracting, multiplying, and dividing rational numbers require that they be seen as *numbers* because in elementary school these operations are defined only for whole numbers. Students may think of a decimal as part of a whole or as a batting average, but such interpretations are not enough for them to understand what is happening when computations are carried out.
- Because students typically range substantially in their rate of learning multiplication facts, many of them have not achieved full fluency by the time their class is discussing multidigit multiplication and division. An advisable tactic is to give such students a multiplication table that they can use to check their multiplications as they go. This aid will permit them to keep up with the class and learn an algorithm. Furthermore, each verification of, or search for, a product in the table creates another learning trial for basic multiplication.
- The difficulties many students have in subtraction noticeably affect division, so understanding and fluency in multidigit subtraction is very important.
- Regardless of the particular method used, students should be able to explain their method; understand that many methods exist; and see the usefulness of methods that are efficient, accurate, and general.
- Calculators should be available at appropriate times as computational tools, particularly when many or cumbersome computations are needed to solve problems. However, when teachers are working with students on developing computational algorithms, the calculator should be set aside to allow this focus.

Questions to Consider . . . *when working with students as they develop or interpret a variety of algorithms*

- Do student understand the multiple meanings and representations of division?
- When exploring or inventing algorithms, do students consider the generalizability of the method?
- Are students able to decompose and recompose the type of number they are operating with?
- Can students explain why the strategy results in the correct answer?

- When analyzing a strategy or learning a new method, do students focus on properties of numbers and the underlying mathematics rather than just memorizing a step-by-step procedure?
- Do students use a variety of estimation strategies to check the reasonableness of the results?

Teacher Sound Bite

"Long division has always been a problem for my students, so I was actually happy to hear that in our texts through to Grade 6, the traditional algorithm would be replaced by one called partial quotients. The strategy probes allow me to get a sense from my seventh-grade classes the number of students still working at a more concrete level such as with Scott's sharing method, and the number of students still being introduced to the traditional method even though it is no longer an expectation."

Additional References for Research and Teaching Implications

AAAS (1993), *Benchmarks for Science Literacy*, pp. 350 and 358.

Bay Area Mathematics Task Force (1999), *A Mathematics Source Book for Elementary and Middle School Teachers*, pp. 71–79.

NCTM (1993b), *Research Ideas for the Classroom: Middle Grades Mathematics*, pp. 99–115 and 137–158.

NCTM (2000), *Principles and Standards for School Mathematics*, pp. 32–36.

NCTM (2003), *A Research Companion to Principles and Standards for School Mathematics*, pp. 84–91 and 114–120.

NRC (2001), *Adding It Up: Helping Children Learn Mathematics*, pp. 231–241.

NRC (2002), *Helping Children Learn Mathematics*, pp. 11–13.

NRC (2005), *How Students Learn Mathematics in the Classroom*, pp. 309–349.

Paulos (1991), *Beyond Numeracy*, pp. 52–55.

> **Curriculum Topic Study**
>
> *What's Your Division Strategy?*
>
> Related CTS Guides: Multiplication and Division, p. 125

STUDENT RESPONSES TO "WHAT'S YOUR DIVISION STRATEGY?"

Sample Responses: Makayla's Method

Student 1: My way had more subtraction stuff since I subtracted 100 six times, but her way still makes sense, it is just less writing down.

Student 2: She just kept subtracting until nothing was left over. The work on the side is what she had to keep track of for what goes into 876.

Sample Response: Tommy's Method

Student 3: Tommy started at 720 and wrote all numbers down that were 12 more again and again. If you count up to the 876 from the 720 it lands on 73, which is the answer.

Sample Response: Scott's Method

Student 4: He made 12 boxes and then put groups of 10 in each box until they were all gone. Each box had 73 inside. I like this way because it is easy to get what's happening.

Sample Response: Allison's Method

Student 5: I am not sure this is right cause 768 – 84 is not 36 but 36 – 36 is 0.

VARIATION: WHAT'S YOUR DIVISION STRATEGY? DECIMALS

Probe 12a

Sam, Julie, and Lisa each divided the number 61.2 by 0.4.

Sam's Method: "I multiplied by the 10, then by the 4." $$\begin{array}{r} 153 \\ 4\overline{)612} \\ \underline{-4} \\ 21 \\ \underline{20} \\ 12 \\ \underline{12} \\ 0 \end{array}$$	**Does each of the methods make sense mathematically? Why or why not?**
Julie's Method: "I subtracted sets of .4." $$\begin{array}{r} 153 \\ .4\overline{)61.2} \\ \underline{-40}\quad .4 * 100 \\ 21.2 \\ \underline{-20}\quad .4 * 50 \\ 1.2 \\ \underline{1.2}\quad .4 * 3 \\ 0 \end{array}$$	
Lisa's Method: "I used estimation and multiplication." 5 know $61.2 \div .5 = 122.4$ so $\div .4$ will be bigger than 122 $100 * .4 = 40$ $50 * .4 = 20$ ~~$5 * .4 = 2$ (62 is too big)~~ $3 * .4 = 1.2$ $20 + 20 + 1.2 = 61.2$ and $100 + 50 + 3 = 153$ so $61.2 \div 0.4 = 153$	

4

Geometry, Measurement, and Data Assessment Probes

Grade Span Bar Key

	Target for Instruction Depending on Local Standards
	Prerequisite Concept/Field Testing Indicates Student Difficulty

Measurement, Geometry, and Data Probes			
Question	**Probe**	**Grade 6–8**	**Grades 9–12**
Are students able to choose the correct measure of a line given a change in the interval?	What's the Measure? p. 107		
Do students understand that figures can have the same perimeter but different areas?	Are Area and Perimeter Related? p. 112		
Do students recognize how a change in the dimensions affects the area of a figure?	What's the Area? p. 117		
Do students recognize how a change in the dimensions affects the volume of a figure?	What's the Capacity? p. 122		
Do students recognize dilations (reduction or contraction and enlargement or magnification) as types of transformation?	Is It Transformed? p. 126		
Are students able to identify needed information in determining whether two figures are similar?	Are They Similar? p. 131		
Do students understand mean and how it is affected by changes to a data set?	What Do You *Mean*? p. 136		
Are students able to move beyond point-by-point graph interpretation?	Name of the Graph? p. 145		
Can students identify correct graphical construction and accurate use of interval scale?	Graph Construction p. 151		

WHAT'S THE MEASURE?

Use the standard or nonstandard tool provided for each line segment to measure its length.

Circle the letter of each line segment that is approximately 2¼ units long.

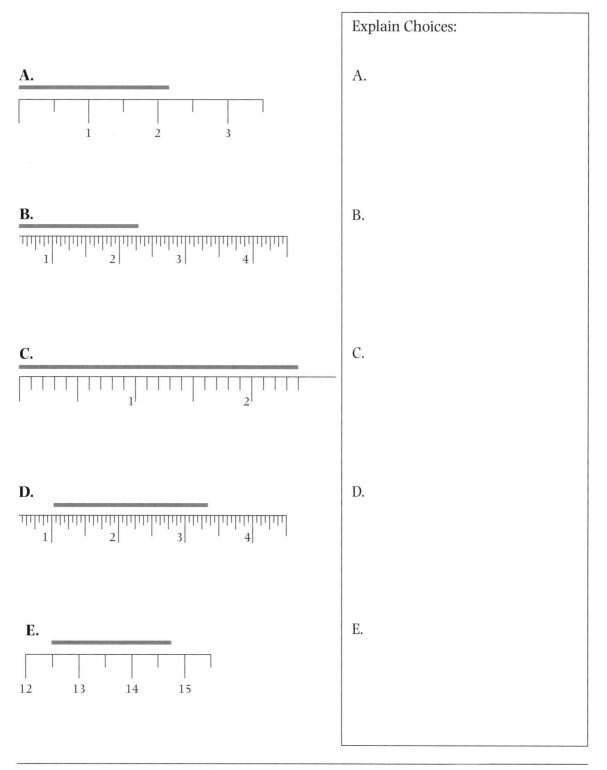

Explain Choices:

A.

B.

C.

D.

E.

TEACHERS' NOTES:
WHAT'S THE MEASURE?

Grade Level for "What's the Measure?" Probe

| 6–8 | 9–12 |

*Q*uestioning for Student Understanding

Are students able to choose the correct measure of a line given a change in the interval or given a non-zero starting point?

*U*ncovering Understandings

What's the Measure? (Content Standard: Measurement)

*E*xamining Student Work

The distracters may reveal common errors made when measuring or lack of understanding when measuring parts of a unit.

- *The correct answers are A, D, and E.* Students who correctly choose only these answers are taking into consideration the starting point and are able to understand one-fourth, given various interval choices. Students who exclude A are not partitioning the $\frac{1}{2}$ intervals indicating $\frac{1}{4}$. Students who exclude D typically do not look at the nonzero starting point. **(See Student Responses 1 and 2)**
- *Distracter B.* Students who choose B typically do not consider the nonzero starting point and give the length as the number on the ruler aligned to the endpoint of the segment. **(See Student Responses 3 and 4)**
- *Distracter C.* Students who choose C are not considering that each interval represents $\frac{1}{10}$, with the length of the line approximately 2 $\frac{1}{2}$ units long. **(See Student Responses 5 and 6)**

*S*eeking Links to Cognitive Research

Children's understanding of zero-point is particularly tenuous. Only a minority of young children understand that any point on a scale can serve as the starting point, and even a significant minority of older children (e.g., fifth grade) respond to nonzero origins by simply reading off whatever number on a ruler aligns with the end of the object (Lehrer et al., 1998a). Many children throughout schooling begin measuring with one rather than zero (Ellis, Siegler, & Van Voorhis, 2001). (NCTM, 2003, p. 183)

Conceptual understanding of measurement includes, among others, understanding of iteration and understanding of the origin. Specific ideas include 1) the need for identical units; 2) partitioning of a unit; 3) conformity on the scale [meaning] that any location on the scale can serve as the origin; 4) mental coordination of the origin and the endpoint of the scale and the resulting measure. Most studies suggest that these understandings of units of length are acquired over the course of the elementary grades. (NCTM, 2003, p. 182)

By middle grades some students still have difficulty recognizing the fundamental ideas of measurement: unit and the iteration of units. Although most were successful with simple problems involving instruments, many could not determine the length of a segment that was not aligned with the zero mark. (NCTM, 1993b, p. 80)

When using conventional tools such as rulers and tape measures for measuring length, students will need instruction to learn to use these tools properly. For example, they will need to recognize and understand the markings on a ruler, including where the "0," or beginning point, is located. (NCTM, 2000, p. 173)

*T*eaching Implications

In order to support a deeper understanding for students in secondary grades in regard to measurement, the following are ideas and questions to consider in conjunction with the research.

Focus Through Instruction

- By constructing their own measurement tools, students can discover important measurement ideas including the partitioning of a unit into smaller units to accommodate more precise length measures.
- An understanding of measurement can serve as a basis for work with fraction and decimal numbers and the idea of scales on a coordinate graph.
- Students need experience with a variety of standard rulers with varying intervals.
- Opportunities to measure length with "broken" rulers can help students learn to compensate for a nonzero starting point.
- Discussion around precision versus accuracy can help students approximate measures of objects that do not match up exactly with marks on a ruler.

Questions to Consider . . . *when working with students as they grapple with the idea of measuring length*

- Do students understand length measure as the result of matching a length with a number of units rather than as a number on the ruler?

- Do students realize the size of the unit determines the number of units that make up the length of an object?
- Do students compensate when translating an object to measure with a "broken" ruler?

Teacher Sound Bite

"Our state tests provide a sheet of tools for student use during the assessment. Every year, the eighth-grade teachers spend time griping about the provided ruler because the 0 mark [is] located quite a bit after the beginning of the outline of the ruler. After giving this probe, I began to realize that maybe it wasn't the ruler that was the problem but the lack of student knowledge to even look for the starting point."

Additional References for Research and Teaching Implications

Curriculum Topic Study
What's the Measure?
Related CTS Guide: Length, p. 171

Bay Area Mathematics Task Force (1999), *A Mathematics Source Book for Elementary and Middle School Teachers*, pp. 27–35.

NCTM (1993b), *Research Ideas for the Classroom: Middle Grades Mathematics*, pp. 79–80.

NCTM (2000), *Principles and Standards for School Mathematics*, pp. 171–174, 243.

NCTM (2003), *A Research Companion to Principles and Standards for School Mathematics*, pp. 180–184.

NRC (2001), *Adding It Up: Helping Children Learn Mathematics*, pp. 281–282.

STUDENT RESPONSES TO "WHAT'S THE MEASURE?"

Sample Responses: A, D, E

Student 1: For A, even though there's no unit marks it measures 2¼. For B, subtract 1 since it starts at one and the unit marks are easy to see. E is the same as A and B. It doesn't start at 0 and there are no tick marks but you can still figure it to be 2¼.

Student 2: If you just look at the line and ignore the numbers you can figure out which ones are a little bit more than two long.

Sample Responses: Inclusion of B

Student 3: B is perfectly 2¼.

Student 4: B because it shows two and the line is as far as the ¼ of two.

Sample Responses: Inclusion of C

Student 5: I counted them and the line went to the fourth mark.

Student 6: The line ends after the first four marks so that is ¼.

VARIATION: WHAT'S THE MEASURE?

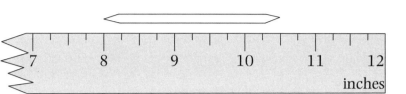

What is the length of the toothpick in the figure above?

A. 10.5 inches
B. 2.5 inches
C. 3.5 inches

Explain your reasoning:

ARE AREA AND PERIMETER RELATED?

Three classmates were having a discussion about two figures that have the same perimeter.

Dakota
Because their perimeters are the same, their areas will also be the same.

Toni
I think their areas could be different depending on the dimensions of the figures.

Marcus
The areas would never be the same because perimeter and area have nothing to do with each other.

Which classmate do you agree with? _____

Explain why you agree with one classmate but disagree with the others.

TEACHERS' NOTES: ARE AREA AND PERIMETER RELATED?

Grade Level for "Are Area and Perimeter Related?" Probe

6–8	9–12

Questioning for Student Understanding

Do students understand that figures can have the same perimeter but different areas?

Uncovering Understandings

Are Area and Perimeter Related? (Content Standard: Geometry and Measurement)

Examining Student Work

The distracters may reveal *common misunderstandings* regarding geometric measurement such as a lack of *conceptual understanding* of the similarities and differences between area and perimeter and not relating a calculated answer as the measurement of an attribute of an object.

- *The correct answer is Toni.* Students who agree with Toni understand that two figures with the same perimeter can have different dimensions and therefore different areas. **(See Student Responses 1 and 2)**
- *Distracter "Dakota."* Students who agree with Dakota typically are incorrectly applying the intuitive rule of Same A–Same B (Stavy & Tirosh, 2000): Multiple figures with the same perimeter must also have the same area because they are the same shape. Since both perimeter and area are ways of stating the size of a shape, this idea may also be the cause of overgeneralizing same shape, same size, and same measures. **(See Student Responses 3 and 4)**
- *Distracter "Marcus."* Students who agree with Marcus typically are taking a procedural approach to comparing area and perimeter. Since the formulas for area and perimeter use different operations, there is no relationship between the figures and measures. **(See Student Responses 5 and 6)**

Seeking Links to Cognitive Research

Students have performance poorly on NAEP items targeting the following measurement topics: choosing the correct numerical expression for the area of a given geometric figure, determining the number of square tiles needed to cover a region of given dimensions, determining the number of boxes of square tiles needed to cover a region of given dimensions, showing a number of different ways a region can be divided to find the area, and determining the surface area of a rectangular solid. (NCTM, 2006)

Many students believe that as the perimeter remains constant, the area will remain constant as well. (Stepans et al., 2005, p. 234)

Although students can often recall standard formulas for finding areas of squares and rectangles, other aspects of area measure remain problematic. . . . Research suggests that many students in elementary school do not "see" the product as a measurement. Even students with experience using square tiles can view the tiles as things to be counted rather than the subdivision of a plane. (NCTM, 2003, p. 185)

Classroom studies point to the importance of helping students go beyond procedural competence to learn about the mathematical underpinnings of measurement. Measuring length, area, volume, or angle affords opportunity for developing ideas about the structure of space such as dimension, array, and curvature. (NCTM, 2003, p. 190)

Filling areas with units to determine a measure has almost no impact on students' understanding of formulas such as L x W for determining area. (Van De Walle, 2007, p. 385)

*T*eaching Implications

In order to support a deeper understanding for students in secondary grades in regard to geometric measurement, the following are ideas and questions to consider in conjunction with the research.

Focus Through Instruction

- Students should be provided opportunities to experiment with area and perimeter using concrete objects.
- Provide concrete opportunities that keep one measure fixed, and ask students to find different values for the other. For example, give students a fixed number of tiles, and ask them to create as many rectangles as possible using all of the tiles and calculate the perimeter of each. Students can also be given a fixed length of string, and be asked to create various shapes and calculate the area of each (Griffin & Madgwick, 2005, p. 54; Van de Valle, 2007, pp. 382–383).
- Composing and decomposing shapes should be used as a method of finding areas for various two-dimensional objects.
- Students should develop formulas through inquiry and investigation.

Questions to Consider . . . **when working with students as they grapple with the idea of area and perimeter**

- Are students able to distinguish correctly between perimeter and area?
- Do students interpret the results of area calculations as a measure, applying appropriate units?
- Do students understand that a number without a unit label has no meaning as a measure?
- Are students able to demonstrate mathematically that two rectangles having the same perimeter do not necessarily have the same area, and that this fact holds true for other two-dimensional figures?
- Do students understand that a square will have a greater area than other non-square quadrilaterals with the same perimeter as the square?

Teacher Sound Bite

"The results of this probe helped me to prepare concrete experiences for students using various shapes with the same perimeter to compare areas, as well as using shapes with the same areas to explore perimeters. I revamped my questioning to focus student thinking on the process involved in finding patterns, rather than just on the mechanics of calculating."

Additional References for Research and Teaching Implications

NCTM (2000), *Principles and Standards for School Mathematics*, pp. 173, 244.

NCTM (2003), *Research Companion to Principles and Standards for School Mathematics*, pp. 180–186.

Stepans et al. (2005). *Teaching for K–12 Mathematical Understanding Using the Conceptual Change Model*, pp. 233–235.

Van de Walle (2007), *Elementary and Middle School Mathematics*, pp. 382–386.

> **Curriculum Topic Study**
>
> *Are Area and Perimeter Related?*
>
> Related CTS Guide: Perimeter, Area, and Volume, p. 175

STUDENT RESPONSES TO "ARE AREA AND PERIMETER RELATED?"

Sample Responses: Toni

Student 1: I saw this on Cyberchase. Just look at a 2 x 3 rectangle perimeter is 2 + 2 + 3 + 3 = 10. Now look at a 1 x 4 rectangle, 1 + 1 + 4 + 4 = 10 too. The 2 x 3 has an area of 6 and the 1 x 4 has an area of 4.

Student 2: I agree with her cuz it depends on what size and shape it is. I learned squarer shapes have more area.

Sample Responses: Dakota

Student 3: Because if the perimeters are the same then they are the same shape and size and the areas are the same.

Student 4: Area has a lot to do with perimeter so I think if the perimeters are the same the areas are the same.

Sample Responses: Marcus

Student 5: Shouldn't say never but area is the space inside and perimeter is the length around. The areas could never be the same.

Student 6: Perimeter and area are different. One you add and one you multiply.

WHAT'S THE AREA?

Square 1:

X units

Square 2:

2X units

Circle the letter of the statement that describes how the area of *Square 1* compares to the area of *Square 2:*

A. Doubles in size

B. Same size

C. Quadruples in size

D. Not enough information to compare

Explain your reasoning:

TEACHERS' NOTES: WHAT'S THE AREA?

Grade Level for "What's the Area?" Probe

6–8	9–12

*Q*uestioning for Student Understanding

Do students recognize how a change in the dimensions affects the area of a figure?

*U*ncovering Understandings

What's the Area? (Content Standard: Geometry and Measurement)

*E*xamining Student Work

The distracters may reveal *common misunderstandings* regarding geometric measurement such as a lack of *conceptual understanding* of how a change in the length of a figure's sides impacts the area of a figure.

- *The correct answer is C, Quadruples in size.* Students who choose C show understanding of the definition of area and of square. Since the side lengths of a square are equivalent, doubling the length of a side gives an area that is four times that of the original square. **(See Student Responses 1 and 2)**
- *Distracter A, Doubles in size:* Students who choose A typically are confusing area and perimeter or are comparing the side lengths and do not consider the effect of the change on the area of the figure. **(See Student Responses 3 and 4)**
- *Distracter B, Same size.* Students who choose B consider only the formula for calculating the area of a figure and do not compare the measures. **(See Student Response 5)**
- *Distracter D, Not enough information to compare.* Students who choose D typically have only a procedural understanding of the area formula. **(See Student Responses 6 and 7)**

*S*eeking Links to Cognitive Research

If students move rapidly to using formulas without an adequate conceptual foundation in area and volume, many students could have underlying confusions that would interfere with their working meaningfully with measurements. (NCTM, 2000, p. 242)

[There is] a distinction between understanding a formula numerically and understanding it quantitatively. (NCTM, 2003, p. 101)

Classroom studies point to the importance of helping students go beyond procedural competence to learn about the mathematical underpinnings of measurement. Measuring length, area, volume, or angle affords opportunity for developing ideas about the structure of space such as dimension, array, and curvature. (NCTM, 2003, p. 190)

Area and perimeter are continually a source of confusion for students. Perhaps it is because both involve regions to be measured or because students are taught formulas for both concepts and tend to get the formulas confused. (Van de Valle, 2007, p. 386)

Students can use measurement to explore the meaning of similarity and later to apply the concept to solve problems. The important observation that the measurements of the corresponding angles of similar shapes are equal is often a starting point for work with similarity. Measurement is also useful for determining the relationships between the side lengths and the perimeters and areas of similar shapes and the surface areas and volumes of similar objects. Students need to understand that the perimeters of pairs of similar shapes are proportional to their corresponding side lengths but that their areas are proportional to the squares of the corresponding side lengths. (NCTM, 2000, p. 244)

*T*eaching Implications

In order to support a deeper understanding for students in secondary grades in regard to geometric measurement, the following are ideas and questions to consider in conjunction with the research.

Focus Through Instruction

- Building an understanding of similar figures requires understanding the relationship among side lengths, perimeter, and area,
- Composing and decomposing shapes should be used as a method of finding areas for various two-dimensional objects and comparing how changing one dimension affects area measures.
- Use of dynamic software programs can allow students to easily manipulate figures, record measurements, and analyze patterns.
- Students should develop formulas through inquiry and investigation.
- Concepts of area and volume should first be developed concretely, with procedures for computation following only when the concepts and some of their practical uses are well understood.
- Students should have many informal experiences in understanding attributes of perimeter, area, and volume before using tools to measure them or relying on formulas to compute measurements.

- The development of formulas to find area and volume should be done by students through active engagement in hands-on experiences.
- Students should make connections between the formula and an actual object.

Questions to Consider . . . *when working with students as they grapple with the idea of surface area and volume*

- Do students recognize how a change in a figure's dimensions can affect its area? Are students able to distinguish between area and perimeter?
- Do students see the connection between side length and area?
- Do students have a conceptual understanding of area, or do they rely on formulas?
- Can student communicate what information is needed to find area, and can they calculate the measure?

Teacher Sound Bite

"I've always been aware of the difficulty students have in choosing correctly between the perimeter and area formula, but this probe highlighted how this problem could impact other ideas such as with comparing two figures. I thought more students would just *see* how four original squares fit inside the new square but so many didn't look at this visually at all, instead moving straight to the formulas."

Additional References for Research and Teaching Implications

Curriculum Topic Study

What's the Area?

Related CTS Guide:
Area, p. 169

NCTM (1993b), *Research Ideas for the Classroom*, pp. 81–82.
NCTM (2000), *Principles and Standards for School Mathematics*, pp. 245–246.
NCTM (2003), *Research Companion to Principles and Standards for School Mathematics*, pp. 184–185.
Van de Walle (2007), *Elementary and Middle School Mathematics*, pp. 382–385.

STUDENT RESPONSES TO "WHAT'S THE AREA?"

Sample Responses: C

Student 1: In a square all sides are equal so if you double one side they all double. Double times double is quadruple.

Student 2: If you just look at it you can see how 4 little squares fit in the bigger square.

Sample Responses: A

Student 3: Say you have 4 sides of 10, that would be 40. Double the sides to get 20 and 4 sides of 20 would be 80 so 80 is double 40.

Student 4: If you double the side you get double the shape.

Sample Response: B

Student 5: Area is always length times width so it wouldn't be different because the shape is bigger.

Sample Responses: D

Student 6: Not enough info because X could be anything so you need the number before you can plug it in the length times width formula.

Student 7: a = l x w and you can't finish it with an x.

WHAT'S THE CAPACITY?

Each of the figures below is constructed from an 8.5 in. × 11 in. sheet of paper as shown.

Figure A   **Figure B**

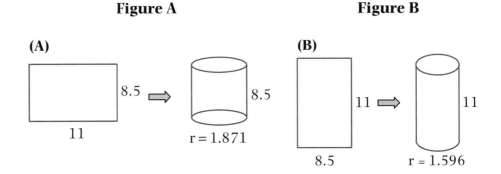

(A)
8.5
11
r = 1.871

(B)
11
8.5
11
r = 1.596

Circle the best response for the figures pictured above.

A. Figure A has a greater volume than Figure B.

B. Figure B has a greater volume than Figure A.

C. The volumes of the figures are the same.

Explain your reasoning:

TEACHERS' NOTES:
WHAT'S THE CAPACITY?

Grade Level for "What's the Capacity?" Probe

6–8	9–12

Questioning for Student Understanding

Do students recognize how a change in the dimensions affects the volume of a figure?

Uncovering Understandings

What's the Capacity? (Content Standard: Geometry and Measurement)

Examining Student Work

The distracters may reveal *common misunderstandings* regarding geometric measurement such as a lack of *conceptual understanding* of how a change in the size of the base and height impacts the volume of a figure, or the *overgeneralization* about the size or shape of the cylinder.

- *The correct answer is A.* Figure A with an approximate volume of 93 cubic units has a greater volume than Figure B with an approximate volume of 88 cubic units. **(See Student Responses 1, 2, and 3)**
- *Distracter B.* Students answering B often are incorrectly applying the intuitive rule of More A–More B (Stavy & Tirosh, 2000): overgeneralizing that taller figures have greater volume. **(See Student Responses 4 and 5)**
- *Distracter C.* Students overgeneralize about the equivalent portion of the figure's net as shown in the diagram and so do not incorporate the size of the base. They often are incorrectly applying the intuitive rule of Same A–Same B (Stavy & Tirosh, 2000): since the initial 8.5×11 rectangle is the same, the volume must be equivalent. **(See Student Responses 6 and 7)**

Seeking Links to Cognitive Research

Findings suggest that, as with area and length measure, students' models of spatial structure influence their conceptions of an object's volume measure. (NCTM, 2003, p. 186)

The intuitive rule, Same A–Same B, is activated in comparison tasks in which two objects are equal in a certain quantity and differ in another quantity. . . . When students start to conserve the area of two sheets of paper, they will also argue that the volumes of the two cylinders are equal. Our data show . . . a very small percentage of the students in the upper grades [6–9] correctly argued about the cylinder with the greater volume. "There is no evidence of a decrease with age in students' incorrect judgments about conservation of volume." (Stavy & Tirosh, 2000, pp. 51–52)

Classroom studies point to the importance of helping students go beyond procedural competence to learn about the mathematical underpinnings of measurement. Measuring length, area, volume, or angle affords opportunity for developing ideas about the structure of space such as dimension, array, and curvature. (NCTM, 2003, p. 190)

Do not expect students to be able to accurately predict which of the two containers holds more. Even adults have difficulty making this judgment. Most groups split roughly in thirds: short and fat, tall and skinny, same. (Van de Walle, 2007, pp. 287–388)

Two types of units can be used to concretely measure volume, solid units and containers (for example, wooden cubes to fill the container or using smaller containers to repeatedly pour and fill the container). Measuring activities for capacity are similar to those for length and area, although estimation of capacity is more difficult. (Van de Walle, 2007, p. 388)

*T*eaching Implications

In order to support a deeper understanding for students in secondary grades in regard to geometric measurement, the following are ideas and questions to consider in conjunction with the research.

Focus Through Instruction

- Students should be provided opportunities to experiment with volume using concrete objects.
- Students need experience composing and decomposing two- and three-dimensional shapes.
- Composing and decomposing shapes should be used as a method of finding volumes for various three-dimensional objects.
- Students should develop formulas through inquiry and investigation.
- Students with prior knowledge about the relationship between perimeter and area (see the "Are Perimeter and Area Related?" probe) are better able to make understand the relationship of surface area to volume.

Questions to Consider . . . *when working with students as they grapple with the ideas of surface area and volume*

- Do students understand the differences between volume and capacity?

- Do students understand how the dimensions of the base and the height of an object impact its volume?
- Over time, are students able to use properties and formulas to justify their answers and check their assumptions?

Teacher Sound Bite

"Students easily jumped to conclusions based on a visual assumption and it was difficult to convince them otherwise. Prior to using this probe, I was not explicit in helping students [connect their] understanding that two or more figures can have the same perimeter but different areas to new ideas concerning surface area and volume."

Additional References for Research and Teaching Implications

NCTM (2000), *Principles and Standards for School Mathematics*, pp. 243–245.

NCTM (2003), *Research Companion to Principles and Standards for School Mathematics*, p. 186.

Stepans et al. (2005), *Teaching for K–12 Mathematical Understanding Using the Conceptual Change Model*, pp. 103+.

Van de Walle (2007), *Elementary and Middle School Mathematics*, pp. 387–388.

> **Curriculum Topic Study**
>
> *What's the Capacity?*
>
> Related CTS Guide:
> Volume, p. 177

STUDENT RESPONSES TO "WHAT'S THE CAPACITY?"

Sample Responses: A

Student 1: Well the rectangle is the same size but in Fig B it is taller and probably has more weight than Figure A.

Student 2: They are almost the same but the short fat one has more volume than a taller skinnier one.

Student 3: I don't know why but I used the formula and A's volume is more than B's.

Sample Responses: B

Student 4: The cylinder looks bigger than the other one.

Student 5: 11 * 1.596 has to be bigger than 1.871 * 8.5.

Sample Responses: C

Student 6: Because the numbers are higher on the height. But I don't really know a lot about volume. I think it is C because when you turn the figure about then they have the same numbers. If you can't flip the figure though it might be B.

Student 7: It is the same, just folded up differently.

IS IT TRANSFORMED?

Circle the example(s) that represent a transformation of the figure.

(A)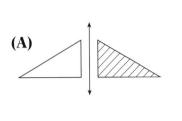

(B)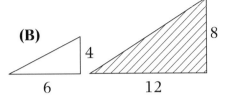

(C)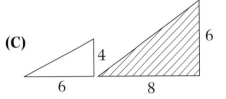

(D)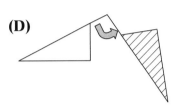

(E)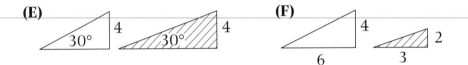

(F)

Explain how you made your choices:

TEACHERS' NOTES: IS IT TRANSFORMED?

Grade Level for "Is It Transformed?" Probe

6–8	9–12

*Q*uestioning for Student Understanding

Do students recognize dilations (reduction or contraction and enlargement or magnification) as types of transformation?

*U*ncovering Understandings

Is It Transformed? (Content Standard: Geometry and Measurement)

*E*xamine Student Work

This probe may reveal a lack of *conceptual understanding* of transformations as motions that include dilations. Students may *overgeneralize* their understanding of translations, reflections, and rotations not changing size to all transformations not changing size.

- *The correct responses are A, B, D, and F.* All of these examples show a transformation of the original figure. Choice A shows a reflection, choice B shows a dilation (magnification), choice D a rotation, and choice F a dilation (contraction). Most students will understand that A and D are correct as they do not change size. These two transformations, along with a translation (not shown) are the three types that students are most familiar with. Many students understand transformations to be a movement of a figure that does not allow the figure to change size; therefore they do not see B and F as transformations. Both dilations, B and D, are transformations that produce an image that is the same shape as the original, but a different size. Dilations keep the angle measure, but side lengths change according to a given scale factor.
- *Distracters C and E.* The students that choose these examples either do not analyze the ratios of the "corresponding" side lengths or have a lack of understanding of magnifications. Each side needs to be increased by the same scale factor, which neither of these figures do.

*S*eeking Links to Cognitive Research

Long before they can use the language of geometry, children become aware of shape. Before entering school, they have had lots of experiences with points, lines, planes, and spaces. In school, students need to extend that knowledge, developing spatial sense and learning to see the world through the eyes of geometry. That can come from activities that require them to use geometry in constructing, drawing, measuring, visualizing, comparing, describing, and transforming things. The progression of experiences should take students from recognizing shapes as wholes to recognizing explicit properties of shapes, and only then to the analysis of relationships among shapes. (AAAS, 1993, p. 222)

Middle-grade students should have had experience with such basic geometric transformations as translations, reflections, rotations, and dilations (including contractions). In high school they will learn to represent these transformations with matrices, exploring the properties of the transformations using both graph paper and dynamic geometry tools. (NCTM, 2000, pp. 314–315)

Transformations can be used to help students understand similarity and symmetry. Work with magnifications and contractions, called dilations, can support students' understanding of similarity. For example, dilation of a shape affects the length of each side by a constant scale factor, but it does not affect the orientation or the magnitude of the angle. (NCTM, 2000, pp. 236–237)

The expanding logical capabilities of students at the middle-grade level enable them to draw inferences and make logical deductions from geometric problems. Students should investigate and use geometric ideas rather than memorize definitions and formulas. Similarity and congruence can be explored through transformations. Figures should be oriented in various positions to aid in forming generalizations that won't be bound to standard orientations. That is made particularly convenient by computer software that performs "flips" and "stretches." Photographs, overhead projectors, and photocopying machines are other common tools for shrinking and stretching shapes. (AAAS, 1993, p. 224)

Although transformation or motion geometry—that is, translation (slide), reflection (flip), rotation (turn), and dilation (stretch or shrink)—is a relatively new approach in the mathematics curriculum in North America, it has been a standard part of informal geometry taught in the middle grades in many parts of the world. Why teach transformation geometry? Transformations bring a spatial-visual aspect to geometry that is as important as logical-deductive aspects. Also, transformation geometry has important real-world applications such as fabric patterns, mirrors, symmetry in nature, photos, and enlargements. (NCTM, 1993b, pp. 212–213)

*T*eaching Implications

In order to support a deeper understanding for students in secondary grades in regard to geometric transformation, the following are ideas and questions to consider in conjunction with the research.

Focus Through Instruction

- When transformations are first introduced, do not generalize them to only include the types that "move" but keep their size. Have discussions that focus on translations (slides), reflections (flips), and rotations (turns) being special kinds of transformations that do conserve their size.
- When exploring dilations, refer to them as transformations. Have discussions on how they compare and contrast to other transformations that the students have worked with in the past.
- Allow students to explore similar triangles through dilations.

Questions to Consider . . . *when working with students as they grapple with the ideas of transformations*

- Do students have a conceptual understanding of transformations?
- Can students communicate accurate ideas about transformations?
- Do students see transformations as "moves," but not as possible scale changes?
- How were students initially introduced to transformations?

Teacher Sound Bite

"After giving this probe to my students, I reflected on what their initial experiences with transformations are. To my knowledge our district introduces translations, reflections, and rotations first. When we discuss these transformations, we tell students that the original shape does not change. I can see that because we don't preface this with the fact that there are other types of transformations, this information can be overgeneralized to all transformations. We as a district need to take a look at the language we use to introduce our students to transformations so that they can understand dilations as valid transformations."

Additional References for Research and Teaching Implications

AAAS (1993), *Benchmarks for Science Literacy*, pp. 222–225, 352.

NCTM (1993c), *Research Ideas for the Classroom: High School Mathematics*, pp. 140–147, 150–152.

NCTM (1993b), *Research Ideas for the Classroom: Middle Grades Mathematics*, pp. 212–214.

NCTM (2000), *Principles and Standards for School Mathematics*, pp. 233, 235–237, 308–309, 314–316.

NCTM (2003), *A Research Companion to Principles and Standards for School Mathematics*, p. 162.

Paulos (1991), *Beyond Numeracy*, pp. 234–236.

Stepans et al. (2005), *Teaching for K–12 Mathematical Understanding Using the Conceptual Change Model*, pp. 233–273.

Curriculum Topic Study
Is It Transformed?
Related CTS Guide: Transformations and Symmetry, p. 164

STUDENT RESPONSES
TO "IS IT TRANSFORMED?"

Sample Responses: A, B, D, and F

Student 1: I think that A, B, D, and F are all transformations. A is a reflection, B is a dilation (I think it is called enlargement), D is a rotation, and F is another dilation (a reduction).

Student 2: I chose A, B, D, and F. A is just flipping it, B is doubling the size, D is rotating it, and F is dividing the sides by 2. Easy as pie!

Student 3: A, B, D, and F are either dilations, flips, or turns.

Sample Responses: A and D (or just A or D)

Student 1: I picked A because it is a reflection and D because it is a rotation. None of the other ones are transformations. They all change size.

Student 2: Choices A and D showed that they move without changing the size. This is what a transformation is.

Student 3: A and D are the only transformations. The triangles in B, C, E, and F are similar, but nothing has been done with them, except for changing their size. A has been reflected and D has been rotated.

Sample Responses: B, C, E, and F

Student 1: I chose B, C, E, and F because they all show a triangle being changed to a smaller or larger triangle. All the other ones just show a change in position.

Student 2: Because transformation means to transform, I chose B, C, E, and F as all of these changed or transformed.

Sample Responses: A, D, and E or All

Student 1: I chose A because it is a flip. I chose D because it is a rotation. I chose E because it is a slide.

Student 2: All of them have a transformation as they all have changed their shape somehow.

ARE THEY SIMILAR?

State whether each pair of triangles are similar
based on the information given. Justify why you
think they are or are not similar.

(1)

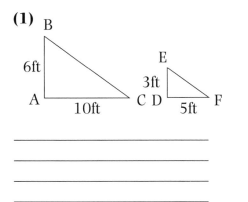

_____
_____
_____
_____

(2)

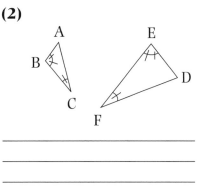

_____
_____
_____
_____

(3) Triangles MNO and PQR have
the following measures:
Angle N = 20°   Angle Q = 20°
Side NO = 10 in   Side QR = 20 in
Side MO = 4 in   Side PR = 8 in

_____
_____
_____
_____

(4) The corresponding three
sides of two triangles are
in proportion to each other.

_____
_____
_____
_____

(5)

(6)

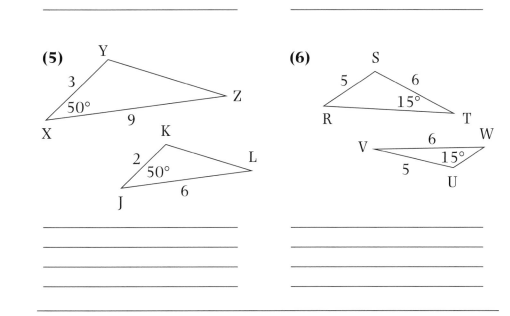

_____
_____
_____
_____

_____
_____
_____
_____

TEACHERS' NOTES: ARE THEY SIMILAR?

Grade Level for "Are They Similar?" Probe

6–8	9–12

Questioning for Student Understanding

Are students able to identify needed information in determining whether two figures are similar?

Uncovering Understandings

Are They Similar? (Content Standard: Geometry and Measurement)

Examining Student Work

The distracters may reveal *common misunderstandings* regarding geometric measurement.

- *The correct answers are 2, 4, and 5.* Students who only choose these sets of triangles are appropriately applying the tests of similarity. The A-A (If two angles in one triangle are congruent with the corresponding two angles of another triangle, the two triangles are similar.) test applies to set 2. The S-S-S (If the three sides of one triangle are proportional to the three corresponding sides of another triangle, the two triangles are similar.) test applies to set 4. The S-A-S (If two sides of one triangles are proportionate to the two corresponding sides of a second triangles and the angles between the two sides of each triangle are equal, the two triangles are similar.) test applies to set 5. **(See Student Response 1)**
- *Distracter 1.* Although two corresponding sides are proportional, not enough information is given in order to apply either the S-A-S test or the S-S-S test. Student who include 1 typically see angles A and D as right angles and they incorrectly apply the S-A-S test. **(See Student Responses 2 and 3)**
- *Distracters 3 and 6.* Although information is given on two corresponding sides and one corresponding angle, the S-A-S test does not apply since the corresponding angles are not between the pair of corresponding sides. Students who include 3 and/or 6 are not considering the positions of the given information. **(See Student Responses 4, 5, 6, and 7)**

Seeking Links to Cognitive Research

According to the van Hiele theory, students progress through levels of thought in geometry: First Level—visual; Second Level—analysis; Third Level—informal deduction; Fourth Level—deduction; Fifth level—rigor. Progress from one of van Hiele's levels to the next is more dependent upon instruction than age. Given traditional instruction, middle school students perform at levels one or two. Despite that, almost 40% of high school graduates finish high school geometry below level two. (AAAS, 1993, p. 352)

The international average for an item on the TIMMS [Trends in International Mathematics and Science Study] on properties of congruent triangles was 27% for 7th graders and 35% for 8th graders. Instruction can help. For example, most students taught to use transformations to learn about congruence advanced a level in the van Hiele hierarchy. . . . If instruction has not developed students' thinking to level 2 or higher, students may only memorize and fail to understand the purpose of proof. (NCTM, 2003, pp. 161, 168)

A strong spatial sense allows students to formulate image-based solutions to mathematics problems. Having a mental image of a parallelogram is fundamental. Without spatial sense, a student may only act mechanically with shapes and symbols that have little meaning. (NCTM, 2002, p. 148)

Teaching Implications

In order to support a deeper understanding for students in secondary grades in regard to similarity, the following are ideas and questions to consider in conjunction with the research.

Focus Through Instruction

- The use of materials such as geoboards, dot paper, multiple-length cardboard strips with hinges, and dynamic geometry software to create and transform two-dimensional shapes can be helpful.
- Students need a solid foundational understanding of ratio and proportion.
- Multiple opportunities should be given to construct similar triangles of various shapes, sizes, and orientation on a coordinate grid or with dynamic software.
- Students should make and record measurements of the sides and angles of parallelograms to observe some of the characteristic properties.
- Students should generate tests for similarity that are correct and consistent with the commonly used ones, and recognize the principal relationships among elements of sets of similar triangles.

- Students should understand the minimal set of sufficient conditions required to determine similarity.
- When students begin the use of specific labeling, care should be taken to accurately represent angles, congruency, and side lengths.

Questions to Consider . . . *when working with students as they grapple with the idea of similarity*

- Can students accurately recognize geometric labeling and symbols?
- Do students identify similar triangles given a variety of known measurements?
- Are students using accurate mathematical language to describe similarity?

Teacher Sound Bite

"I gave the probe prior to the geometry unit in order to gauge a starting point. Overall my tenth-graders seemed to have a handle on the various notations used to label various angles and sides and most mentioned similarity as same shape, different size. The majority of the students had difficulty deciding when the information provided proved similarity. As we progressed through the unit, I capitalized on the examples and non-examples strategies, having the students generate many examples to scale of each of the tests and many non-examples to scale of SSA and SS. I returned the original probe to students at the end of the unit and asked them to check for errors. It was a nice way to make it clear to students what they learned."

Additional References for Research and Teaching Implications

Curriculum Topic Study

Are They Similar?

Related CTS Guide:
Congruence and
Similarity, p. 152

NCTM (1993c), *Research Ideas for the Classroom: High School Mathematics,* pp. 140–147.
NCTM (2000), *Principles and Standards for School Mathematics,* pp. 234–235, 310–315.
NCTM (2003), *A Research Companion to Principles and Standards for School Mathematics,* pp. 151–156, 160, 164, 170.
Stepans et al. (2005), *Teaching for K–12 Mathematical Understanding Using the Conceptual Change Model,* pp. 233–238.

STUDENT RESPONSES TO "ARE THEY SIMILAR?"

Sample Response: 2, 4, and 5

Student 1: 2—All three angles are equal so the triangles are same shape but can be scaled up or scaled down. 4—similar to 2 but opposite. If the sides are to scale the angles have to be equal. 5—3 to 2 is 9 to 6 simplified and the angle in between them is equal.

Sample Responses: Inclusion of 1

Student 2: Yes the angles look the same but one triangle is bigger.

Student 3: They are both right triangles and EDF is half the size of BAC.

Sample Responses: Inclusion of 3

Student 4: Yes, they are the same exact triangle with two different names.

Student 5: They are congruent and congruent is still similar—special case.

Sample Responses: Inclusion of 6

Student 6: They both have two sides and a same angle so yes.

Student 7: If you flip it up you can tell the angles labeled 15 degrees are in different spots. I'm pretty sure that means they are not similar.

WHAT DO YOU *MEAN?*

Each statement below can be preceded by one of the following statements:

The mean is always . . .
The mean is sometimes . . .
The mean is never . . .

Read each statement and indicate **A** (always), **S** (sometimes), or **N** (never):

Statement	Justify Response
1. ☐ the value obtained by dividing the sum of a set of data points by the number of data points in the set.	
2. ☐ equal to the value of the term in the middle.	
3. ☐ equivalent to the value of the mode.	
4. ☐ changed when the same amount is added to each of the data points.	
5. ☐ affected when a 0 is added as one of the data points.	
6. ☐ one of the data points in the original set.	

TEACHERS' NOTES: WHAT DO YOU *MEAN?*

Grade Level for the "What Do You *Mean?*" Probe

6–8	9–12

*Q*uestioning for Student Understanding

Do students understand mean and how it is affected by changes to a data set?

*U*ncovering Understandings

What Do You Mean? (Content Standard: Data Analysis)
Variation: *What Do You Mean?*

*E*xamining Student Work

This probe may uncover a lack of *conceptual understanding* of mean and measures of center. Although students compute the mean of a data set fairly well using the "add-and-divide" algorithm, many have difficulty understanding the mean in context or how changing values of the data set change or do not change the value of the mean.

- *The correct responses are 1—always, 2—sometimes, 3—sometimes, 4—always, 5—sometimes, and 6—sometimes.*
- *Distracter 1.* This is the algorithm for computing the mean. Some students will confuse the mean with the median (or mode) and think this is the algorithm for finding the median (or mode). Other students know this algorithm as one for "finding the average," not for finding the mean. This confusion seems to be about terminology used to describe measures of center. **(See Student Responses 1, 2, and 3)**
- *Distracter 2.* The correct response is, "The mean is sometimes equal to the value of the term in the middle." Students learn the median is the middle term of a data set when placed in ascending order. Many believe that the mean can never be the middle term. An example where the mean is the middle term of a data set is {2, 3, 5, 7, 8}. Other students confuse the mean and the median and think that the statement in choice 2 is always true. An example where it is not true is {1, 2, 5, 7, 9, 12} in which the mean is 6. **(See Student Responses 4 and 5)**
- *Distracter 3.* The correct response is, "The mean is sometimes the value of the mode." Some students believe the mean cannot be one of the data points because in many cases it is not. As the mode is part of the data set, they do not see it as a valid value for the mean. An example of this being true is in the set {3, 5, 6, 7, 8, 9, 9, 10, 15, 18}. The mode and the mean are both 9 in this set. **(See Student Responses 6 and 7)**

- *Distracter 4.* The correct response is, "The mean is always changed when the same amount is added to each of the data points." Many students do not understand that adding a constant to all values in a data set changes the measures of center by that constant. Because this is an "always" statement, many students find this difficult as they try to find a counterexample. This concept needs to be taught with much exploration and a foundation that allows for conceptual understanding to occur. Another area of confusion for students is that the measures of spread are not affected by adding the same amount to each of the data points. Students sometimes confuse measures of center with measures of spread. **(See Student Responses 8 and 9)**

- *Distracter 5.* The correct response is, "The mean is sometimes affected when a 0 is added as one of the data points." Many students misinterpret a 0 data point as one that has no bearing on the mean, median, or mode. They see it as not having value, so therefore it does not affect the mean. Examples of data sets that would not see a change would be when all of the data points are 0 or if the mean itself is 0. (This case would need to have negative and positive numbers as part of the data set.) **(See Student Responses 10, 11, and 12)**

- *Distracter 6.* The correct response is, "The mean is sometimes one of the data points in the original set." Students are taught that the median (and mode) is one of the data points but not necessarily so with the mean. In many of the data sets students analyze, the mean is not one of the data points. This can lead them to believe that it never is. An example of the mean not being one of the data points is in the set $\{2, 4, 6, 9, 12, 15\}$. The mean for this set is 8. Examples where the mean is part of the data set are $\{4, 4, 4, 4, 4, 4\}$ and $\{2, 3, 5, 7, 8\}$. The means for these data sets are 4 and 5, respectively. Both of these numbers belong to the respective data sets. **(See Student Responses 13 and 14)**

Seeking Links to Cognitive Research

The concept of mean is quite difficult for students of all ages to understand, even after several years of formal instruction. Several difficulties have been documented in the literature: Students of all ages can talk about the algorithm for computing the mean and relate it to limited contexts, but cannot use it meaningfully in problems (Mokros & Russell, 1992; Pollatsek, Lima, & Well, 1981); upper elementary- and middle-school students believe that the mean of a particular data set is not one precise numerical value but an approximation that can have one of several values (Mokros & Russell, 1992); some middle-school students cannot use the mean to compare two different-sized sets of data (Gal et al., 1990); high-school students may believe the mean is the usual or typical value (Garfield & Ahlgren, 1988); students (or adults) may think that the sum of the data values below the mean is equivalent to the sum above the mean (rather than that the total of the deviations below the mean is equal to the total above) (Mokros & Russell, 1992). (AAAS, 1993, pp. 353–354)

Research involving students from middle school through college suggests that few students know much more about means than how to compute them (Cai, 1998; Pollatski, Lima, & Well, 1987). Thus, even children who can compute the mean often do not understand why the computation works or what the result represents. Although the add-and-divide algorithm is relatively simple to execute, developing a conceptual underpinning that allows one to use the mean sensibly is surprisingly difficult. (NCTM, 2003, p. 204)

In the middle grades, students should learn to use the mean, and continue to use the median and the mode, to describe the center of a set of data. Although the mean often quickly becomes the method of choice for students when summarizing a data set, their knack for computing the mean does not necessarily correspond to a solid understanding of its meaning or purpose (McClain, 1999). Students need to understand that the mean "evens out" or "balances" a set of data and that the median identifies the "middle" of a data set. They should compare the utility of the mean and the median as measures of center for different data sets. As several authors have noted (e.g., Uccellini, 1996; Konold, in press), students often fail to apprehend many subtle aspects of the mean as a measure of center. Thus, the teacher has an important role in providing experiences that help students construct a solid understanding of the mean and its relation to other measures of center. (NCTM, 2000, pp. 250–251)

Students need to think about measures of center in relation to the spread of a distribution. In general, the crucial question is, How do changes in data values affect the mean and median of a set of data? To examine this question, teachers could have students use a calculator to create a table of values and compute the mean and median. Then they could change one of the data values in the table and see whether the values of the mean and median are also changed. These relationships can be effectively demonstrated using software through which students can control a data value and observe how the mean and median are affected. For example, using software that produces line plots for data sets, students could plot a set of data and mark the mean and median on the line. The students could then change one data value and observe how the mean and median change. By repeating this process for various data points, they can notice that changing one data value usually does not affect the median at all, unless the moved value is at the middle of the data set or moves across the middle, but that every change in a value affects the mean. Thus the mean is more likely to be influenced by extreme values, since it is affected by the actual data values, but the median involves only the relative positions of the values. Other similar problems can be useful in helping students understand the different sensitivities of the mean and median; for example, the mean is very sensitive to the addition or deletion of one or two extreme data points, whereas the median is far less sensitive to such changes. (NCTM, 2000, p. 251)

Students should be able to explain why adding a constant to all observed values in a sample changes the measures of center by that constant but does not change the measures of spread or the general shape of the distribution. They should also understand why multiplying each observed value by the same constant multiplies the mean, median, range, and standard deviation by the same factor. (NCTM, 2000, pp. 327–328)

Students have difficulty with three properties of mean. The first is that the sum of the deviations from the average is zero. This property is important, for example, in estimating the mean of a set of data. The second difficult property [is] misunderstanding the impact that a zero can have on the mean. Errors on this property center on the misunderstanding that zero means "nothing," when in fact it is a legitimate piece of data. Every middle-grade teacher has probably had the experience of trying to explain to a student why he or she has received a lower than expected grade on a report card. Carefully entering the numbers into a calculator (particularly when one of the numbers is zero) and recomputing the average grade only results in a perplexed look on the student's face when the result in the display matches the grade on the report card. It is also interesting that 30% of preservice teachers thought that adding zero to a set of data would not change the value of the mean. The third troublesome property of the mean is that the average is representative of the values that were averaged. This property is one of the most difficult for students to understand, but it is important because of its value in interpreting the computed mean of data. The mean is not necessarily part of the data it represents. Rather, it is an abstraction that may be troublesome to visualize. (NCTM, 1993b, pp. 87–88)

Students should make distributions for many data sets, their own and published sets, which have already inspired some meaningful questions. The idea of a middle to a data set should be well motivated—say by asking for a simple way to compare two groups—and various kinds of middle should be considered. The algorithm for the mean can be learned but not without recurrent questions about what it conveys—and what it does not. (AAAS, 1993, p. 228)

Research suggests students should be introduced first to location measures that connect with their emerging concept of the "middle," such as the median, and later in the middle-school grades, to the mean. Premature introduction of the algorithm for computing the mean divorced from a meaningful context may block students from understanding what averages are for (Mokros & Russell, 1992; Pollatsek et al., 1981). (AAAS, 1993, p. 354)

The concept of a simple mean is more difficult for students to grasp than the simplicity the computational algorithm suggests. Apparently slight shifts in terminology cause great differences in performance. For example, only about 6% of seventh-grade students were able to calculate a mean for given data. When the same data were presented in a problem that required finding an average, about 51% of the students were successful. Students seem more familiar with "average" than "mean." You could ask your students to compute an average and a mean to see if they also are more familiar with "average." (NCTM, 1993b, p. 87)

*T*eaching Implications

In order to support a deeper understanding for students in secondary grades in regard to mean, the following are ideas and questions to consider in conjunction with the research.

Focus Through Instruction

- Rather than providing students with data and having them compute a mean, provide students with a mean (say, 20) and have them construct data sets with that mean. With an even number of items in the data set, students will quickly discover a balancing strategy. For example, 18 is two less than 20 so it should be paired with 22, which is two more than 20. Constructing data sets with an odd number of items, then, provides a greater challenge. (NCTM, 1993b, p. 87–88)
- As students progress in their understanding of measures of center and spread, utilize the above teaching strategy to include more stipulations on the data sets.
- Have students construct data sets for a given mean and require the inclusion of a zero to force students to consider the impact of a zero. (NCTM, 1993b, p. 88)
- Complete understanding of the mean may involve being able to picture the mean as a middle or balance point. A balance beam where the mean acts as a fulcrum balancing a distribution of weights may help some students understand the concept. (NCTMb, 1993, p. 89)

Questions to Consider . . . *when working with students as they grapple with the idea of mean*

- Do students know the term "mean" versus "average"?
- Can students explain why the algorithm for finding the mean works and what the resulting number represents?
- Can students communicate an understanding about the similarities and differences among mean, median, and mode?
- Do students understand what adding a value of 0 (and other values) to a data set does to the measures of center? To the measures of spread?
- Do students see how the mean, median, and mode are used in real-world situations, and are they able to communicate an understanding of which ones are more beneficial to the information that is needed?

Teacher Sound Bite

"I always thought that my students had a good understanding of mean, but after giving them this probe I now see that they have a good understanding of how to compute the mean using the algorithm. This is far from what my expectations were. I now see that we need to take a few steps back and explore some data sets that bring some of these examples into our conversations around measure of center. I will also start giving my students certain information about a data set (the mean, mode, median, etc.) and have them come up with some examples and non-examples of data sets for the given information."

Additional References for Research and Teaching Implications

Curriculum Topic Study
What Do You Mean?
Related CTS Guide: Measures of Center and Spread, p. 181

AAAS (1993), *Benchmarks for Science Literacy*, pp. 228–229, 353–354.

Huff (1954), *How to Lie With Statistics*, pp. 27–36.

Paulos (1991), *Beyond Numeracy*, pp. 141–143.

NCTM (1993c), *Research Ideas for the Classroom: High School Mathematics*, p. 188.

NCTM (1993b), *Research Ideas for the Classroom: Middle Grades Mathematics*, pp. 87–90, 226.

NCTM (2000), *Principles and Standards for School Mathematics*, pp. 50, 176, 179–180, 248, 250–251, 327–328, 342–344.

NCTM (2003), *A Research Companion to Principles and Standards for School Mathematics*, pp. 202–209.

Stepans et al. (2005), *Teaching for K–12 Mathematical Understanding Using the Conceptual Change Model*, pp. 189–230.

STUDENT RESPONSES TO "WHAT DO YOU *MEAN?*"

Sample Responses: #1

Student 1: A: Because that's the formula—it's what mean means.

Student 2: A: That is the process for finding the mean.

Student 3: N: That would be finding the average. The mean is the number that comes up the most.

Sample Responses: #2

Student 4: S: You could have something like 2, 4, 4, 4, 6, in which the mean and median are both in the middle.

Student 5: N: Because it isn't like the median, which is in the middle. It is always to one side of the middle.

Sample Responses: #3

Student 6: S: It depends on the numbers, by chance the mean and mode could be the same. What if you have 3 3 3 3 3 3, that's an obvious one.

Student 7: N: They just aren't the same thing.

Sample Responses: #4

Student 8: A: It would raise the mean of course, 1 2 3 add 4 to get 5 6 7. The mean has to be different.

Student 9: N: I don't think that it would change because the value is being added to all of them.

Sample Responses: #5

Student 10: A: It would lower the mean just like when you forget your homework it hurts your grade.

Student 11: S: It depends on the situation. Sometimes 0 is just a placeholder.
Student 12: N: 0 never matters with the mean.

Sample Responses: #6

Student 13: S: It just depends on the numbers, like 3 4 5 it is 4 but with 3 4 it is 3.5.

Student 14: A: The mean always is one of the numbers. It is the number most often seen.

VARIATION: **WHAT DO YOU** *MEAN?*

Each statement below can be preceded by one of the following statements:

The mean is always . . .
The mean is sometimes . . .
The mean is never . . .

Read each statement and indicate **A** (always), **S** (sometimes), or **N** (never):

Statement	Justify Response
1. ☐ the number that represents a typical value within a set of data	
2. ☐ the value obtained by dividing the sum of a set of data points by the number of data points in the set	
3. ☐ equal to the value of the term in the middle	
4. ☐ affected when there is an outlier	
5. ☐ the balance point of the set of data	
6. ☐ equivalent to the value of the mode	
7. ☐ half of the range	
8. ☐ changed when the same amount is added to each of the data points	
9. ☐ a fair share distribution	
10. ☐ affected when a 0 is added as one of the data points	
11. ☐ one of the data points in the original set	

NAME OF THE GRAPH?

Bob made the graph below.

Which of these could be the title for the graph?

A. Number of students who walked to school the last 5 days
B. Number of students in 10 clubs
C. Either of these could be the title.

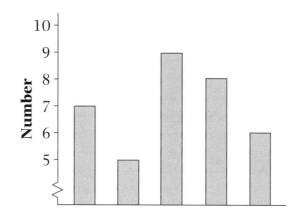

Explain your thinking:

TEACHERS' NOTES: NAME OF THE GRAPH?

Grade Level for "Name of the Graph?" Probe

6–8	9–12

*Q*uestioning for Student Understanding

Are students able to move beyond point-by-point graph interpretation?

*U*ncovering Understandings

Name of the Graph? (Content Standard: Data Analysis)

*E*xamining Student Work

The distracter in this probe may reveal *common errors* in graphical interpretation.

- *The correct answer is A.* The independent variable is the days (X values), and the dependent variable is how many students walked to school (Y values).
- *Distracter B.* Some students will choose this example because they see the 10 on the Y axis representing the 10 clubs described. These students usually lack practice in analyzing graphical representation and making choices about dependent versus independent variables.
- *Distracter C.* Most students realize that the graph shown can represent the information described in choice A, but many also misinterpret it to include choice B. They either use the 10 on the Y axis for the number of clubs, or think that each of the five bars includes 2 clubs each. Many students that choose C reason that the word "number" on the Y axis does not specify number of what, so it could mean days, clubs, or students. They do not feel they have enough labeling information to accurately make a choice.

*S*eeking Links to Cognitive Research

Students read graphs point-by-point and ignore their global features. This has been attributed to algebra lessons where students are given questions that they could easily answer from a table of ordered pairs. They are rarely asked questions about maximum and minimum values; intervals over which a function increases, decreases, or levels off; or rates of change. (AAAS, 1993, p. 351)

A new view of mathematical representations in general and graphing in particular has slowly emerged in the past decade. Instead of being isolated curricular items to be taught and tested as ends in themselves, graphs along with diagrams, charts, number sentences, and formulas, are increasingly seen as "useful tools for building understanding and for communicating both information and understanding" (NCTM, 2000). As such, graphs and other representations have come to play an increasingly important role in mathematical activities in school. (NCTM, 2003, p. 250)

Reading graphs is not a trivial task. Many graphs that are produced for commercial publications are in fact designed to magnify differences that may or may not be important. Students need to learn when information is accurately portrayed. For seventh graders, prior knowledge of mathematics (e.g., 1 centimeter is less than 1 inch), of the topic of a graph (e.g., understand that height refers to "tallness" rather than the "oldness"), and of graphical form (e.g., the tallest bar in a bar graph represents the greatest quantity) are all important for comprehending information in a graph. Significant predictors of graph comprehension were reading achievement, mathematics achievement, and prior knowledge of mathematics content. These results may not seem surprising, but they point up the complexity of graph comprehension as a cognitive task. Teachers must address the acquisition of supporting skills as graphing is taught. (NCTM, 1993b, p. 91)

One technique useful for helping students understand that their mental image of an event is not necessarily what will show up on a graph is to have them deal with several graphs simultaneously. Discussion of why one graph is better than another will expose both correct and incorrect conceptions. (NCTM, 1993, p. 91)

Both processes (interpretation and modeling) depend on the ability of the students to associate, using their own words, situation facts with the corresponding graphical features. For Swan [1985], interpretation amounts to "listening to what graphs say" and modeling corresponds to "how to talk with them." What is required from the students is more than being capable of focusing on one single point. The students' ability to deal with such processes depends on the familiarity they would have developed with *global features of graphs*—those involving more than one point to be comprehended. If students are not specifically trained to handle graphs and their global features at school, it is no surprise that students meet difficulties in interpretation or modeling tasks. (NCTM, 1993, pp. 92–93)

In an *interpretation task,* students start with an external representation (a graph, for example) and try, using words, to specify a situation that fits the representation. Graphical interpretation is a progressive integration of the various pieces of interpretation conveyed by the graph with the underlying situational background. This means that the situation guides the interpretation, and this is where we must look for mistakes. Indeed, situations are often characterized by objects or pictures suggested by the verbal descriptions introducing the graphs. Concrete elements belonging to or associated with the situations often contaminate the interpretation in the sense that they will determine the meaning attached to parts of the graphical representation. (NCTM, 1993, pp. 93–94)

Little is known about how graphic skills are learned and how graph production is related to graph interpretation. Microcomputer-Based Laboratories (MBLs) are known to improve the development of students' abilities to interpret graphs. (AAAS, 1993, p. 351)

*T*eaching Implications

In order to support a deeper understanding for students in secondary grades in regard to graphical interpretation, the following are ideas and questions to consider in conjunction with the research.

Focus Through Instruction

- Have students analyze a variety of graphs that were created by other sources: students, newspapers, the Internet, etc.
- Have students work with several graphs simultaneously. Have them compare and contrast them. Have them write a heading (or description) for each graph.
- Have students verbalize what the X and Y axes are representing.
- Have students find different graphical representations for situations, then compare and contrast the different graphs.

Questions to Consider . . . *when working with students as they grapple with the idea of graphical interpretation*

- Do students have an understanding of dependent and independent variables?
- Do students understand the labels for the axes?
- Do students use a variety of graphic representations?
- Are students only creating graphs, or are they also analyzing graphs of other sources?

Teacher Sound Bite

"Most of my students chose A or C, but not all of the students who chose A had reasoning that truly backed up their choice. . . . [E]ven though many of them got the right answer, I am not confident that they truly understand graphical representations. I am going to continue assessing them on these types of graphs (and others) to give me a better understanding of their progress and use them as a focus for student discussions to foster a better understanding of graphs. I am going to pull from a variety of graphs and places that we find them."

Additional References for Research and Teaching Implications

AAAS (1993), *Benchmarks for Science Literacy*, pp. 297, 351.

NCTM (1993c), *Research Ideas for the Classroom: High School Mathematics*, pp. 92–94.

NCTM (1993b), *Research Ideas for the Classroom: Middle Grades Mathematics*, pp. 91–93, 226.

NCTM (2000), *Principles and Standards for School Mathematics*, pp. 49–50, 176–180, 248–253.

NCTM (2003), *A Research Companion to Principles and Standards for School Mathematics*, pp. 202, 250–260.

Stepans et al. (2005), Teaching for K–12 Mathematical Understanding Using the Conceptual Change Model, pp. 189–230.

> **Curriculum Topic Study**
>
> *Name of the Graph?*
>
> Related CTS Guide: Line Graphs, Bar Graphs, and Histograms, p. 179; Graphic Representation, p. 196

STUDENT RESPONSES TO "NAME OF THE GRAPH?"

Sample Responses: A

Student 1: A is right because there are 5 bars so 5 days. As for the numbers up the Y axis, they show the number of students.

Student 2: This graph must show the number of students who walked to school in the last 5 days. It couldn't represent the number of students in 10 clubs, because there are only 5 bars. You would need 10 if there were 10 clubs. By the process of elimination, A is correct.

Student 3: I chose A, because there are only 5 bars shown in the graph, so the number of students who walked to school in the last 5 days would work. I don't think B would work as good since there are only 5 bars and there would be 10 different clubs. So since I don't think B would work, then C isn't an option.

Sample Responses: B

Student 4: I think it is B because there is a 10 going up the right side of the graph and there are 10 clubs in B. Seems to work fine.

Student 5: If you add them up you get 35 students. There would be more students than that who walked to school in the last 5 days, so it would have to be B, the number of students in 10 clubs.

Student 6: It would have to be B because it couldn't be A. If it was there would only be 1 bar as opposed to 5.

Sample Responses: C

Student 7: I chose C because the X axis is not labeled.

Student 8: My thinking is that C is correct because there is no label on the Y axis as to what the number means. And there is nothing at all written on the X axis so at this point there really could be any title.

Student 9: It could be either of the answers but we don't know for sure, because they don't give the dependent variable. You wouldn't be able to title it at all without it.

Student 10: I chose C because it is possible for them both because the graph shows both. It shows the number of clubs and the number of students of the last 5 days.

Student 11: C because they don't have any specifics to what the graph is pertaining to.

GRAPH CONSTRUCTION

Circle each coordinate graph that has been set up appropriately.

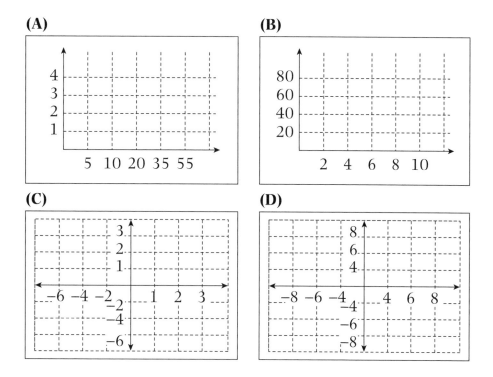

Explain why you chose/did not choose each of the coordinate graphs.

TEACHERS' NOTES: GRAPH CONSTRUCTION

Grade Level for "Graph Construction" Probe

6–8	9–12

Questioning for Student Understanding

Can students identify correct graphical construction and accurate use of interval scale?

Uncovering Understandings

Graph Construction (Content Standard: Data Analysis)

Examining Student Work

The distracters may reveal *common errors* using interval scale in graph construction. Some students construct different scales for the positive and negative portions of the graph, believe that the scales on the X and Y axes need to be the same, or do not have intervals that are evenly labeled. There may also be *misunderstandings* that a coordinate graph needs to show all of the quadrants.

- *The correct answer is B.* This coordinate graph (of the first quadrant) has scales that are correctly constructed on the X and Y axes. Because it only has the first quadrant shown, many students will inaccurately think that this is a graph used only for bar graphs or histograms. Other students will not choose this graph because the scales on the X and Y axes are not the same, but this is not a requirement of coordinate graphs—the only requirement is that the positive and negative scales are the same.
- *Distracter A.* The scales on the Y axis are correct, but the scales on the X axis of this choice are incorrect. On the X axis, the scales start out in multiples of 5, then jump from 20 to 35 to 55. Some students think this is not an accurate representation of a coordinate graph, not because of the incorrect scale, but because it only shows the first quadrant.
- *Distracter C.* This choice shows the scales of the positive values (X and Y axes) constructed the same and the scales of the negative values (X and Y axes) constructed the same. This is incorrect, as the scales of the positive and negative values of the same axis have to be the same. The X axis and Y axis values do not.
- *Distracter D.* Although this graph constructs the positive and negative scales of each axes the same, the scales start out incorrectly. Both the X

and Y axes jump from the origin to the value of 4, then after that only jump by multiples of 2. Many times, graphs will not start out using the scale of the axis, but will be labeled with a "zig-zag" line to show this break in scale.

Seeking Links to Cognitive Research

When constructing graphs, middle-school and high-school students have difficulties with the notions of interval scale and coordinates even after traditional instruction in algebra (Kerslake, 1981; Leinhardt et al., 1990; Vergnaud & Errecalde, 1980; Wavering, 1985). For example, some students think it is legitimate to construct different scales for the positive and the negative part of the axes. Alternately, students think that the scales on the X and Y axes must be identical, even if that obscures the relationship. When interpreting graphs, middle-school students do not understand the effect that a scale would have on the appearance of the graph. (AAAS, 1993, p. 351)

Among the most common misconceptions concerning graphs are the following:

Use of different scales for the positive and negative parts of the line

Placement of axes to intersect at a point other than the origin

Difficulty with continuity—for example, viewing a line as having a finite number of points

Leinhardt, Zaslavsky, and Stein have also found that most of these "misconceptions" are actually taught, or at least implied, by the kinds of graphing experiences in most elementary school textbooks. For example, students rarely construct a set of axes themselves; mostly they work with line graphs and bar graphs that use discontinuous axes. The activities they mainly engage in are plotting ordered pairs, and perhaps joining the resulting points with lines, or interpreting already constructed bar graphs and line graphs within given "real-world" situations. Students need more experience in constructing graphs, including drawing and marking the axes. Instruction must also emphasize the connection between an equation and its graph and the continuity of most graphs in algebra. (NCTM, 1993c, p. 115)

Students are capable of reading and plotting points on graphs, but they may be doing so in a rote manner. They often do not have the ability to construct axes (Leinhardt, Zaslavsky, & Stein, 1990). They may use coordinates to indicate lengths of segments on the graph. Student may interpret graph points as having density and may have difficulty with the idea that there are, for example, more points on a line than those the students graphed themselves. Students' ability to work on scale on graphs is often minimal. For example, they may believe that it is legitimate to use different scales on the positive and negative portions of the axes. In summary, dealing with a graph as an abstraction with a large amount of convention and notation to be learned is a nontrivial task (Leinhardt et al., 1990). All these areas need sustained instructional attention. (NCTM, 2003, p. 166)

Deciding on plot scales and on what data should be included in their plots poses a number of interesting challenges to students. Some students described in Russell et al. (2002a) thought that plot scales should not extend beyond the range of observed values, whereas others argued that the scales should extend to include values that could have occurred or far enough at least to make a pleasant boundary. (NCTM, 2003, p. 201)

*T*eaching Implications

In order to support a deeper understanding for students in secondary grades in regard to graph construction, the following are ideas and questions to consider in conjunction with the research.

Focus Through Instruction

- When using graphical representation, use a variety of graphs and "windows."
- When creating histograms, allow students to see that, although we draw these types of graphs in the first quadrant and the other quadrants are not usually shown, they are "still there."
- Allow students to construct their own scale, and have them discuss their choice in groups to analyze for accuracy.
- Use graphing technology to explore the correct use of scales.
- Use graphing technology to illustrate what different changes in scale do to the "look" of graphs.

Questions to Consider . . . *when working with students as they grapple with the idea of graph construction*

- Do students use the same scale for the positive and negative parts of the axes?
- Do students understand that the scale of the X and Y axes do not have to be the same?
- Can students communicate the meaning behind the scales that they choose or ones already constructed?
- Can students defend their choices in scale (or ones already constructed)?
- Do students have an opportunity to explore different graphical representations for situations?
- Do students understand that histograms are created in the first quadrant of a coordinate graph?

- Do students understand that when the first quadrant of a coordinate graph is the only one shown, it does not mean that the graph is a bar graph?

Teacher Sound Bite

"The biggest surprise I found with the results of this probe is that several of my students thought that choices A and B were only used for bar graphs and were not coordinate graphs. I will need to use a wide variety of windows for my students in the future. I will also need to take more time to have some discussions about graphs and scale to allow for students to communicate their understanding and lack of understanding."

Additional References for Research and Teaching Implications

AAAS (1993), *Benchmarks for Science Literacy*, p. 351.

NCTM (1993b), *Research Ideas for the Classroom: Middle Grades Mathematics*, pp. 93–94, 226.

NCTM (1993c), *Research Ideas for the Classroom: High School Mathematics*, pp. 113–115.

NCTM (2000), *Principles and Standards for School Mathematics*, pp. 49–50, 176–180, 248–253.

NCTM (2003), *A Research Companion to Principles and Standards for School Mathematics*, pp. 166–167, 201–202, 250–260.

Stepans et al. (2005), *Teaching for K–12 Mathematical Understanding Using the Conceptual Change Model*, pp. 189–230.

Curriculum Topic Study

Scale Interval Graphs

Related CTS Guide: Graphic Representation, p. 196

STUDENT RESPONSES TO "GRAPH CONSTRUCTION"

Sample Responses: Graph B

Student 1: The correct graph is B. A is not correct because it jumps integers. Instead of going 5, 10, 15, 20, it went 5, 10, 20, 35. B is set up right because the integers stay the same throughout (on both the X and Y axes). C is not correct because it says –2 when it should say –1. It throws off the whole graph. D is also not correct because the integers jump to 4 to start, then go up by 2's. There needs to be a 2 between 0 and 4.

Student 2: I did not choose graph A because the bottom coordinates don't make sense at all. You can't go from 5, 10 then jump to 20. You would get all mixed up. Graph B makes sense because there are equal increments of numbers and it is easy to understand.

Sample Response: Graph A

Student 3: I chose A and B because these graphs are like the ones we use in class.

Sample Response: Graph C

Student 4: I chose C because it has the positive and negative numbers on it and the numbers go in a pattern that makes sense.

Sample Responses: Graph D

Student 5: I did not choose A because it is a bar graph and the numbers aren't the same on each side. I did not choose B because it is a bar graph. I did not choose C as a coordinate graph because all of the numbers are not the same. I chose D as a coordinate graph because it is set up properly and the numbers are correct.

Student 6: I picked B and D because they have the same kind of spacing in the numbers. On B it goes 2, 4, 6, 8, 10 (on the bottom) and 20, 40, 60, 80 (going up). On D it just has all the same numbers.

Student 7: I picked D. In A the numbers on the Y axis are by 1's and the numbers on the X axis are by 5's. In B the Y axis is by 10's and the X axis is by 2's. Because of this, neither one is right. In C the negative numbers start at 2 while the positive numbers start at 1. D is correct because the whole graph is the same and starts with the same numbers.

Student 8: I chose D because coordinate graphs have four lines, not 2 so A and B would not fit. Coordinate graphs have positive and negative numbers and they have to have the same negative numbers and positive numbers so C can't be it. So it should be D.

Student 9: I think that D is the only one because they have to have the same numbers (the X and Y have to be the same) and they have to have positive and negative numbers.

Student 10: Well I chose D because we played a game last year and it was set up the same way.

Sample Responses: No Choice

Student 11: I don't think any of them are set up properly because A and B are set up as bar graphs, C has 1, 2, 3 for positives then 2, 4, 6 for the negatives. And if you count by 2's for graph D you should start with 2 not 4.

Student 12: I did not choose any of these graphs, even though C and D got close, they are supposed to start at 0.

5

Algebra Assessment Probes

Grade Span Bar Key

■	Target for Instruction Depending on Local Standards
▨	Prerequisite Concept/Field Testing Indicates Student Difficulty

Algebra Probes			
Question	**Probe**	**Grade 6–8**	**Grades 9–12**
Are students able to identify equivalent expressions in the form of familiar formulas?	Equal or Not Equal? p. 158	■	▨
Do students misuse "key words" when writing expressions?	Is It the Same as a + b? p. 165	■	▨
Do students correctly apply knowledge of equality and relationships among quantities?	M & N's? p. 170	■	▨
Do students understand how to evaluate an expression of the form ax?	What's the Substitute? p. 175	■	▨
Do students understand the operation implied by concatenation of literal symbols and numbers?	Is It True? p. 180	■	▨
Do students understand appropriate methods and notations when solving for an unknown?	Solving Equations p. 187	■	▨
Are students able to identify various representations of an inequality?	Correct Representation of the Inequality? p. 194	■	▨
Are students able to identify when a literal symbol is being used as a variable?	Is It a Variable? p. 200	■	▨
Do students correctly use the distributive law when multiplying algebraic binomials?	Binomial Expansion? p. 207	■	▨
Do students recognize the characteristics of the graph of a quadratic function?	Is It Quadratic? p. 213	■	■

157

Probe
1

EXPRESSIONS: EQUAL OR NOT EQUAL?

Decide whether the following sets of expressions are equal or not equal, and then explain your reasoning behind each choice.

A

πr^2 and $2\pi r$

Equal   or   not equal?

Explain:

B

$2(l+w)$ and $2l + w$

Equal   or   not equal?

Explain:

C

lwh and hwl

Equal   or   not equal?

Explain:

TEACHERS' NOTES: EXPRESSIONS: EQUAL OR NOT EQUAL?

Grade Level for "Expressions: Equal or Not Equal?" Probe

6–8	9–12

*Q*uestion for Student Understanding

Are students able to identify equivalent expressions in the form of familiar formulas?

*U*ncovering Understandings

Expressions: Equal or Not Equal? (Content Standard: Algebra)

*E*xamining Student Work

The first example may expose a lack of *conceptual understanding* of exponents and *common errors* students have working with them. The second example may reveal a lack of *conceptual and procedural understanding* of parenthesis and *common errors* students have manipulating them. The third example may reveal a lack of *conceptual understanding* of variables and the commutative law and *common errors* students have using the commutative law with variables.

- *The correct responses are A—not equal, B—not equal, and C—equal.* **(See Student Responses 1, 2, 3, 4, 8, 9, 10, 11, 15, and 16)**
- *Distracter A.* Students who choose equal in example A usually see powers as multiplication between the base and the exponent as in $x^2 = 2$ times x $(2x)$ instead of $x^2 = x$ times x. In the given example of the area of a circle, the correct equality would be $r^2 = rr$. **(See Student Responses 5, 6, and 7)**
- *Distracter B.* Students' choice of equal in example B shows a lack of understanding of the distribution law. In the perimeter of a rectangle example, $2(l + w)$, the 2 was only distributed to the l and not the w. The correct distribution would be $2l + 2w$. **(See Student Responses 12, 13, and 14)**
- *Distracter C.* In example C, a choice of not equal shows a lack of understanding of the commutative law over multiplication or a lack of conceptual understanding of variables. Some students believe that changing locations of variables (numbers) in multiplication may change the results. Some students might not have a clear understanding of variables and confuse them with place value. **(See Student Responses 17 and 18)**

Seeking Links to Cognitive Research

Students should begin to develop their skill in producing equivalent expressions and solving linear equations in the middle grades, both mentally and with paper and pencil. They should develop fluency in operating with symbols in their high school years, with by-hand or mental computation in simple cases and with computer algebra technology in all cases. In general, if students engage extensively in symbolic manipulation before they develop a solid conceptual foundation for their work, they will be unable to do more than mechanical manipulation. The foundation for meaningful work with symbolic notation should be laid over a long time. (NCTM, 2000, p. 39)

Being able to operate with algebraic symbols is also important because the ability to rewrite algebraic expressions enables students to re-express functions in ways that reveal different types of information about them. (NCTM, 2000, p. 301)

High school students should develop an understanding of the algebraic properties that govern the manipulation of symbols in expressions, equations, and inequalities. They should become fluent in performing such manipulations by appropriate means—mentally, by hand, or by machine—to solve equations and inequalities, to generate equivalent forms of expressions or functions, or to prove general results. (NCTM, 2000, p. 297)

It is obvious that students have problems in performing arithmetic operations on algebraic expressions. Perhaps this is partially due to the difficulties they have in thinking of a letter as representing a number. (NCTM, 1999, p. 186)

Students often find algebra concepts and the manipulation of the algebraic symbols difficult. The difficulty may not so much be with the mathematical ideas themselves but rather with the mode of instruction (Piaget, 1971). Students need extensive experience with concrete models to develop their own internal mental images of a concept. When mathematical symbols are finally introduced, they can be accepted as a code to represent ideas that a child already understands. (NCTM, 1999, p. 189)

A number of recent studies have shown how selected modifications of elementary school mathematics might support the development of algebraic reasoning. One approach infuses elementary mathematics with a systematic use of problems requiring students to generalize, to determine values of a literal term that satisfy quantitative constraints (with or without equations), or to treat numbers in algebraic ways. For example, students might be asked to determine how many ways the number 4 can be written using a given number of 1s and the four basic operations. Since each expression must equal 4, students must distinguish among the different possibilities on the basis of their symbolic form rather than their value when evaluated. (NRC, 2001, p. 262)

Some older students make errors in writing totals and products that were not made by younger students. They wrote h10, meaning "h plus 10," assuming that conjoining meant addition. When they had to write "x times 4" they wrote x^4. Younger students did not make this mistake because they had not learned the notation for powers. Some older students think of exponents as an instruction to multiply, without having a clear idea of what is being multiplied. (NCTM, 1999, p. 310)

In mathematical equations (and expressions), the signals for ordering are not those of ordinary language. They include parentheses (which are not used as we are using them here in the ordinary language way) and more subtle signals that must be deduced from a knowledge of formal rules for the procedures of operations. Natural-language rules are no help in reading mathematical expressions. (NCTM, 1999, p. 311)

Parentheses and other bracketing symbols should provide a perceptual aid for unitizing. However, there are three common behaviors that seem to neutralize the suggestive effect of parentheses. Some students apparently ignore or overlook bracketing symbols, as in $4(n + 5) = 4n + 5$. Other students, perhaps in response to the order-of-operations exhortation to "do what's in parentheses first," focus on parentheses to the exclusion of the overall structure of the expression. And finally, the equation-solving advice to "clear the parentheses first" may prompt many students to overlook the variable unit in their haste to eliminate grouping symbols. As with many rules of thumb, we need to show students some situations in which the usual rules are not the most efficient way to proceed. (NCTM, 1999, p. 332)

Many errors related to expressions seem to involve an interaction between (a) overgeneralizing on the part of the student and (b) the highly abstract nature of the field properties, especially the associative or distributive law. For example, one of the most common errors is to simplify an expression like $4 + 3n$ to $7n$. One explanation for this kind of error is that, in arithmetic, students learn to operate on numbers until they obtain a single number as the answer. Then, in algebra they may feel uncomfortable leaving an expression with a visible operation sign as the final answer, so they perform whatever operations they can on the available numbers (and/or letters) to reduce the expression to a single term. (NCTM, 1999, pp. 335–336)

In the course of modeling problem situations, students often develop different but equivalent expressions. By exploiting these occurrences as opportunities to compare and analyze for meaning, teachers can foster symbol sense. (Driscoll, 1999, p. 126)

*T*eaching Implications

To support a deeper understanding for students in secondary grades in regard to these algebraic concepts, the following are ideas and questions to consider in conjunction with the research.

Focus Through Instruction

- Check that your students clearly distinguish products and powers in arithmetic and the ways of writing them in arithmetic and algebra. Most teachers explain that ab means "a multiplied by itself b times," which is easily conflated with "a multiplied by b." (NCTM, 1999, p. 312)
- Most students will need extensive experience in interpreting relationships among quantities in a variety of problem contexts before they can work meaningfully with variables and symbolic expressions. Relationships among quantities can often be expressed symbolically in more then one way, providing opportunities for students to examine the equivalence of various algebraic expressions. (NCTM, 2000, pp. 225–226)
- Do not reject algebraic expressions students correctly construct in favor of simpler equivalent ones. Opportunities to compare and analyze the advantages different expressions offer can be missed by doing so. (Driscoll, 1999, p. 126)
- Allow students to use different methods to check their results, including algebraic technology.
- Area models are a tool for visualization of algebraic concepts. For example students can move from numerical representations like $7 \times 13 = 7 \times 10 + 7 \times 3$ to algebraic representations like $a(b + c) = ab + ac$. In the area model, $a(b + c)$ would be viewed as one rectangle and $ab + ac$ would be viewed as two connected rectangles. (NCTM, 1999, p. 165)
- Encourage students to substitute numbers into the expressions to help them see if equality holds true.
- Allow students to work with partners or in groups to discuss the correct or incorrect reasoning behind each example.
- Pull from other formulas to give students practice with algebraic manipulation.
- Allow students to write rules differently in class. Do not insist that all expressions be simplified. Allow students to discuss classmates' rules for the same problem and let them discuss whether they are equivalent and what makes them so/not so.

Questions to Consider . . . *when working with students as they grapple with equivalent expressions*

- Can students give non-algebraic (numerical) examples to back up their reasoning of the algebraic equality/inequality?
- In students' prior work with formulas and expressions, have they learned about concepts through meaningful work with models, or have they been given them to use or memorize?
- Can students verbalize what the formulas mean? Can they verbalize the manipulation of the expressions?

- Can students not only choose the incorrect manipulations but also see the mistake that was made?
- Can students calculate the perimeter of a rectangle in three ways that yield equivalent expressions? For example, the perimeter of a 7×4 rectangle can be calculated in the following ways: $2(7 + 4)$, $(2 \times 7) + (2 \times 4)$, and $7 + 7 + 4 + 4$. (NRC, 2001, p. 272)
- Do students have a clear conceptual understanding of variables?

Teacher Sound Bite

"My initial reaction to giving this probe was that it would be too easy for my students, as we have been working with all of these concepts for months. Well, I was very surprised by the results I ended up with. Many of my students picked the wrong choice. Their reasoning is what surprised me most, as it showed that there are a lot of misunderstandings in my classroom over these topics. I think I am going to use this probe as a basis for classroom discussions to start building a foundation of understanding."

Additional References for Research and Teaching implications

AAAS (1993), *Benchmarks for Science Literacy*, pp. 25–29, 215, 217–221, 351–352.

Driscoll (1999), *Fostering Algebraic Thinking*, pp. 115–162.

National Research Council (2001), *Adding It Up*, pp. 255–280.

NCTM (1993b), *Research Ideas for the Classroom: Middle Grades Mathematics*, pp. 179–196, 226.

NCTM (1993c), *Research Ideas for the Classroom: High School Mathematics*, pp. 119–139.

NCTM (1997), *Algebraic Thinking*, pp. 52–58, 59, 141, 165, 186–187, 189, 219, 310–312, 325, 330–336.

NCTM (2000), *Principles and Standards for School Mathematics*, pp. 37–40, 67–71, 158–159, 222–223, 225–227, 280–285, 296–297, 301.

NCTM (2003), *A Research Companion to Principles and Standards for School Mathematics*, pp. 116–117, 120, 123–124, 130–131, 138–140.

Stepans et al. (2005), *Teaching for K–12 Mathematical Understanding Using the Conceptual Change Model*, pp. 31–50, 149–163.

Curriculum Topic Study

Expressions: Equal or Not Equal?

Related CTS Guide:
Expressions and Equations, p. 136; Exponents, p. 118; Formulas, p. 137

STUDENT RESPONSES TO "EXPRESSIONS: EQUAL OR NOT EQUAL?"

Sample Responses: Not equal for A (correct)

Student 1: These are not equal because πr^2 is the area of a circle and 2 r is just twice the radius times π.

Student 2: Not equal because squared is not the same as multiplied by 2.

Student 3: Not equal. $2\pi r = 2$ times π times the radius, $\pi r^2 =$ times the radius times the radius.

Student 4: Not equal. This is so because when you multiply 2 times a number it only doubles it. The square is multiplying a number times itself.

Sample Responses: Equal for A

Student 5: These are equal because they are both equations to find the area of a circle.

Student 6: A is equal because it doesn't matter what order you multiply, the answer will be the same.

Student 7: Equal because there is a 2 in the first one so you have to multiply by 2.

Sample Responses: Not equal for B (correct)

Student 8: They are not equal because if you put numbers in place of the letters and you do the math, the answers are different.

Student 9: It is not equal. 2(l + w) = 2l + 2w, not 2l + w.

Student 10: The expression 2(l + w) equals the sum of l + w times 2. The expression 2l + w equals 2 times l plus w.

Student 11: To make these equal you would have to have 2l + 2w because the distributive property has to go all the way through.

Sample Responses: Equal for B

Student 12: These are equal because you can use the distributive property to get the same answer.

Student 13: The two are equal because the l is being multiplied by 2.

Student 14: They are equal as both are the same, but one has parenthesis.

Sample Responses: Equal for C (correct)

Student 15: They are equal because they have the same letters being multiplied together, just in a different order.

Student 16: No matter the order of multiplication, the products are the same.

Sample Responses: Not Equal for C

Student 17: These are not equal because the numbers could be different so the answers would be different.

Student 18: Not equal. If you put numbers in, it shows that they are not equal. For example: 258 does not equal 852.

IS IT THE SAME AS A + B?

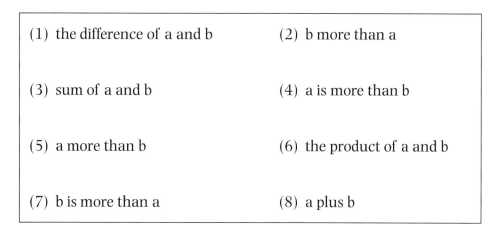

Circle all statements that can be represented by the expression a + b.

(1) the difference of a and b	(2) b more than a
(3) sum of a and b	(4) a is more than b
(5) a more than b	(6) the product of a and b
(7) b is more than a	(8) a plus b

Explain how you made your choices:

TEACHERS' NOTES: IS IT THE SAME AS A + B?

Grade Level for "Is It the Same as a + b?" Probe

6–8	9–12

Questioning for Student Understanding

Do students misuse "key words" when writing expressions?

Uncovering Understandings

Is It the Same as a + b? (Content Standard: Algebra)

Examining Student Work

The distracters may reveal a lack of *conceptual understanding* of key words used to describe mathematical situations. The focus of this probe is on addition and words that might or might not describe the operation.

- *The correct responses are 2, 3, 5, and 8.* "a + b" symbolically represents two numbers, a and b, being added together. Response 3 is the result (sum) of adding a and b. Response 8 uses "plus" for adding. Responses 2 and 5 describe adding a number to another number. Some will not choose 5 because when written "a + b," the "b" is the number being added on, but using the commutative law of addition, we can also say "b + a" without changing the result. **(See Student Responses 1, 2, 3, 4, 5, and 6)**
- *Distracter 1.* The word "difference" is used in this choice to check for students' understanding of words that describe subtraction.
- *Distracters 4 and 7.* These choices combine the word "is" with "more than" to check for understanding of descriptors of inequality statements. Many students get confused over these two choices and have difficulty seeing the difference between 2 and 7, and between 4 and 5. In some cases this difficulty arises from a lack of concentrated reading, but in many cases there is a lack of understanding of the meaning of these statements. Another difficulty that arises is that the word "is" is often used in sentences to denote the word "equals." **(See Student Responses 7, 11, and 12)**
- *Distracter 6:* "Product" is used instead of "sum" to see if students can distinguish between the descriptors used for the results of multiplying versus adding. **(See Student Responses 8, 9, and 10)**

Seeking Links to Cognitive Research

One of the major reasons that students today do not succeed in algebra is that they do not correctly interpret the technical language of mathematics.

Attention to language has numerous implications for both content and instruction. Although being attentive to language is a broad and perhaps vague directive, the basic routine for organizing both content and instruction should be moving from the descriptive language of students to the more technical language of mathematics. (NCTM, 1999, p. 54)

Discussion gives students a means of articulating aspects of a situation, which helps the speaker clarify thoughts and meanings. Verbalizing helps develop technical understanding because the descriptive talk and explanations must be worked toward communicating with mathematical terms and symbols. (NCTM, 1999, p. 55)

Though looking for key words can be a useful problem-solving heuristic, it may encourage over-reliance on a direct, rather than analytical mode for translating word problems into equations. The fact that so many textbook problems lend themselves to direct translation is seductive. (NCTM, 1999, p. 332)

*T*eaching Implications

To support a deeper understanding for students in secondary grades in regard to these algebraic concepts the following are ideas and questions to consider in conjunction with the research.

Focus Through Instruction

- Students should be required to write descriptive statements for such relations as $S/6 = P$, $S + P = 6$, $S = 6P$, $P = 6S$, $(6S)/P = T$, $6S + P = T$. (NCTM, 1999, p. 54)
- Discuss how vocabulary is used differently within mathematics and outside mathematics as in science, social studies, and so forth.
- Middle school students should have many opportunities to use language to communicate their mathematical ideas . . . to reach agreement about the meanings of words, and to recognize the crucial importance of commonly shared definitions and notations. (NCTM, 1999, p. 61)
- Encourage students to record answers in mathematical statements and in English sentences written out in full and share their answers. (NCTM, 1999, p. 73)

Questions to Consider . . . *when working with students as they grapple with translating literal expressions*

- Do students know the meaning of key words that describe operations?
- Are students aware of what the word "is" means in a mathematical statement?
- Are students familiar with inequalities and their different representations?
- Do students have multiple opportunities to translate algebraic expressions to English and vice versa?

Teacher Sound Bite

"The biggest surprise I had when looking at my students' responses to this probe was that they confused "product" with addition. I am not sure where this comes from but will need to clarify this. I was aware of the confusion with the word "is," but this probe allowed me some insight as to why they were thinking of the statements using "is" as addition instead of inequalities. I also want to do some more work with variables, what we can assume about them and what we cannot assume. I am not sure that my students have a good grasp of their meaning and how to use them."

Additional References for Research and Teaching Implications

Curriculum Topic Study
Is It the Same as a + b?
Related CTS Guide: Expressions and Equations, p. 136

AAAS (1993), *Benchmarks for Science Literacy*, pp. 25–29, 215, 217–221.

Driscoll (1999), *Fostering Algebraic Thinking*, pp. 115–162.

NCTM (1993b), *Research Ideas for the Classroom: Middle Grades Mathematics*, pp. 179–196, 226.

NCTM (1993c), *Research Ideas for the Classroom: High School Mathematics*, pp. 79–82, 119–139.

NCTM (1997), *Algebraic Thinking*, pp. 10, 52–58, 61–62, 73, 141, 150, 161, 181, 189, 304, 325–326, 332.

NCTM (2000), *Principles and Standards for School Mathematics*, pp. 37–40, 158–162, 222–223, 225–226, 280–285.

NCTM (2003), *A Research Companion to Principles and Standards for School Mathematics*, pp. 138–140, 276–279.

NRC (2001), *Adding It Up*, pp. 255–280.

Stepans et al. (2005), *Teaching for K–12 Mathematical Understanding Using the Conceptual Change Model*, pp. 31–50, 149–163.

STUDENT RESPONSES TO "IS IT THE SAME AS A + B?"

Sample Responses

Student 1: Well it is easier to explain why I didn't pick certain ones than why I did pick the ones I did. So I didn't pick the difference of a and b because that denotes subtracting, b is more than a denotes that b > a, a is more than b denotes a > b, and product denotes a times. As you can see, none of these mean a plus b or a added to b. (circled 2, 3, 5, and 8)

Student 2: Numbers 3 and 8 mean addition. The commutative property of addition makes it possible to add "b" to "a" or "a" to "b" and they will have the same sum. (circled 2, 3, 5, and 8)

Student 3: I only chose 3 and 8 because the other ones describe subtracting, multiplication, or division.

Student 4: I chose 3 and 8 because it looks like an addition sentence.

Student 5: There is not enough information for any of the others. I picked number 8 because a plus b is the exact same as a + b.

Student 6: Number 8 because that is what it says, a + b. It couldn't be any more clear.

Student 7: Sum and plus both mean to add and more than also means to add, but because the word "than" is in there you have to switch the variables. (circled 2, 3, 7, and 8)

Student 8: Well the only ones that make sense to me were the product and plus because you have to add a and b and these mean add. (circled 6 and 8)

Student 9: I chose all of the ones that meant adding a and b, or what the outcome of a + b would be. (circled 2, 3, 6, and 8)

Student 10: I picked 3, 6, and 8 because this means a plus b. It has nothing to do with how much larger a is than b or b is than a.

Student 11: I made the choices "sum of a and b" and "a plus b" because that is what the question asks. B could be more than a and a could be more than b . . . we don't know that they are. (circled 2, 3, 4, 5, 7, and 8)

Student 12: I picked the ones that said more than because you don't know which one is bigger, so I picked all of them. "a + b" and "sum of a and b" explain the expression. (circled 2, 3, 4, 5, 7, and 8)

M & N'S?

For the equation m = 15 + n, which of the following would be true if n ≠ 0?

(A) m is greater than n.

(B) n is greater than m.

(C) m = 15

(D) There is not enough information to tell whether m or n is greater.

Explain your choice:

TEACHERS' NOTES: M & N'S?

Grade Level for "M & N's?" Probe

6–8	9–12

*Q*uestioning for Student Understanding

Do students correctly apply knowledge of equality and relationships among quantities?

*U*ncovering Understandings

M & N's? (Content Standard: Algebra)

*E*xamining Student Work

The distracters may reveal a lack of *conceptual understanding* of equality and variables. They may also reveal a lack of *conceptual understanding* of relationships described in an algebraic equation. In some cases, an *overgeneralization* of the use of the equal sign from the elementary grades occurs.

- *The correct response is A.* In this equation, any number can be substituted for n (positive or negative) and m will always be 15 more than the number n. **(See Student Responses 1, 2, 3, and 4)**
- *Distracter B* is often chosen by students who do not consider the equality statement and the relationship that is expressed between the two variables. They see that the equation shows "15 more" on the right-hand side of the equation and misunderstand this to mean that the variable sharing the same side of the equation with the 15 would be greater. **(See Student Response 5)**
- *Distracter C* is mostly used by students who read this equation as "m is equal to 15, then add n." This happens with those students who do not have a conceptual understanding of this equation as representing a relationship between m and n. They instead read the = as "gives" or "makes" as used in arithmetic. **(See Student Responses 6 and 7)**
- *Distracter D* is chosen by students who do not have an understanding of variable and/or of equality. It is also chosen by students who do not see that a relationship is being described in the equation. **(See Student Responses 8, 9, 10, 11, 12, and 13)**

*S*eeking Links to Cognitive Research

Students' interpretation of equations can be influenced by prior experiences in arithmetic. Their background of arithmetic has been built on a foundation in which the equals sign means "gives" or "makes," as in "3 plus 5 gives 8." (NCTM, 1999, p. 310)

Many students think that since letters stand for unknown numbers, they can not tell which is greater by looking at an equation that shows their relationship. (NCTM, 1999, p. 311)

It is essential that students become comfortable in relating symbolic expressions and equations containing variables to verbal, tabular, and graphical representations. (NCTM, 2000, p. 223)

Most students will need extensive experience in interpreting relationships among quantities in a variety of problem contexts before they can work meaningfully with variables. An understanding of the meanings and uses of variables develops gradually as students create and use symbolic expressions and relate them to verbal, tabular, and graphical representations. (NCTM, 2000, p. 225)

In general, the use of spreadsheets has been found to be an effective way to develop several notions involved in the representational activities of algebra. It encourages discussion of the role of a letter as both a variable and an unknown; it provides meaningful experience in creating algebraic expressions; and it puts the focus squarely on the representation of quantitative relationships. (NRC, 2001, p. 265)

*T*eaching Implications

To support a deeper understanding for students in secondary grades in regard to these algebraic concepts, the following are ideas and questions to consider in conjunction with the research.

Focus Through Instruction

- Students should be given time to explore and discuss many different types of situations that can be modeled algebraically.
- Encourage students to create a table of values or a graphical representation to compare the variables. This also helps students to see that different types of representation can be more helpful in different problem situations.
- Allow students to discuss what they know about the equation and relationship. Have them share with others in class.
- Foster discussions around equality and how it was used in arithmetic.

Questions to Consider . . . *when working with students as they grapple with relationships between variables*

- Do student have an understanding of equality and the = sign?
- Do students use tables and graphs to check their thinking and compare different solution methods and results?

- Are students looking at the equation as a linear relationship between two variables?
- Can students verbalize what the equation states about the relationship between the variables?

Teacher Sound Bite

"This diagnostic probe opened my eyes as to what my students were thinking about relationships described in algebraic equations. Once I looked at their reasoning, I decided it was time to take a more in-depth look at describing relationships with algebraic equations. I am going to have them use multiple representations and compare and contrast them with [those of] other classmates. I am also going to have students have conversations about the relationships and reason out loud to allow a deeper understanding of this topic."

Additional References for Research and Teaching Implications

AAAS (1993), *Benchmarks for Science Literacy,* pp. 25–29, 215, 217–221, 351–352.

Driscoll (1999), *Fostering Algebraic Thinking,* pp. 115–162.

NCTM (1993b), *Research Ideas for the Classroom: Middle Grades Mathematics,* pp. 179–196, 226.

NCTM (1993c), *Research Ideas for the Classroom: High School Mathematics,* pp. 79–82, 119–139.

NCTM (1997), *Algebraic Thinking,* pp. 52–58, 61, 73–74, 141, 150–161, 168–174, 299–327, 331.

NCTM (2000), *Principles and Standards for School Mathematics,* pp. 37–40, 158–159, 222–223, 225–227, 280–285.

NCTM (2003), *A Research Companion to Principles and for School Mathematics,* pp. 116–117, 120, 125, 138–140.

NRC (2001), *Adding It Up,* pp. 255–280.

Stepans et al. (2005), *Teaching for K–12 Mathematical Understanding Using the Conceptual Change Model,* pp. 31–50, 149–163.

> **Curriculum Topic Study**
>
> *M & N's?*
>
> Related CTS Guide: Linear Relationships, p. 139; Variables, p. 146

STUDENT RESPONSES TO "M & N'S?"

Sample Responses: A

Student 1: m is always 15 more than n.

Student 2: I picked A, because no matter what number n is, you have to add 15 to n to get m. Therefore m will always be 15 more than n.

Student 3: m is greater than n because m minus n equals 15. Since 15 is not a negative number, m must in fact be greater than n.

Student 4: A is the correct answer because no matter what n is, a positive or a negative, m is still going to be greater than n.

Sample Response: B

Student 5: n is greater than m because when you add the 15, the number gets higher.

Sample Responses: C

Student 6: I chose m = 15 because it is part of the equation.

Student 7: C is the correct answer because the problem says m = 15.

Sample Responses: D

Student 8: I don't know what m equals until I know what n equals.

Student 9: I chose d because it doesn't tell you what m is, therefore you won't be able to figure 15 + n.

Student 10: D is correct because the m might be smaller or larger than n.

Student 11: I chose d because n could equal anything. It could be more than 15 or less than 15 or it could be the number 15.

Student 12: D, because n could be represented by a negative or positive . . . there isn't enough info to decipher whether it is positive or negative.

Student 13: D is the answer I chose because m and n are letters not numbers so we do not know the value of the letters.

WHAT'S THE SUBSTITUTE?

When you substitute ½ for x in 4x and simplify the results, what is the correct answer?

A. 4½

B. 2

C. 8

Explain your reasoning:

TEACHERS' NOTES: WHAT'S THE SUBSTITUTE?

Grade Level for "What's the Substitute?" Probe

6–8	9–12

$\underline{Q}$uestioning for Student Understanding

Do students understand how to evaluate an expression of the form "ax"?

$\underline{U}$ncovering Understandings

What's the Substitute? (Content Standard: Algebra)

$\underline{E}$xamining Student Work

The distracters in this probe may uncover *common errors* using the concatenation rules of algebra. They may also reveal an *overgeneralization* of conjoining numbers with fractions in arithmetic to conjoining numbers with variables in algebra.

- *The correct response is B.* The concatenation of 4x indicates multiplication between 4 and the value of x (4 times x). In this example, x is given as ½, therefore 4 times ½ is 2. **(See Student Responses 1, 2, 3, 4, 5, and 6)**
- *Distracter A.* Students sometimes associate the conjoining of numbers in arithmetic with those in algebra. When mixed numbers are written, it signifies addition between the whole number and the fraction as in 4½ = 4 plus ½. Students generalize this "rule" to algebraic terms, where it actually means multiplication. **(See Student Responses 7–12)**
- *Distracter C.* Although this response is less used by students, a few will still see it as a correct answer. Most of the students who choose this have a lack of conceptual or procedural knowledge of fractions along with concatenation. **(See Student Responses 13, 14, and 15)**

$\underline{S}$eeking Links to Cognitive Research

Students should be required to explain some of the typical conflicts between the language of arithmetic, with which they are familiar, and the more technical language of algebra, which they will need to master. In algebra we see that: a x b means the same as ab, but in arithmetic $3 \times 5 \neq 35$; and ab = ba, but $35 \neq 53$. In arithmetic we find that $7 + \frac{1}{2} = 7\frac{1}{2}$ and $4 + 0.75 = 4.75$, but in algebra 2a + b does not mean 2ab. Students should explain why not. If the sources of difficulty are misconceptions between written language and algebraic language, then the students should be confronted with these trouble spots prior to algebra. (NCTM, 1999, p. 54)

An obstacle students have is that of the different meaning associated with concatenation in algebra. In arithmetic, the juxtaposition of two numbers denotes addition (43 = 40 + 3; 4½ = 4 + ½); in algebra, concatenation denotes multiplication (4a = 4 times a). (NCTM, 1999, p. 169)

The fact that the conjoining of terms to denote addition does appear in arithmetic—in mixed fractions (e.g., 2½ = 2 + ½) and also implicitly in place value (e.g., 43 = 4 tens + 3 units)—may lead students to view the situation similarly in algebra. (NCTM, 1999, p. 302)

The concept of variable is central to mathematics teaching and learning in junior and senior high school. Understanding the concept provides the basis for the transition from arithmetic to algebra and is necessary for the meaningful use of all advanced mathematics. Despite the importance of the concept, however, most mathematics curricula seem to treat variables as primitive terms that—after some practice of course—will be understood and used in a straightforward way by most students. Mirroring the textbook presentations, we mathematics teachers are frequently seen at the chalkboard manipulating a's, b's, x's, and y's in an easy and almost automatic way. In fact, it is easy to do so without keeping in mind the multiple connotations, meanings, and uses of the terms we manipulate. (NCTM, 1999, p. 150)

Quite often, algebraic expressions are introduced by stating that they involve variables and that "a variable is a letter that stands for one or more numbers." Such formal definitions may be adequate for mathematics teachers but they often fail to provide meaning for the beginning student. (NCTM, 1999, p. 168)

There is a very natural tendency of students to interpret an algebraic expression new to them in terms of the only numerical frame of reference they possess, that of arithmetic. (NCTM, 1999, p. 173)

Students have insufficient opportunities to practice representation with arithmetic and, therefore, do not make connections between symbols and numbers. (Stepans et al., 2005, p. 151)

*T*eaching Implications

To support a deeper understanding for students in secondary grades in regard to these algebraic concepts the following are ideas and questions to consider in conjunction with the research.

Focus Through Instruction

- Introduce new ideas about variables and symbols gradually as they appear in the curriculum.
- Encourage students to discuss and reflect on new ideas and compare/ contrast them with prior experiences and knowledge.

- Give students ample time and opportunity to build on their prior experiences and move from working in an arithmetic framework to working with variables in algebra.
- Provide experiences that allow students to work within a familiar context when first learning about variables.

Questions to Consider . . . *when working with students as they grapple with evaluating algebraic expressions*

- Do students conceptually understand literal symbols and variables?
- Are students transitioning from working in an arithmetic platform to an algebraic one?
- Can students communicate their understanding of the meaning of conjoining terms (in arithmetic and algebra)?
- Do students transfer their procedural skills from one problem to another?

Teacher Sound Bite

"I never truly understood why so many students kept adding in this type of situation until I looked at research on this concept. When I look back and see how they learned about place value and adding fractions, their confusion is more understandable. This probe has helped me to be aware of what students are thinking when they see a number and variable next to each other, especially when we substitute a fraction in for the variable. I now feel I have a better understanding of how to move their thinking from where they are to a better understanding of this topic."

Additional References for Research and Teaching Implications

Curriculum Topic Study
What's the Substitute?
Related CTS Guide: Variables, p. 146

AAAS (1993), *Benchmarks for Science Literacy*, pp. 25–29, 215, 217–221, 351–352.

Driscoll (1999), *Fostering Algebraic Thinking*, pp. 115–162.

NCTM (1993b), *Research Ideas for the Classroom: Middle Grades Mathematics*, pp. 104, 179–196, 226.

NCTM (1993c), *Research Ideas for the Classroom: High School Mathematics*, pp. 119–139.

NCTM (1997), *Algebraic Thinking*, pp. 52–58, 59, 141, 150–161, 168–174, 299–327, 331.

NCTM (2000), *Principles and Standards for School Mathematics*, pp. 37–40, 158–159, 222–223, 225–227, 280–285.

NCTM (2003), *A Research Companion to Principles and for School Mathematics*, pp. 116–117, 120, 125, 138–140.

NRC (2001), *Adding It Up*, pp. 255–280.

Stepans et al. (2005), *Teaching for K–12 Mathematical Understanding Using the Conceptual Change Model*, pp. 31–50, 149–163.

STUDENT RESPONSES
TO "WHAT'S THE SUBSTITUTE?"

Sample Responses: B

Student 1: When I substituted ½ for x, I got $\frac{4}{1} \times \frac{1}{2} = \frac{4}{2} = 2$ so I reduced $\frac{4}{2} = 2$, so 2 is my answer.

Student 2: If you substitute ½ in, you get 4(½), which means 4 times ½. I am sure that we know that ½ of 4 = 2.

Student 3: I think B is correct because when you multiply 4 by ½ it's just like counting ½ 4 times: ½ + ½ + ½ + ½ = 1 + 1 = 2.

Student 4: ½ of 4 is 2. It's like dividing 4 by 2.

Student 5: The way I got this answer was by changing ½ to .5 and doing 4 x .5 and it got me 2.

Student 6: 2 is ½ of 4.

Sample Responses: A

Student 7: I chose A, because if you add ½ you are adding half not a whole number.

Student 8: Because you just take the x out and where the x was, you put ½.

Student 9: Because you just add them.

Student 10: A, because when you put ½ where x is, it makes 4 ½.

Student 11: Because you can't simplify 4 ½ any more.

Student 12: 4 + a ½ is 4 ½.

Sample Responses: B

Student 13: Because if you split 4 in half it is like doing 4 × 2.

Student 14: 4 times half of 4 is 2 so 4 × 2 = 8.

Student 15: When x is beside a number that means you would multiply. So if you multiply 4 × ½ (½ of 4 is 2), 4 × 2 would equal 8.

IS IT TRUE?

If m = 5, circle all of the statements below that are true for the expression 3m.

A. 3m = 35

B. 3m = 8

C. 3m = 3 + 5

D. 3m = 3 meters

E. 3m = 15

F. 3m = 3 times 5

G. 3m means the slope is ³/₅

H. 3m = 3 miles

Explain your reasoning for each circled statement:

TEACHERS' NOTES: IS IT TRUE?

Grade Level for "Is It True?" Probe

6–8	9–12

*Q*uestioning for Student Learning

Do students understand the operation implied by concatenation of literal symbols and numbers?

*U*ncovering Understandings

Is It True? (Content Standard: Algebra)

*E*xamining Student Work

The distracters may reveal *common errors* in using the rules of concatenation in algebra the same way they are used in arithmetic. They may also reveal a lack of *conceptual understanding* of literal symbols and variables.

- *The correct responses are E and F.* Students who choose E and F are using the correct operation, multiplication, to evaluate the expression "3m." Many students only choose E, reasoning that the answer in F, "3 times 5," was not completely simplified. There are also students who choose E and/or F along with numerous other responses. These students do not show an understanding of what "3m" means, as they think it could mean numerous things. **(See Student Responses 1, 2, 3, and 4)**
- *Distracter A.* Students who choose this option are using "m" in terms of place value. Another misconception can also arise from this in that many students use letters in terms of place value and alphabetical rank (3a is 31 because a is the first letter of the alphabet, 3d is 34 because d is the fourth letter). (NCTM, 1999, p. 173) **(See Student Responses 5 and 6)**
- *Distracters B and C.* These distracters are chosen by students who think a variable next to a number implies addition. Many of these students are considering the rules of concatenation with mixed numbers when reasoning about this. In students' prior experiences two numbers next to each other, as in 3 ½, has implied addition ("3 and ½" or "3 plus ½"). **(See Student Response 7)**
- *Distracters D and H.* Some students see letters as abbreviations for something, as in "m" is used for "miles" and "meters," "l" for "liters," and so forth. Students frequently mistake letters that are being used as variables for abbreviations. This shows a lack of understanding of the multiple uses of letters as symbols. **(See Student Responses 8 and 9)**

- *Distracter G.* Many students learn that the letter "m" in math class represents the slope of an equation. Further conversations with students may reveal that the misunderstanding in choosing this response can be with variables, slope, or reading directions. **(See Student Response 10)**
- Frequently students will choose several answers. They reason that "3m" could have different meanings. It could mean addition, multiplication, or division. **(See Student Responses 11 and 12)**
- Other students will choose A, C, F, and G because these responses have a 3 and 5 in the answer. **(See Student Responses 13 and 14)**
- Some students do not think any of the choices are correct. They reason that a number and a variable cannot be multiplied together. **(See Student Response 15)**

Seeking Links to Cognitive Research

One of the most obvious differences between arithmetic and algebra, of course, is in the latter's use of letters to represent values. Letters also appear in arithmetic, but in a quite different way. The letters "m" and "c," for instance, may be used in arithmetic to represent "meters" and "cents," rather than representing *the number of* meters or *the number of* cents, as in algebra. Confusion over this change in usage may result in a "lack of numerical referent" problem in students' interpretation of the meaning of letters in algebra. (NCTM, 1999, p. 303)

Working with variables and equations is an important part of the middle-grades curriculum. Students' understanding of variable should go far beyond simply recognizing that letters can be used to stand for unknown numbers in equations (Schoenfeld & Arcavi, 1988). An understanding of the meanings and uses of variables develops gradually as students create and use symbolic expressions and relate them to verbal, tabular, and graphical representations. (NCTM, 2000, p. 225)

Research shows that students can work with variables without fully understanding the power and flexibility of literal symbols. Because variables operate much like the numbers of arithmetic, and because conceptually they resemble pronouns in ordinary language, most students can acquire some facility in routine algebraic manipulations. However, there is evidence that students' early impressions about variables may impede their construction of a sufficiently general concept. For example, students who first encounter variables as names (as in person A, person B) may assume that letters are like abbreviations. This assumption is reinforced when we use the mnemonic device of choosing as variables the first letter of the name of the objects we are talking about, as in *a* to represent some number of apples. (NCTM, 1993c, pp. 122, 123)

The most common notational shortcut in algebra is the omission of the operation sign for multiplication. Because variables have no place value, we can denote multiplication by concatenating (linking) literal symbols with numerals, other literal symbols, or parentheses, as in $3a = 3 \times a$ or $3(^1/_2) = 3 \times ^1/_2$. However, students are used to interpreting concatenation in arithmetic as implying addition as in $32 = 30 = 2$ or $3 \, ^1/_2 = 3 + ^1/_2$. It takes [students] awhile to internalize these conflicting conventions and of course the fact that both arithmetic and algebraic conventions operate simultaneously in algebra does nothing to alleviate the confusion. (NCTM, 1993c, p. 124)

Students have difficulty understanding how symbols are used in algebra (Kieran, 1992). They are often unaware of the arbitrariness of the letters chosen to represent variables in equations (Wagner, 1981). Middle-school and high-school students may regard the letters as shorthand for single objects, or as specific but unknown numbers, or as generalized numbers before they understand them as representations of variables (Kieran, 1992). (AAAS, 1993, p. 351)

Students are frequently presented with equations or symbolic expressions that do not relate to their concrete experiences and verbal explanations. (Stepans et al., 2005, p. 151)

The first step toward understanding [algebra] is for students to learn about symbols, including that the use of symbols is widespread, takes many forms, and is not the exclusive property of algebra or mathematics. (AAAS, 1993, p. 215)

*T*eaching Implications

To support a deeper understanding for students in secondary grades in regard to these algebraic concepts, the following are ideas and questions to consider in conjunction with the research.

Focus Through Instruction

- "Emphasize that letters in algebraic expressions stand for numbers, not for names of things" (NCTM, 1999, p. 312). Use letters other than the first letter of a word to represent a certain number of that item.
- Recognize that students come to algebra with prior experiences about symbols, some of which interfere with their understanding of variables. Generate discussions about the subtle and not-so-subtle ways symbols are used in math and other disciplines.
- Introduce ideas gradually and give students time to go from writing "3 times m" or "$3 \times m$" to "3m." Sometimes this is taught in less than a class period and students are expected to regularly write 3m thereafter. The introduction of this topic can and maybe should be delayed and the product written out in full for a substantial period of the students' early work in algebra. (NCTM, 1999, p. 302)

- When reading 3m out loud, teachers and students should say "3 times m" instead of just "3m." This will reinforce the multiplicative meaning.
- Present variables in situations that require algebraic thinking instead of giving assignments that are repetitive application of a specific procedure. (Stepans et al., 2005, p. 151)
- Use algebraic notation frequently as a language for generalizing and writing formulas. Give students practice with variables wherever possible.
- Include classroom discussion around the topic. Ask students whether the multiplication sign in 5×8 can be removed the way we can in algebraic expressions such as $3 \times m$ (3m).

Questions to Consider . . . *when working with students as they grapple with the interpretation of algebraic expressions*

- Do students clearly distinguish the different ways in which terms are written in algebra compared to arithmetic?
- Can students explain in words the relationships they see?
- Have students developed an initial understanding of several different meanings and uses of variables through representing quantities in a variety of problem situations? (NCTM, 2000, p. 223)
- Do students realize that a letter can behave like a numeral and be subject to numerical operations, but also realize that a letter behaves very differently from a numeral with regard to the juxtaposition convention?
- Can students tell when symbols are being used as abbreviations instead of variables?
- Do students realize that letters do not have specific values that depend on their position in the alphabet?

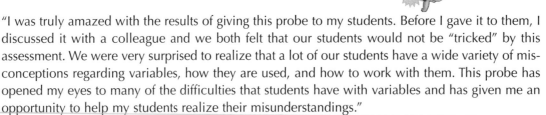

Teacher Sound Bite

"I was truly amazed with the results of giving this probe to my students. Before I gave it to them, I discussed it with a colleague and we both felt that our students would not be "tricked" by this assessment. We were very surprised to realize that a lot of our students have a wide variety of misconceptions regarding variables, how they are used, and how to work with them. This probe has opened my eyes to many of the difficulties that students have with variables and has given me an opportunity to help my students realize their misunderstandings."

Additional References for Research and Teaching Implications

Curriculum Topic Study

Is It True?

Related CTS Guide:
Variables, p. 146

AAAS (1993), *Benchmarks for Science Literacy*, pp. 25–29, 215, 217–221, 351–352.

Driscoll (1999), *Fostering Algebraic Thinking*, pp. 115–162.

NCTM (1993b), *Research Ideas for the Classroom: Middle Grades Mathematics*, pp. 179–196, 226.

NCTM (1993c), *Research Ideas for the Classroom: High School Mathematics*, pp. 119–139.

NCTM (1997), *Algebraic Thinking*, pp. 52–58, 59, 141, 150–161, 168–174, 299–327, 331.

NCTM (2000), *Principles and Standards for School Mathematics*, pp. 37–40, 158–159, 222–223, 225–227, 280–285.

NCTM (2003), *A Research Companion to Principles and Standards for School Mathematics*, pp. 116–117, 120, 125, 138–140.

NRC (2001), *Adding It Up*, pp. 255–280.

Stepans et al. (2005), *Teaching for K–12 Mathematical Understanding Using the Conceptual Change Model*, pp. 31–50, 149–163.

STUDENT RESPONSES TO "IS IT TRUE?"

Sample Responses: E and F

Student 1: I picked E and F because 3m means 3 × 5 or the answer to 3 × 5 which is 15. When there is a letter after a number, it means multiply.

Student 2: E and F are correct because if you put the 5 in, it would be 3(5) and that equals 15 or you could say 3(5) = 3 times 5.

Student 3: E because 3m means multiply so 3 × 5 = 15 and F because it is the same as E but in words.

Student 4: E because it would be like saying there are 3 m's, which would be like 3 5 = 15. F because it would be like saying 3 m's and each m = 5 so it would be 3 5, just writing it all out.

Sample Responses: A

Student 5: I think A is correct because if you put 3 and 5 side by side it is the number 35.

Student 6: A because in 3m the m is 5, then it would be 35 because you replace the m with a 5 and it reads 35.

Sample Response: B and C

Student 7: I circled B and C because m = 5 so I thought that 3m would be the same as 3 + 5 or the answer to 3 + 5, which would be 8.

Sample Responses: D and H

Student 8: I think that D and H are right because m in length equals miles and can also equal meters.

Student 9: I chose D and H because both words start with m. But I think it is 3m = miles because in mph, m means miles.

Sample Responses: Multiple Choices

Student 10: I chose E, F, and G. E and F are correct because 3m = 3 × 5. G is also correct because 3m means the slope is $^3/_5$.

Student 11: I chose B, C, E, and F. B and C because 3m = 3 + 5 and 3 + 5 = 8. E and F because m = 5 and 3 × 5 = 15. When m = 5 then 3m could mean 8 (+) or 15 (×).

Student 12: A, C, E, and F are the ones I circled because I thought that if 5 = m then all the possibilities are ×, ÷, -, and + so that means all 4 of them are used.

Student 13: I circled the ones that had a five in each statement (A, C, E, F, and G).

Student 14: I circled A, C, F, and G because they all had something to do with 3 and 5.

Student 15: I think that none of them are correct because you can't times a number by variables.

SOLVING EQUATIONS

Probe
6

Will, Haley, and Andy each solved the equation x + 23 = 140. Whose process, notation, and answer is correct?

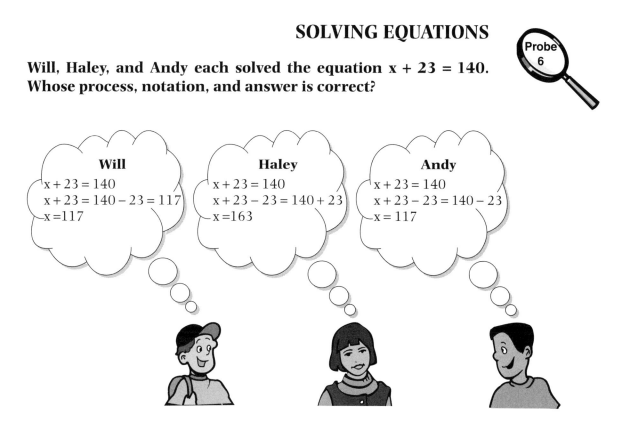

Will

$x + 23 = 140$
$x + 23 = 140 - 23 = 117$
$x = 117$

Haley

$x + 23 = 140$
$x + 23 - 23 = 140 + 23$
$x = 163$

Andy

$x + 23 = 140$
$x + 23 - 23 = 140 - 23$
$x = 117$

Explain the reasoning for your choice and why the others may or may not make sense mathematically:

TEACHERS' NOTES: SOLVING EQUATIONS

Grade Level for "Solving Equations" Probe

6–8	9–12

*Q*uestioning for Student Understanding

Do students understand appropriate methods and notations when solving for an unknown?

*U*ncovering Understandings

Solving Equations (Content Standard: Algebra)

*E*xamining Student Work

The distracters may reveal a lack of *conceptual understanding* of equivalency, a lack of *procedural understanding* of solving equations, or an *overgeneralization* of the meaning of the equal sign as "gives" or "makes."

- *The correct response is Andy.* Andy uses an appropriate process and has the correct answer. His process of solving the equation subtracts 23 from both sides, which honors equivalency in the equation. **(See Student Response 1)**
- *Distracter "Will."* Will recognizes that to solve this equation, 23 needs to be subtracted from the left side of the equation. What Will does not seem to have an understanding of is the notion of the equal sign or equivalency. He uses the = sign for a partial-answer approach in which he works from left to right. **(See Student Responses 2, 3, 4, 5, and 6)**
- *Distracter "Haley."* Haley also recognizes that 23 needs to be subtracted from the left side. She correctly subtracts 23 from the left, but instead of also subtracting it from the right, she adds it. Many students make this error and sometimes think that what is added to one side must be subtracted from the other or vice versa. **(See Student Responses 7 and 8)**

*S*eeking Links to Cognitive Research

A one-dimensional focus in elementary school mathematics classes on "undoing operations" can sometimes be counterproductive to students' developing an understanding of a) an equation as a balanced entity and b) the solving procedure of performing the same operation on both sides of the equation. By a *one-dimensional focus on undoing operations,* we mean an undue emphasis on interpreting open sentences, such as + 7 = 15, not as the "number that when added with 7 gives 15" but rather as the number that results from subtracting 7 from 15. In other words, the focus is on the undoing operation of subtraction, not on the given operation of addition. (NCTM, 1999, pp. 61–62)

Students' interpretation of equations can be influenced by prior experiences in arithmetic. Their background of arithmetic has been built on a foundation in which the equals sign means "gives" or "makes," as in "3 plus 5 gives 8." Teachers see evidence of this interpretation when students working with multistep calculations frequently use the equals sign for partial answers, moving from left to right, as in $3 + 5 = 8 \times 7 = 56 + 2 = 28$. This restricted but familiar use for the equals sign is an obstacle to understanding equations. (NCTM, 1999, p. 310)

When doing a sequence of computations, students often treat the equal sign as a left-to-right directional signal. For example, consider the following problem:

Daniel went to visit his grandmother, who gave him $1.50. Then he bought a book for $3.20. If he has $2.30 left, how much money did he have before visiting his grandmother?

In solving this problem, sixth graders will often write $2.30 + 3.20 = 5.50 - 1.50 = 4.00$, tacking the second computation onto the result of the first. Since $2.30 + 3.20$ equals 5.50, not $5.50 - 1.50$, the string of equations they have written violates the definition of equality. To modify their interpretation of the equality sign in algebra, students must come to respect the true meaning of equality as a statement that the two sides of an equation are equal to each other. (NRC, 2001, pp. 261–262)

Students typically begin solving simple equations long before they enter a formal algebra course, but a clear vision of the structural differences between equations and expressions may be obstructed by their experience with the equal sign in arithmetic. Students do so much computing of answers in arithmetic, they may come to regard the equal sign as a kind of operation sign—a "write-the-answer" sign—rather than a statement of equivalence. (NCTM, 1999, pp. 332–333)

Beginning algebra students use various intuitive methods for solving algebraic equations. Some of these methods may help their understanding of equations and equation solving. Students who are encouraged initially to use trial-and-error substitution develop a better notion of the equivalence of the two sides of the equation and are more successful in applying more formal methods later on. By contrast, students who are taught to solve equations only by formal methods may not understand what they are doing. Students who are taught to use the method of "transposing" are found to only mechanically apply the change side/change sign rule. (AAAS, 1993, p. 352)

Students of all ages can often solve algebraic equations without a deeper understanding of what a solution is. For example, middle- and high-school students do not realize that an incorrect solution, when substituted into the equation, will yield different values for the two sides of the equation. (AAAS, 1993, p. 352)

In algebra, the equal sign may still signal writing an answer, as in simplifying an expression: $2x + 5 + 3x - 7 = 5x - 2$. But in solving equations, the equal sign is explicitly a relation sign, and students are asked to operate on the whole relation to find a sequence of equivalent relations. Lingering confusion between simplifying expressions and solving equations is betrayed when students refer to the (often numerical) right-hand side of an equation as "the answer" or when they simplify an expression, look at the "equation" they have thereby written, and begin solving it, only to wonder what happened to x, when all the x terms subtract out. Perhaps textbook authors should distinguish between the two uses of the equal sign in algebra by consistently using " " to denote identically equivalent expressions (axiomatic properties, simplified expressions, multiplication/factoring identities, equivalent equations, etc.) and "=" to denote the limited equality of an equation or function. Then, for example, students who are wont to solve equations by chaining successive, equivalent equations together with equal signs could quite properly write: $7x - 3 = 5x + 5 = 2x - 3 = 5 = 2x = 8 = x = 4$. (NCTM, 1999, p. 333)

As with expressions, the errors in solving equations are familiar ones, perhaps the most common being variations of the sign error: $x + 37 = 150 \rightarrow x + 37 - 10 = 150 + 10$. Interviews with students reveal that this error may not always be the result of carelessness or confusion with the transposition rule but may sometimes reflect a belief system that attributes validity to some operations that are not mathematically valid. In the example above, for instance, some students seem to believe in [a] fairness ("redistribution") principle: Whatever is taken away from one side of an equation should be added to the other side. (NCTM, 1999, p. 336)

Many textbooks use the word *equation* in arithmetic and in algebra without distinction. This can lead to some unnecessary confusion for the student. Introducing the term *arithmetic identities* leaves us free to use *equation* in the algebraic sense. We must distinguish between an equation in arithmetic and one in algebra. (NCTM, 1999, pp.183–185)

*T*eaching Implications

To support a deeper understanding for students in secondary grades in regard to these algebraic concepts, the following are ideas and questions to consider in conjunction with the research.

Focus Through Instruction

- Students can learn the concepts behind solving equations in more concrete ways. For example, the equation $x + 2 = 9$ can be represented concretely using cups (for variable x) and chips (for constants 2 and 9). (NCTM, 1999, p. 165)

- Use algebra tiles and other manipulatives to model equation-solving processes. Equation mats are also helpful in helping students honor equality while solving equations.
- Spreadsheets and graphing utilities can be used to help solve equations and/or check students' solutions for accuracy. They also encourage students to solve equations by graphing the left-hand side and the right-hand side as functions and determining for what x-value the functions are equal. Students can then perform transformations on the equation and see whether the transformed functions still intersect at the same point or along the same vertical line (same x-value). Explorations of this sort are fun and instructive, and we may find that they help students better understand which transformations preserve the equivalence of equations and why. (NCTM, 1999, pp. 336–337)
- Although many students use the horizontal format with working with operations on arithmetic identities, solving equations in a vertical notation might be preferable. (NCTM, 1999, p. 186)
- Fluency in manipulating symbolic expressions can be enhanced if students understand equivalence and are facile with the order of operations and the distributive, associative, and commutative properties. (NCTM, 2000, p. 227)
- Have classroom discussions around equivalence. Have students decide and defend why some methods preserve equivalence and others do not. (NCTM, 2003, p. 123)

Questions to Consider . . . *when working with students as they grapple with solving equations*

- Do students understand equivalency and what the = sign means in algebra?
- What are students' prior experiences with solving numerical equations? Algebraic equations?
- Do students use the horizontal or vertical approach when solving equations?
- Do students check their answers?
- Can students verbalize what they are doing when solving equations?

Teacher Sound Bite

"This has always been an issue with my students. I like to call work like 'Will's' . . . a run-on sentence. Many students do not have a true understanding of equivalency, although they can go through the steps of solving an equation. I would like to see students have a better conceptual understanding of equality before we show them the procedural ways to solve equations. I think we put too much emphasis on solving equations and not enough on analyzing equations and looking at the relationships that are being defined."

Additional References for Research and Teaching Implications

<table>
<tr><td>

Curriculum Topic Study

Solving Equations

Related CTS Guide:
Expressions and Equations,
p. 136; Equivalence, p. 194

</td><td>

AAAS (1993), *Benchmarks for Science Literacy*, pp. 25–29, 215, 217–221, 351–352.

Driscoll (1999), *Fostering Algebraic Thinking*, pp. 115–162.

NCTM (1993b), *Research Ideas for the Classroom: Middle Grades Mathematics*, pp. 179–196, 226.

NCTM (1993c), *Research Ideas for the Classroom: High School Mathematics*, pp. 79–82, 119–139.

NCTM (1997), *Algebraic Thinking*, pp. 10, 52–58, 61–62, 141, 150, 165, 181, 183–189, 219, 268, 310, 312, 325–326, 332–338, 350–351.

</td></tr>
</table>

NCTM (2000), *Principles and Standards for School Mathematics*, pp. 37–40, 158–159, 222–223, 225–227, 296–297.

NCTM (2003), *A Research Companion to Principles and Standards for School Mathematics*, pp. 116–117, 120, 123–124, 130–131, 138–140.

NRC (2001), *Adding It Up*, pp. 255–280.

Stepans et al. (2005), *Teaching for K–12 Mathematical Understanding Using the Conceptual Change Model*, pp. 31–50, 149–163.

STUDENT RESPONSES TO "SOLVING EQUATIONS"

Sample Response: Andy

Student 1: Andy would be right because he is the only one who showed that you have to subtract 23 from both sides in order to get x by itself. Will was close only he didn't show that you had to subtract it from both sides, only one. Haley made the mistake of subtracting 23 from one side only to add it to the other side.

Sample Responses: Will

Student 2: Andy's solution to the equation is correct because he subtracted 23 from both sides and got x = 117. Will's answer is also correct because he subtracted 23 from 140 and got x = 117 too. Haley's answer is wrong because she subtracted 23 from the left side, but added 23 to the right and got x = 163 instead of x = 117.

Student 3: Will's makes sense because all he did was subtract 23 from 140. Haley got the wrong answer. Andy made extra steps that he didn't have to do.

Student 4: Will's is right because you do end up getting the right answer, he just doesn't show all his work. Haley just did it wrong because she subtracted the 23 and added it on the other side when she needed to subtract it on both. Because of that she got the wrong answer. Andy has his right because all his steps are there and he has them where they need to be and he showed all his work and ended up with the right answer. So in the end, Andy's is right because he showed all his work and steps.

Student 5: Haley's answer is wrong because she added 23 to 140. Andy's is correct but he just added one more step in the problem: $x + 23 = 140$, $x + 23 - 23 = 140 - 23$ (since $23 - 23$ cancels on the left side you don't need to write it), you can just write $x = 140 - 23$ and you end up with $x = 117$.

Student 6: I think that Will is right because you have to subtract 23 from 140 in order to find an answer that will work with the equation.

Sample Responses: Haley

Student 7: I chose Haley because her problem makes more sense to me because she did the same steps that I would do to figure out what x equals.

Student 8: I think that Haley is correct because when I substitute 163 in for x then the problem works out. [The student shows the following work substituted in the second line of Haley's answer.] $163 + 23 - 23 = 140 + 23$, $163 = 140 + 23$, $163 = 163$.

CORRECT REPRESENTATION OF THE INEQUALITY?

Circle the answer(s) that represent the following statement:
"Children 12 and under get in free."

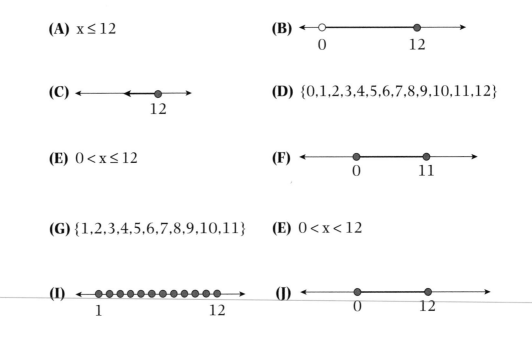

(A) $x \leq 12$

(B) [number line: open circle at 0, closed circle at 12, segment between]
   0   12

(C) [number line: closed circle at 12 with arrow pointing left]
   12

(D) $\{0,1,2,3,4,5,6,7,8,9,10,11,12\}$

(E) $0 < x \leq 12$

(F) [number line: closed circles at 0 and 11, segment between]
   0   11

(G) $\{1,2,3,4,5,6,7,8,9,10,11\}$

(E) $0 < x < 12$

(I) [number line: closed dots from 1 to 12]
   1   12

(J) [number line: closed circles at 0 and 12, segment between]
   0   12

Explain your choices:

TEACHER'S NOTES: CORRECT REPRESENTATION OF THE INEQUALITY?

Grade Level for "Correct Representation of the Inequality?" Probe

6–8	9–12

*Q*uestioning for Student Understanding

Are students able to identify various representations of an inequality?

*U*ncovering Understandings

Correct Representation of the Inequality? (Content Standard: Algebra)

*E*xamining Student Work

The distracters in this probe may reveal a lack of *conceptual understanding* of verbal, graphic, and symbolic representations of inequalities. Many students are not familiar with variable use in these types of situations and have difficulties transferring statements into graphical representation. *Misunderstandings* and *common errors* dealing with sets and what they represent might also be discovered through students' explanations and discussions of age and how it can be represented in different situations.

- *The correct responses are B and E.* Examples B and E both show all ages 12 and under. This includes the age of 12, but not the age of 0. The reason that 0 was not included as a correct answer is that a child would not yet be born. This, of course, leaves room for discussion and teachers will need to choose whether to include 0 for their students' age and grade level. Both of these choices have shown levels of confusion with students of varying ages. Students are sometimes unsure of choice B because of the open and closed circles denoting whether the point is included (or not) in the graph. Choice E uses an inequality symbol, which in many cases is not understood by students. **(See Student Responses 1 and 2)**
- *Distracters A and H.* Choices A and H are used to check students' understanding of symbolic representation of inequalities. Students at all levels might not understand where the variable x comes from and what it has to do with the situation. Other students do not understand the inequality notation. Both of these show a lack of conceptual knowledge about inequalities or variables and symbols. Even though A and C both represent the same inequality, many students choose the graphic (C), but not the algebraic form (A). **(See Student Responses 10, 11, and 12)**
- *Distracters C, F, and J.* These choices use the number line and open and closed circles denoting the inclusion or omission of a point on the line.

Many students choose C and J (along with B), as these number lines show the number 12 on them. Some students do not realize that in choice F, the number 12 is not included as a point, and that in choice C, although the number 12 is included, negative numbers are also included. Other students only look at the right side of the number line and ignore where the age starts. The arrows on the number line (signifying that the line goes to infinity) might cause confusion for some students. A number of students think the arrows are part of the solution. The source of this mis-understanding might be caused by a lack of use in the classroom—drawing number lines without arrows. This probe was not written to ana-lyze this, but as there are many students that misuse the arrows, it is another misunderstanding that should be addressed in the classroom. **(See Student Responses 3, 4, 5, 6, 7, 10, 11, and 12)**

- *Distracter I.* Although this distracter uses a number line like C, F, and J, it is visually different and uses specific points rather than a line to denote ages. Many students choose this because there are 12 "dots" on the line, which they see as representing the "12" in the problem. Other students choose this without regard to the fact that most children will not be exactly 1, 2, 3, . . . 12, (other than those who go on their birthday), but will be an age in between, and therefore the solution on the graph needs to be a line. **(See Student Responses 3, 8, 9, 12, and 13)**
- *Distracters D and G.* Choices D and G are similar to choice I in that they only show the ages of those having their birthday on the day they go to the movies. These choices can be used to have great discussions on age, what it means to be "8" or "10," and how all of their ages would be represented graphically. Some students choose D and not G, as the number 12 is not included in choice G. **(See Student Responses 3, 4, 6, 10, 12, and 13)**

Seeking Links to Cognitive Research

It is essential that middle grade students become comfortable in relat-ing symbolic expressions containing variables to verbal, tabular, and graphical representations of numerical and quantitative relationships. (NCTM, 2000, p. 223)

An important part of learning mathematics is learning to use the lan-guage, conventions, and representations of mathematics. Teachers should introduce students to conventional mathematical representa-tions and help them use those representations effectively by building on the students' personal and idiosyncratic representations when neces-sary. It is important for teachers to highlight ways in which different rep-resentations of the same objects can convey different information and to emphasize the importance of selecting representations suited to the par-ticular mathematical tasks at hand. (NCTM, 2000, pp. 362–363)

Visual representations can be used to create a shared world of under-standing and meaning. Different modes of making meaning are [the following]:

1. By using graphs, students can explore aspects of a context that are not otherwise apparent.

2. The process of representing a context can lead to questions about the context itself.

3. Using a graph to analyze a well-understood context can deepen a student's understanding of a graph and graphing.

4. Students can construct new entities and concepts in a context by beginning with important features of a graph.

5. Students can elaborate their understanding of both a graph and its context through an iterative and interactive process of exploring both.

6. A group can build shared understanding through joint reference to the graph of phenomena in a context. (NCTM, 2003, pp. 252–256)

*T*eaching Implications

To support a deeper understanding for students in secondary grades in regard to these algebraic concepts, the following are ideas and questions to consider in conjunction with the research.

Focus Through Instruction

- Provide students with ample practice at the translation process itself, isolated from all other aspects of problem solving. (NCTM, 1999, p. 324)
- Allow classroom time for discussion on set theory and the different representations of inequalities.
- Have students defend their choices with other students, and have students question each other for complete understanding.
- Give students symbolic and graphic inequalities and have them either verbalize or write what they mean in English.
- Practice "reading" graphs in a variety of contexts, including linear and nonlinear equalities and inequalities.
- Give students practice with picking out non-examples along with examples, and allow time for discussions on the reasoning behind their choices.

Questions to Consider . . . *when working with students as they grapple with using and interpreting various representations and uses of inequalities*

- Are students correctly drawing a number line?
- When using a number line, do students use and understand open and closed circles?
- Do students understand variables, and can they use them to represent a variety of situations?

- Do students know symbolic representation for inequalities (<, >, ≤, and ≥)?
- Can students compare and contrast different forms of representation of inequalities?
- Do students understand sets?
- Can students pick out non-examples and give an explanation for why they are non-examples?

Teacher Sound Bite

"This probe has shown me that my students definitely need to explore open versus closed circles on a graph, symbolic notation for equalities and inequalities (≤ and ≥), and the meaning of x as a variable. I am going to spend more time openly discussing these concepts and bring out the misunderstanding to the class as a whole. There are too many concepts that students are not completely understanding to move on without re-examining where they are at this point. We will take a much deeper look at multiple representations, using words, graphs, and algebra and in the process re-defining inequalities in terms that will hopefully bring forth a better understanding of them."

Additional References for Research and Teaching Implications

Curriculum Topic Study

Correct Representation of the Inequality?

Related CTS Guide: Expressions and Equations, p. 136; Creating Representations, p. 202

AAAS (1993), *Benchmarks for Science Literacy*, pp. 25–29, 215, 217–221, 351–352.

Driscoll (1999), *Fostering Algebraic Thinking*, pp. 115–162.

NCTM (1993b), *Research Ideas for the Classroom: Middle Grades Mathematics*, pp. 179–196, 226.

NCTM (1993c), *Research Ideas for the Classroom: High School Mathematics*, pp. 79–82, 119–139.

NCTM (1997), *Algebraic Thinking*, pp. 10, 52–58, 73, 141, 181, 189, 324–326.

NCTM (2000), *Principles and Standards for School Mathematics*, pp. 37–40, 67–71, 222–229, 280–285, 296–297, 362–363.

NCTM (2003), *A Research Companion to Principles and Standards for School Mathematics*, pp. 116–117, 123–124, 138–140, 250–260.

NRC (2001), *Adding It Up*, pp. 255–280.

Stepans et al. (2005), *Teaching for K–12 Mathematical Understanding Using the Conceptual Change Model*, pp. 31–50, 149–163.

STUDENT RESPONSES TO "CORRECT REPRESENTATION OF THE INEQUALITY?"

Sample Responses

Student 1: I chose B and E because they show all ages between 0 and 12, including 12. I was going to choose J instead of B, but then thought that a 0-year-old wouldn't be born yet or he would have to be at least a few minutes old to go to the movies!

Student 2: This was a little confusing because I did not know if I should include 0. If 0 is included then I would choose J. If 0 is not included, I would choose B and E. I think that 0 should not be included though, as a baby wouldn't be here yet. D and I could be used if you were only looking at whole ages.

Student 3: D, I, and J are correct because they show 0–12 and not 0–11.

Student 4: I chose A, B, C, D, and J because it said 12 and under. That means kids that are 12 and under 12 get in free so it would be 0–12 because a child might be 9 months or anything under 1.

Student 5: I am not sure which ones are right but I think C is wrong because it says 12–0 and the problem says 0–12.

Student 6: I chose B, C, D, and I, but I think C is the best answer because it has a 12 with an arrow pointing backwards, which is what is says . . . 12 and under.

Student 7: I think C is correct because people can also be under 0 years old.

Student 8: I picked I because it is showing a line segment with 12–1. This is showing that 12–1 get in free. All the ones with 12–0 are incorrect. No one is 0 years old.

Student 9: I chose I because the problem said 1–12 and there are 12 dots in I.

Student 10: I chose B, D, H, I, and J. I didn't choose A and E because I do not know what   means. C is not right because it goes into the negatives, and in F and G the 12 should be included.

Student 11: What does x mean? I chose B, C, and D because they all showed 12 and they all went under 12.

Student 12: My choices are D, I, and J. A doesn't make sense. In B, the arrows of the graph go into the negatives. E doesn't make sense. F and G don't go to 12. H doesn't make sense. All the others make sense and go to 12.

Student 13: I picked D and I because they have 0–12 in a clear way. I didn't pick the other ones because they weren't as clear as D and I.

IS IT A VARIABLE?

Circle the letter of each situation that contains a variable.

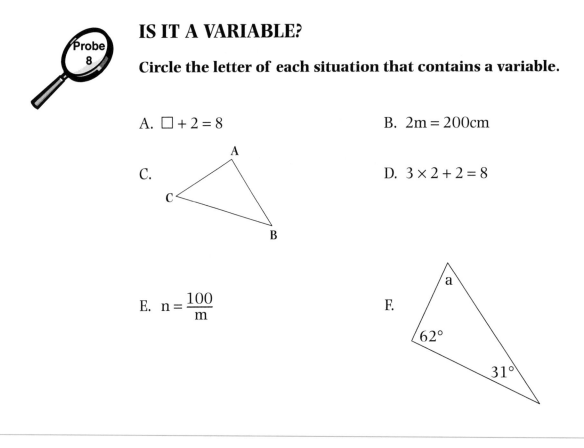

A. $\square + 2 = 8$

B. $2m = 200cm$

C.

D. $3 \times 2 + 2 = 8$

E. $n = \dfrac{100}{m}$

F.

Explain why each letter that you circled contains a variable:

TEACHERS' NOTES: IS IT A VARIABLE?

Grade Level for "Is It a Variable?" Probe

6–8	9–12

*Q*uestioning for Student Learning

Are students able to identify when a literal symbol is being used as a variable?

*U*ncovering Understandings

Is It a Variable? (Content Standard: Algebra)

*E*xamining Student Work

The distracters may reveal a lack of *conceptual understanding* of variables and literal symbols used in mathematics. Many *common errors* students make with variables deal with mistaking all literal symbols used in mathematics for variables. Literal symbols are widely used in mathematics and other disciplines in ways other than as variables, which can cause difficulties for many students.

- *The correct responses are A, E, and F.* These examples use a symbol (letter) for an unknown number (A and F) or a relationship (E). Although many students will correctly choose these examples, their explanation of why the letters are considered variables may be lacking in conceptual understanding of variables. Other students will correctly communicate what a variable is, but show a lack of understanding by choosing the wrong examples. This shows what is referred to as miscommunicated understanding versus communicated misunderstanding in *Dynamic Classroom Instruction* (Bright & Joyner, 2004). **(See Student Responses 1, 2, and 3)**
- *Distracter B.* Students often mistake units of measure (abbreviations) for variables. In this case, "m" and "cm" are literal symbols used as abbreviations for "meters" and "centimeters." Students see this equation as one similar to $2x = 200y$ where both x and y can be solved for. **(See Student Responses 5, 6, and 11)**
- *Distracter C.* Labels on various geometric shapes are often thought to represent variables when they are actually denoting positions or points. **(See Student Responses 8, 9, 10, and 12)**
- *Distracter D.* The four operations signs are sometimes mistaken for variables, especially with x, as it is used to denote multiplication and often as a variable in algebra. Some students see the numbers "varying" and consider this as signifying "variables." **(See Student Responses 5, 6, 8, and 10)**

Seeking Links to Cognitive Research

Our multiple uses of the term variable make it hard for students to understand. (NCTM, 1999, p. 152)

The concept of variable is both variable and elusive. It is hard to describe and a good deal harder to learn. (NCTM, 1999, p. 155)

Students have difficulty understanding how symbols are used in algebra (Kieran, 1992). They are often unaware of the arbitrariness of the letters chosen to represent variables in equations (Wagner, 1981). Middle-school and high-school students may regard the letters as shorthand for single objects, or as specific but unknown numbers, or as generalized numbers before they understand them as representations of variables (Kieran, 1992). (AAAS, 1993, p. 351)

The concept of variable is one of the most fundamental ideas in mathematics, from elementary school through college. This concept is so important that its invention constituted a turning point in the history of mathematics. However, research indicates that students experience difficulty with the concept of variable, a difficulty that might partially be explained by the fact that within mathematics, variables can be used in many different ways. (NCTM, 1999, p. 157)

Research indicates a variety of student difficulties with the concept of variable (Kieran, 1983; Kuchemann, 1978; Wagner & Parker, 1993), so developing [an] understanding of variable over the grades is important. In the elementary grades, students typically develop a notion of variable as a placeholder for a specific number, as in __ + 2 = 11. Later, they should learn that the variable x in the equation $3x + 2 = 11$ has a very different use from the variable x in the identity $0 \times x = 0$ and that both uses are quite different from the use of r in the formula $A = r^2$. A thorough understanding of variable develops over a long time, and it needs to be grounded in extensive experience (Sfard 1991). (NCTM, 2000, p. 39)

Some of the different uses of literal symbols are: labels (f, y in $3f = 1y$, i.e., 3 feet in 1 yard), constants (, e, c), unknowns (x in $5x - 9 = 91$), generalized numbers (a, b in $a + b = b + a$), varying quantities (x, y in $y = 9x - 2$), parameters (m, b in $y = mx + b$), abstract symbols (e, x in $e \cdot x = x$). Much of the difficulty students encounter with variables may be related to their inability to recognize the correct role of the literal symbol. (NCTM, 1999, p. 160)

Students are told that in algebra, letters stand for numbers. However, they see letters used with other meanings. Letters are used in many contexts, both within and outside mathematics, as abbreviated words or as labels: "p. 6" means "page 6"; cm means "centimeters"; and <ABC labels an angle in a geometric figure, with the letters A, B, and C denoting positions or points. Quantities are frequently denoted by the initial letters of their names. Teachers talk about m as the "mass" and t as the "time taken"; they make statements like "Let C denote the "circumference" and "We'll use C to stand for the cost." (NCTM, 1999, p. 310)

In arithmetic, "3m" is read as "3 meters," and statements such as "3m = 300 cm" are interpreted as "3 meters are equivalent to 300 centimeters." In algebra, too, reading the variable letters as "labels" in this way often appears to be correct. Reading the statement "$a = l \times w$" as [a] shorthand version of the verbal statement "area = length x width" is perhaps hard to distinguish from a reading of the statement as a relationship between the appropriate measures or variables. The apparent correctness of the literal reading of the algebraic statement (area = the measure of the length times the measure of the width) in this instance may well encourage students to do likewise with terms of the "5y" kind. (NCTM, 1999, p. 302)

The concept of variable, pervasive as it is in mathematics, is difficult and often not understood. Even adult veterans of algebra may think of variables only by imagining particular numerical values for them. Letter names for variables may be taken to stand for single units (P to stand for professor rather than some number of professors). Variables should not be approached through abstract definition but rather through real-world situations familiar to students in which they can understand, perhaps even be interested in, the multiple possibilities for value. (AAAS, 1993, p. 219)

Working with letter symbols is challenging, in part, because of a set of fundamental obstacles that can get in the way of understanding the very concept of symbolic expression. Included in such obstacles are the following: differences between natural language and algebraic expression, multiple meanings attached to letter symbols, and cognitive difficulty [in] translating to algebraic expressions. (Driscoll, 1999, pp. 118–119)

Though generations of beginning algebra students have grumbled at the introduction of variables, their use isn't any more abstract than the use of pronouns, to which they bear a strong conceptual resemblance. And just as pronouns make communication easier and more flexible, variables allow much greater generality than does restricting our mathematical discourse to constants. (Paulos, 1991, p. 260)

Teaching Implications

To support a deeper understanding for students in secondary grades in regard to these algebraic concepts, the following are ideas and questions to consider in conjunction with the research.

Focus Through Instruction

- The dynamic aspects of the variable concept should be stressed whenever it is appropriate and feasible. (NCTM, 1999, p. 155)
- Students should be given many opportunities to discuss and reflect on the many different uses of variables and literal symbols.
- Discussions about variables and literal symbols help students develop more conceptual understanding of the topic.
- Students should learn to distinguish when letters are used as labels referring to concrete entities or, alternately, as variables standing abstractly for some number or number of things. An important step, however, is that we, as mathematics educators, should be aware of the distinctions ourselves. . . . We need to be aware of the myriad ways symbols are used and recognize the particular characteristics they exhibit in various contexts. Next, we need to alert students to the properties of literal symbols and point out which characteristics may be similar to words or numerals and which characteristics are unique to the literal symbols themselves. (NCTM, 1999, pp. 315, 319)
- When communicating with variables, teachers and students should completely and correctly read/write the translation. For example, "$P = 2l + 2w$" should be read "the perimeter is equal to two times the measure of the length plus two times the measure of the width."
- Use algebraic notation more often. Use it when revising and extending students' knowledge of arithmetic; spread it through other topics in the mathematics course as a useful and precise language for generalizing and for writing formulas. (NCTM, 1999, p. 312)
- When students are writing rules, they should be left to decide on their own the variables to use in the rule statement. Many times students will not use the initial letter since they are choosing variables to represent numerical values, not abbreviation. (NCTM, 1999, pp. 303–304)
- With technology using the symbol * for multiplication, students should be introduced to this in place of the word "times" instead of "x."

Questions to Consider . . . *when working with students as they grapple with the various uses of symbols*

- Do students realize the different roles that literal symbols play in mathematics? Do they know which ones are considered variables?
- Do students know the correct translation of the variables (and symbols) used in algebra?

- Can students communicate what a variable is, what a literal symbol is, and give examples and non-examples of both?
- Can students compare how literal symbols are used in and outside of mathematics?

Teacher Sound Bite

"Most of my students are using variables in algebra and can solve for unknowns, but this probe has helped me see how they certainly lack a true understanding of symbols and variables. Symbols are used in so many areas that it can be very confusing for students and teachers to keep track of their many uses and correctly use them in mathematics. I think having class discussions around this whole idea—how symbols are used in and outside of mathematics—would be very beneficial for me and my students."

Additional References for Research and Teaching Implications

AAAS (1993), *Benchmarks for Science Literacy*, pp. 25–29, 215, 217–221, 351–352.

Driscoll (1999), *Fostering Algebraic Thinking*, pp. 115–162.

Bright & Joyner (2004), *Dynamic Classroom Assessment, Facilitator's Guide*, pp. 81–91.

Paulos (1991), *Beyond Numeracy*, p. 260.

NCTM (1993b), *Research Ideas for the Classroom: Middle Grades Mathematics*, pp. 179–196, 226.

NCTM (1993c), *Research Ideas for the Classroom: High School Mathematics*, pp. 119–139.

NCTM (1997), *Algebraic Thinking*, pp. 52–58, 59, 141, 150–161, 168–174, 299–327, 331.

NCTM (2000), *Principles and Standards for School Mathematics*, pp. 37–40, 158–159, 222–223, 225–227, 280–285.

NCTM (2003), *A Research Companion to Principles and Standards for School Mathematics*, pp. 116–117, 120, 125, 138–140.

NRC (2001), *Adding It Up*, pp. 255–280.

Stepans et al. (2005), *Teaching for K–12 Mathematical Understanding Using the Conceptual Change Model*, pp. 31–50, 149–163.

Curriculum Topic Study
Is It a Variable?
Related CTS Guide: Variables, p. 146

STUDENT RESPONSES TO "IS IT A VARIABLE?"

Sample Response: A, E, and F

Student 1: I picked A, E, and F because a variable is something that you put in an equation to substitute for a number.

Student 2: A, E, and F because the letters stand for numbers.

Student 3: I chose the letters A and F because you have to find out what number the letter indicates.

Sample Response: Picked All

Student 4: I picked all of them: A because it is missing a number, B because cm is a measurement symbol so m has to be a variable, I guessed on C and D, E because m is a variable, and F because it is missing an angle measurement.

Sample Response: Variety of Choices

Student 5: Each letter that I have circled (A, B, D, E, and F) contains a variable to substitute for the unknown number that we are trying to figure out.

Student 6: I chose A, B, D, E, and F because they all contain a letter representing the number you need to find.

Student 7: I chose B, D, E, and F because they all had a letter in them or a label for measurement.

Student 8: I chose C, D, E, and F because they all have a letter in a place you need information.

Student 9: I chose C, E, and F. A variable is portrayed as a letter in these examples. They have letters that aren't abbreviations.

Student 10: The reason I chose C, D, and F is because letters are variables and each of the situations contains a variable.

Student 11: I chose A, B, and E because they are all in equations.

Student 12: I chose A, C, E, and F because they are variables and not units or symbols of multiplication signs.

Student 13: D is the only correct one because the numbers "vary" in this problem.

BINOMIAL EXPANSION

Students were asked to multiply (a + b)(a + b). Four students multiplied it differently as shown below.

Lizzy
(a + b)(a + b)
a² + b²

Adam
(a + b)(a + b)
a² + ab + ba + b²
a² + 2ab + b²

Kate
(a + b)(a + b)
2a + 2b

Jeff
(a + b)(a + b)
2ab

Who do you agree with? Why?

TEACHERS' NOTES: BINOMIAL EXPANSION

Grade Level for "Binomial Expansion" Probe

6–8	9–12

Questioning for Student Understanding

Do students correctly use the distributive law when multiplying algebraic binomials?

Uncovering Understandings

Binomial Expansion (Content Standards: Algebra)

Examining Student Work

The distracters may reveal a lack of *conceptual* and *procedural understanding* of the distributive law or *common errors* with the use of parentheses. Students may *overgeneralize* work from arithmetic in performing mathematical operations and obtaining answers.

- *The correct method and answer are Adam's.* Adam correctly multiplied $(a + b)$ $(a + b)$. Most students who agree with Adam see this as a problem that uses the distributive law (twice). Some students learn this as the FOIL (first, outer, inner, last) method. **(See Student Responses 1, 2, 3, and 4)**
- *Distracter "Lizzy."* Students who agree with Lizzy's process seem to understand that parentheses denote multiplication, but only see the multiplication of "like terms" to be valid. They are following the pattern of $(xy)^2 = x^2 y^2$. **(See Student Responses 5 and 6)**
- *Distracter "Kate."* Kate's process is picked by students who ignore the parentheses, see everything as addition, and add "like terms," or in this case "double" them as there are two a's and two b's. **(See Student Response 7)**
- *Distracter "Jeff."* Jeff's process is the one that is least often picked. Students who choose this process misunderstand the use of parentheses and operations with variables and combine everything together. This might stem from an overgeneralization from work in arithmetic where students learn to operate on numbers until they obtain a single number as the answer. Many students feel uncomfortable with leaving more than one term in an answer. **(See Student Response 8)**

Seeking Links to Cognitive Research

Visual demonstrations can help students analyze and explain mathematical relationships. Geometric models are also useful in representing algebraic relationships. For example, using the area model to visualize $(a + b)^2 = a^2 + 2ab + b^2$ makes it easier for students to remember processes when eventually solving procedurally. (NCTM, 2000, p. 238)

Parenthesis and other bracketing symbols should provide a perceptual aid for unitizing. However, there are three common behaviors that seem to neutralize the suggestive effect of parenthesis. Some students apparently ignore or overlook bracketing symbols, as in $4(n + 5) = 4n + 5$. Other students, perhaps in response to the order-of-operations exhortation to "do what's in parenthesis first," focus on parenthesis to the exclusion of the overall structure of the expression. And finally, the equation-solving advice to "clear the parenthesis first" may prompt many students to overlook the variable unit in their haste to eliminate grouping symbols. As with many rules of thumb, we need to show students some situations in which the usual rules are not the most efficient way to proceed. (NCTM, 1999, p. 332)

Many errors related to expressions seem to involve an interaction between (a) overgeneralizing on the part of the student and (b) the highly abstract nature of the field properties, especially the associative or distributive law. For example, one of the most common errors is to simplify an expression like $4 + 3n$ to $7n$. One explanation for this kind of error is that, in arithmetic, students learn to operate on numbers until they obtain a single number as the answer. Then, in algebra they may feel uncomfortable leaving an expression with a visible operation sign as the final answer, so they perform whatever operations they can on the available numbers (and/or letters) to reduce the expression to a single term. (NCTM, 1999, pp. 335–336)

The expression $(x + y)^2$ is often converted to $x^2 + y^2$ following the pattern of $(xy)^2 = x^2y^2$. Of course, writing $(x + y)^2 = (x + y)(x + y)$ and using the distributive law (twice) helps clarify where the missing middle term $2xy$ comes from, in contrast to $(xy)^2$, which converts to x^2y^2 using only the commutative and associative laws. (NCTM, 1999, p. 336)

In general, if students engage extensively in symbolic manipulation before they develop a solid conceptual foundation for their work, they will be unable to do more than mechanical manipulation. The foundation for meaningful work with symbolic notation should be laid over a long time. (NCTM, 2000, p. 39)

Being able to operate with algebraic symbols is also important because the ability to rewrite algebraic expressions enables students to re-express functions in ways that reveal different types of information about them. (NCTM, 2000, p. 301)

*T*eaching Implications

To support a deeper understanding for students in secondary grades in regard to these algebraic concepts, the following are ideas and questions to consider in conjunction with the research.

Focus Through Instruction

- Area models are a tool for visualization of algebraic concepts. For example, students can move from numerical representations like $7 \times 13 = 7 \times 10 + 7 \times 3$ to algebraic representations like $a(b + c) = ab + ac$. In the area model, $a(b + c)$ would be viewed as one rectangle and $ab + ac$ would be viewed as two connected rectangles. Later, students can move from numerical representations like 13 x 13 to algebraic representations like $(x + y)^2 = x^2 + 2xy + y^2$. The area $(x + y)^2$ would be viewed as one square, whereas $x^2 + 2xy + y^2$ is viewed as the sum of one square, two rectangles, and another square. (NCTM, 1999, p. 165)
- Algebra tiles are a tool that students can use to model area and visualize the distributive law.
- Simply telling students that their conceptual understanding of a particular mathematical topic is incorrect and then giving them an explanation is often not sufficient to extirpate the misconception. Research literature consistently indicates that misconceptions are deeply seated and not easily dislodged; in many instances, students appear to overcome a misconception only to have the same misconception resurface a short time later. This phenomenon is probably a result of the fact that when students construct learning, they become attached to the notions they have constructed (Resnick, 1983). Therefore students must actively participate in the process of overcoming their misconceptions. (NCTM, 1999, p. 325)
- By comparing different solution methods, students learn which manipulations make sense and thereby may develop more general procedures. (NCTM, 2003, p. 116)
- Algebraic operations should be explored as operations in concrete situations that later develop into meaningful operations on more formal equations. (NCTM, 2003, p. 116)
- Technology, such as graphing calculators, that links expressions and graphs has the potential to give students visual feedback that emphasizes the various meanings of equivalence. (NCTM, 2003, p. 131)
- Students can use graphing calculators or software to compare the different answers graphically to see which one corresponds to the graph of $(x + y)^2$.

Questions to Consider . . . *when working with students as they grapple with ideas related to multiplying polynomials*

- Do students see binomial expansion as an area problem, an algebraic one, or both?
- How did students originally learn about binomial expansion and other related topics (conceptually or procedurally)?
- Can students solve a binomial expansion problem using manipulatives, such as algebra tiles?
- Can students represent the original expression and possible simplified representations graphically?
- Do students use numerals to check their choice, and can they explain verbally what is happening mathematically with the numerals?

Teacher Sound Bite

"I was surprised to find out how many of my students still do not have an accurate understanding of using parentheses and the distributive law when multiplying algebraic binomials. I assumed that a fair amount of practice would have them on target with this process. After seeing their answers and looking at research, I have decided to explore this problem conceptually and use the area model to connect the algebraic expression with a concrete experience for them. I wish the area model would have been used to introduce this concept . . . even before we added variables."

Additional References for Research and Teaching Implications

AAAS (1993), *Benchmarks for Science Literacy*, pp. 25–29, 215, 217–221, 351–352.

Driscoll (1999), *Fostering Algebraic Thinking*, pp. 115–162.

NCTM (1993b), *Research Ideas for the Classroom: Middle Grades Mathematics*, pp. 179–196, 226.

NCTM (1993c), *Research Ideas for the Classroom: High School Mathematics*, pp. 119–139.

NCTM (1997), *Algebraic Thinking*, pp. 52–58, 59, 141, 150, 165, 172, 189, 219, 268, 302, 312, 325, 330–336.

NCTM (2000), *Principles and Standards for School Mathematics*, pp. 37–40, 67–71, 158–159, 222–223, 225–227, 238–239, 280–285, 296–297, 301.

NCTM (2003), *A Research Companion to Principles and Standards for School Mathematics*, pp. 116–117, 120, 123–124, 130–131, 138–140.

NRC (2001), *Adding It Up*, pp. 255–280.

Stepans et al. (2005), *Teaching for K–12 Mathematical Understanding Using the Conceptual Change Model*, pp. 31–50, 149–163.

Curriculum Topic Study
Binomial Expansion
Related CTS Guide: Expressions and Equations, p. 136

STUDENT RESPONSES TO "BINOMIAL EXPANSION"

Sample Responses: Adam's Method

Student 1: Adam is correct because he shows when you multiply a and b, not only a and a.

Student 2: Adam is 100% correct. First Adam wrote out the problem, then he multiplied a × a and a × b. He simplified it to write $a^2 + ab$, then he did the same thing with b. When he was done with that it was wrote out $a^2 + ab + ba + b^2$. He put it all together to get $a^2 + 2ab + b^2$.

Student 3: I agree with Adam because to multiply (a + b)(a + b), you have to use the distributive property and then add like terms. He is the only one that did that.

Student 4: I agree with Adam. He followed the FOIL (first, outside, inside, last) method to make sure that all of the variables were multiplied together to get the complete answer.

Sample Responses: Lizzy's Method

Student 5: Lizzy is right because she multiplies them together while the others don't.

Student 6: I agree with Lizzy, because it looks right and when you multiply two variables together they will just add together.

Sample Response: Kate's Method

Student 7: Kate is right because you would multiply 2 times each letter to double it so the answer would be right.

Sample Response: Jeff's Method

Student 8: Jeff is the only one who combined them all together.

IS IT QUADRATIC?

Probe
10

Circle the graphs that represent a quadratic function.

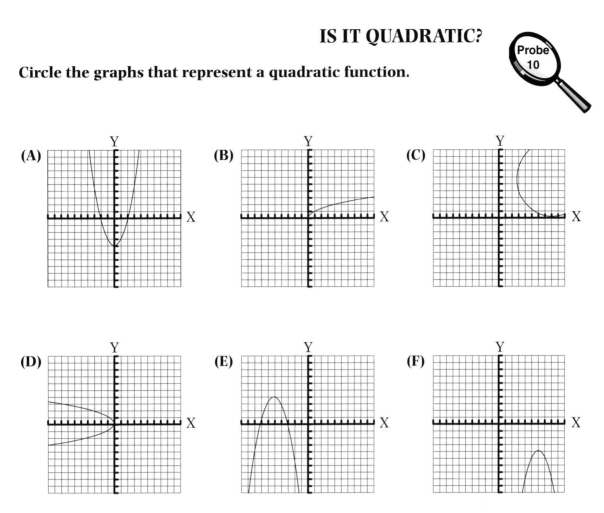

Explain your reasoning why each is or is not a function:

A.

B.

C.

D.

E.

F.

TEACHERS' NOTES: IS IT QUADRATIC?

Grade Level for "Is It Quadratic?" Probe

6–8	9–12

*Q*uestioning for Student Understanding

Do students recognize the characteristics of the graph of a quadratic function?

*U*ncovering Understandings

Is It Quadratic? (Content Standard: Algebra)

*E*xamining Student Work

The distracters of the probe are used to check students' understanding of the attributes of quadratic functions when represented graphically. The distracters are used to show a lack of *conceptual understanding* of (1) functions and (2) quadratics. These same distracters can also be used to show a lack of *procedural understanding* of the use of the vertical line test.

- *The correct answers are A, E, and F.* The graphs of these relations show quadratic functions in a variety of forms. Many students have a fairly good understanding of quadratic graphs and representations, but lack conceptual understanding of functions and what it means to be a function. A definition of function that is useful for graphs is "a set of ordered pairs (x, y) in which each value of x is paired with exactly one value of y" (University of Chicago School Mathematics Project, 1998). The definition for functions in general is a relation between two sets that associates a unique element of the second with each element of the first (Borowski & Borwein, 1991).
- *Distracter B:* This graph shows a function, but not a quadratic function. It was created using $\sqrt{x}$ or $x^{\frac{1}{2}}$. Many students will consider this graph a quadratic function because it passes the "vertical line test."
- *Distracter C.* This graph was created using the inverse of a quadratic. Many students will reason that this relation is not a quadratic function, not because it is not a function, but because it is not a quadratic, as they cannot "see the whole graph." They have only worked with quadratics that are visually "complete."
- *Distracter D.* This relation is similar to distracter C, but actually shows the form of a parabola. Many students will consider this a quadratic function that is "on its side."

Seeking Links to Cognitive Research

Some early research on concepts related to function indicates that students construct the formal concept of function in stages, beginning with the notion of a function rule, and progressing through vocabulary and symbolism, graphical representation, operations on functions, and internal properties of specific functions. (NCTM, 1999, p. 333)

As they progress from preschool through high school, students should develop a repertoire of many types of functions. In the middle grades, students should focus on understanding linear relationships. In high school, they should enlarge their repertoire of functions and learn about the characteristics of classes of functions. (NCTM, 2000, p. 38)

Many college students understand the notion of function only as a rule or formula such as "given n, find 2^n for $n = 0$, 1, 2, and 3." By the middle grades, students should be able to understand the relationships among tables, graphs, and symbols and to judge the advantages and disadvantages of each way of representing relationships for particular purposes. As they work with multiple representations of functions— including numeric, graphic, and symbolic—they will develop a more comprehensive understanding of functions. (NCTM, 2000, p. 38)

The set-theoretic definition of *function* that appears in many algebra textbooks does not convey the richness of the function concept in a very meaningful way. By and large, students' intuition about what constitutes a function corresponds more to the first functions they encounter than to the formal definition. That is, students generally believe that functions should be linear, or at the very least, continuous, smooth, and definable by a single formula. To help students construct a more complete conceptualization, we need to augment the introduction of simple examples with a variety of other kinds of functions, as well as nonexamples of functions. (NCTM, 1999, p. 334)

Students' first introduction to functions should emphasize the versatility of functions to describe the relationship among two or more sets of objects. Mathematics teachers should encourage students to develop their capability to discover mathematical relations embedded in any piece of information. (NCTM, 1999, p. 206)

Students should practice using tabular, graphical, and symbolic representations of functions and translating among them—and they should be called upon to describe their tables, graphs, and equations in clear English. With the help of calculators and computers, they should explore the effects of changing terms in an equation on the general behavior of its graph. Computing technology enables schools to provide a richer set of algebra experiences for all students than ever before. Students should spend less time plotting curves point by point but more time interpreting graphs, exploring the properties of graphs, and determining how those properties relate to the forms of the corresponding equations. Of course, students should continue to plot a few points to check the reasonableness of their graphs. (NCTM, 2000, p. 220)

Central to the changes in graphing has been an increased awareness of the visual aspects of mathematics, in how the things we see and the way we see them are intimately tied to what we say and do and, therefore, how we think. This new interest in visuality in mathematics and how changes in the way we see things can be fostered has promoted new points of view from which to address the problem of the persistent errors students make in graphing. At the same time, the growing realization of the complexities and importance of graphing has led to a more flexible and diverse approach to teaching graphs as a representational form. The focus is no longer on using a single visual representation of a given mathematical situation but on employing many visual displays, of several kinds, one of which might be a conventional graph, and having students participate in the choices and evaluation of the representations used. Cumulatively, all these changes have led to an increase in the importance of graphing in school mathematics. Graphing is no longer a topic consisting of a few skills and procedures to be taught once and for all. As a means of communication and of generating understanding, graphing must repeatedly be encountered by students as they move across the grades from one area of school mathematics to another. (NCTM, 2003, p. 260)

Helping students to distinguish features of a function's graph that are indigenous to the graph itself from features that are not indigenous [is] important. To help students take a global approach to thinking about function graphs, in addition to their thinking about them in pointwise fashion, teachers can engage students in discussions that focus attention on how quantities vary, and how the variations are represented in the graphs. (Driscoll, 1999, p. 150)

*T*eaching Implications

To support a deeper understanding for students in secondary grades in regard to these algebraic concepts the following are ideas and questions to consider in conjunction with the research.

Focus Through Instruction

- Before the vertical line test is introduced, allow ample time for students to explore relations and functions and have discussions on their conceptual meaning. Make sure students know that functions are special types of relations. Have students communicate understanding in a variety of ways.

- Instead of "showing" students the vertical line test, allow them to come up with it on their own and make sure they communicate an understanding of what the vertical line is testing.
- Verbalizing helps develop technical understanding because the descriptive talk and explanations must be worked toward communicating with mathematical terms and symbols. (NCTM, 1999, p. 55)
- Students should use technological tools to represent and study the behavior of polynomial, exponential, rational, and periodic functions, among others. They should learn to combine functions, express them in equivalent forms, compose them, and find inverses where possible. (NCTM, 2000, p. 297)

Questions to Consider . . . *when working with students as they grapple with ideas related to quadratic functions*

- Do students have an understanding of the definitions of relations and functions?
- Can students pick out a variety of relations and functions, not just quadratic?
- Do students see the graphs as a relationship between two sets?
- Can students describe the graphs in terms of relationships?
- For those students using the vertical line test to determine which relations are functions, do they understand why the vertical line test works and what it is testing for?
- Do students use other forms of representation (tables, equations, etc.) to analyze graphs?

Teacher Sound Bite

"Many of my students used the vertical line test for functions (some didn't use it correctly) but didn't seem to have a true conceptual understanding of what a function is (or isn't). Unfortunately I showed them the "trick" of using the vertical line test as the book we use introduces it fairly soon in our exploration of quadratic functions. I wish I could go back and have them explore graphs of functions and those of non-functions to allow them to get a better foundation of the meaning of function before they automatically use the vertical line test. Although they already know the vertical line test, we are going to re-examine what a function is and hopefully have some class discussions that will re-focus their understanding of functions."

Additional References for Research and Teaching Implications

AAAS (1993), *Benchmarks for Science Literacy*, pp. 25–29, 215, 217–221, 351.

Driscoll (1999), *Fostering Algebraic Thinking*, pp. 115–162.

NCTM (1993b), *Research Ideas for the Classroom: Middle Grades Mathematics*, pp. 93–94, 226.

NCTM (1993c), *Research Ideas for the Classroom: High School Mathematics*, pp. 128–129, 155–160.

Curriculum Topic Study

Is It Quadratic?

Related CTS Guide:
Functions, p. 138; Graphic Representation, p. 196

NCTM (1997), *Algebraic Thinking*, pp. 10, 52–58, 141, 189, 206, 325–326, 333–338, 351–357.

NCTM (2000), *Principles and Standards for School Mathematics*, pp. 37–40, 67–71, 222–229, 280–285, 296–305.

NCTM (2003), *A Research Companion to Principles and for School Mathematics*, pp. 116–117, 123–124, 130–132, 138–140, 250–260.

NRC (2001), *Adding It Up*, pp. 267–270.

Stepans et al. (2005), *Teaching for K–12 Mathematical Understanding Using the Conceptual Change Model*, pp. 31–50, 149–163.

STUDENT RESPONSES TO "IS IT QUADRATIC?"

Sample Responses: Graph A

Student 1: A is a quadratic function because it is a graph of a parabola that opens up.

Student 2: This is a function because it passes the vertical line test.

Student 3: A is not a function because it does not pass the vertical line test.

Sample Responses: Graph B

Student 4: B is a quadratic function as it is a half of a parabola that opens sideways.

Student 5: B is not a quadratic function because it does not make a parabola.

Student 6: B is not a quadratic because it is just a line or a half of a curve.

Student 7: It is because it passes the vertical line test.

Student 8: No because it doesn't pass the vertical line test.

Sample Responses: Graph C

Student 9: This is not a function because the equation would be $x = y^2$ instead of $y = x^2$.

Student 10: No because it doesn't have a line of symmetry.

Student 11: No because this is not the shape of a function.

Student 12: No because it doesn't have a distinct vertex.

Student 13: No because it opens sideways.

Sample Responses: Graph D

Student 14: No . . . it has the right curve but is facing the wrong way.

Student 15: Yes, it is a quadratic function on its side.

Student 16: Yes, it passes the vertical line test.

Student 17: No because it does not pass the vertical line test.

Sample Responses: Graph E

Student 18: Yes, this is a parabola of the form $y = -x^2 + bx + c$.

Student 19: Yes because it has 2 x-intercepts.

Student 20: Yes, it is an upside-down curve with a vertex in it.

Sample Responses: Graph F

Student 21: Yes, it is. Even though it's in the corner it still shows the curve shape and vertex.

Student 22: Yes, it is just an inverted parabola.

Student 23: This is not a quadratic function because it is not shown fully.

Resource A

Note Template

__Q__uestioning for Student Understanding

_____

__U__ncovering Understandings

_____

Adaptations made to the probe:

_____

__E__xamining Student Thinking

_____

__S__eeking Links to Cognitive Research

Source:

_____

Findings:

_____

Source:

_____

Findings:

_____

Source:

_____

Findings:

_____

T*eaching Implications*

Source:

_____

Findings:

_____

Source:

_____

Findings:

_____

Source:

_____

Findings:

_____

Summary of Instructional Implications/Plan of Action:

_____

Results of Instruction:

_____

Results of Instruction:

References

Alexander, B. (1997). *Explore quadratic functions with the TI-83 or TI-82.* Richmond Hill, Ontario, Canada: Bob Alexander.

American Association for the Advancement of Science. (1993). *Benchmarks for science literacy.* New York: Oxford University Press.

Anthony, G. J., & Walshaw, M. A. (2004). Zero: A "none" number? *Teaching Children Mathematics, 11*(1), 38–42.

Askew, M., & Wiliam, D. (1995). *Recent research in mathematics education 5–16.* London: HMSO Publications.

Barton, M., Heidema, C., & Jordan, D. (2002). Teaching reading in mathematics and science. *Educational Leadership, 60*(3), 24–28.

Bay Area Mathematics Task Force. (1999). *A mathematics sourcebook for elementary and middle school teachers.* Novato, CA: Arena Press.

Borowski, E. J., & Borwein, J. M. (1991). *Dictionary of mathematics.* New York: HarperCollins.

Bright, G., & Joyner, J. (2004). *Dynamic classroom assessment: Linking mathematical understanding to instruction.* Vernon Hills, IL: ETA/Cuisenaire.

Burns, M. (2005). Looking at how students reason. *Educational Leadership: Assessment to Promote Learning, 63*(3), 26–31.

Davies, A. (2000). *Making classroom assessment work.* Courtenay, BC, Canada: Connections Publishing.

Driscoll, M. (1999). *Fostering algebraic thinking: A guide for teachers, Grades 6–10.* Portsmouth, NH: Heinemann.

DuFour, R., & Eaker, R. (1998). *Professional learning communities at work.* Bloomington, IN: National Educational Service. Quotation retrieved April 17, 2008, from http://ksde.org/Default.aspx?tabid=136.

Frayer, D., Frederick, W. C., & Klausmeier, H. J. (1969). *A schema for testing the level of cognitive mastery.* Madison: Wisconsin Center for Education Research.

Griffin, P., & Madgwick, S. (2005). *Multiplication makes bigger and other mathematical myths.* Sowton, UK: DCS Publications.

Hiebert, J. (1997). *Making sense: teaching and learning mathematics with understanding.* Portsmouth, NH: Heinemann.

Huff, D. (1954). *How to lie with statistics.* New York: Norton.

Keeley, P., & Rose, C. (2007). *Mathematics curriculum topic study: Bridging the gap between standards and practice.* Thousand Oaks, CA: Corwin Press.

Leahy, S., Lyon, C., Thompson, M., & Wiliam, D. (2005). Classroom assessment: Minute by minute, day by day. *Educational Leadership: Assessment to Promote Learning, 63*(3), 19–24.

Loucks-Horsley, S., Love, N., Stiles, K., Mundry, S., & Hewson, P. (2003). *Designing professional development for teachers of science and mathematics.* Thousand Oaks, CA: Corwin Press.

McTighe, J., & O'Conner, K. (2005). Seven practices for effective learning. *Educational Leadership: Assessment to Promote Learning, 63*(3), 10–17.

Mestre, J. (1989). Hispanic and Anglo students' misconceptions in mathematics. *ERIC Digest.* Appalachia Educational Laboratory. ERIC Identifier: ED313192.

National Council of Teachers of Mathematics. (1993a). *Research ideas for the classroom: Early childhood mathematics.* New York: Macmillan.

National Council of Teachers of Mathematics. (1993b). *Research ideas for the classroom: Middle grades mathematics.* New York: Macmillan.

National Council of Teachers of Mathematics. (1993c). *Research ideas for the classroom: High school mathematics.* New York: Macmillan.

National Council of Teachers of Mathematics. (1999). *Algebraic thinking.* Reston, VA: Author.

National Council of Teachers of Mathematics. (2000). *Principles and standards for school mathematics.* Reston, VA: Author.

National Council of Teachers of Mathematics. (2002). *Reflecting on NCTM's principles and standards in elementary and middle school mathematics.* Reston, VA: Author.

National Council of Teachers of Mathematics. (2003). *Research companion to principles and standards for school mathematics.* Reston, VA: Author.

National Council of Teachers of Mathematics. (2006). *Teachers engaged in research: Inquiry into mathematics classrooms, Grades 9–12.* Greenwich, CT: Information Age Publishing.

National Research Council. (2001). *Adding it up: Helping children learn mathematics.* Washington, DC: National Academy Press.

National Research Council. (2002). *Helping children learn mathematics.* Washington, DC: National Academy Press.

National Research Council. (2005). *How students learn: Mathematics in the classroom.* Washington, DC: National Academy Press.

Naylor, S., & Keogh, B. (2000). *Concept cartoons in science education.* Sandbach, UK: Millgate House Education.

Paulos, J. A. (1991). *Beyond numeracy.* New York: Vintage.

Rose, C., Minton, L., & Arline, C. (2007). *Uncovering student thinking in mathematics: 25 formative assessment probes.* Thousand Oaks, CA: Corwin Press.

Sowder, J. (1992). Making sense of numbers in school mathematics. In G. Leinhardt, R. Putman, & R. Hattrup (Eds.), *Analysis of arithmetic for mathematics teaching* (pp. 1–51). Hillsdale, NJ: Lawrence Erlbaum.

Stavy, R., & Tirosh, D. (2000). *How students (mis-) understand science and mathematics.* New York: Teachers College Press.

Stepans, J. I., Schmidt, D. L., Welsh, K. M., Reins, K. J., Saigo, B. W. (2005). *Teaching for K–12 mathematical understanding using the Conceptual Change Model.* St. Cloud, MN: Saiwood Publications.

Tomlinson, C. (1999). *The differentiated classroom: Meeting the needs of all learners.* Alexandria, VA: Association for Supervision and Curriculum Development.

University of Chicago School Mathematics Project. (1998). *Functions, statistics, and trigonometry.* Glenview, IL: Scott Foresman/Addison-Wesley.

University of Kansas. (2005). *Dynamic mathematics assessment.* Retrieved December 31, 2005, from http://www.specialconnections.ku.edu/~specconn/page/instruction/math/pdf/patternanalysis.pdf.

U.S. Department of Education, National Assessment Governing Board. (2003). Cognitive abilities. *Mathematics Framework for the 2003 National Assessment of Educational Progress.* Retrieved December 31, 2005, from http://www.nagb.org/pubs/math_framework/ch4.html.

Van de Walle, J. A. (2007). *Elementary and middle school mathematics* (6th ed.). Boston: Pearson.

Watson, J. M. (2006, July). Issues for statistical literacy in the middle school. In A. Rossman & B. Chance (Eds.), *Proceedings from the 7th International Conference on Teaching Statistics*, Salvador, Bahia, Brazil. Retrieved October 15, 2007, from http://www.ime.usp.br/~abe/ICOTS7/Proceedings/PDFs/InvitedPapers/6C1_WATS.pdf.

Watson, J. M. (2003). *Statistical literacy at the school level: What should students know and do? Bulletin of the International Statistical Institute*, Berlin, 68–71. Retrieved October 15, 2007, from http://www.stat.auckland.ac.nz/~iase/publications/3/3516.pdf.

Wheeler, M., & Feghali, I. (May 1983). Much ado about nothing: Preservice elementary school teachers' concept of zero. *Journal for Research in Mathematics Education, 14*(3), 147–155.

Yetkin, E. (2003). Student difficulties in learning elementary mathematics. *Eric Digest.* ERIC Clearinghouse for Science Mathematics and Environmental Education. ERIC Identifier: ED482727.

Index

CORWIN PRESS

The Corwin Press logo—a raven striding across an open book—represents the union of courage and learning. Corwin Press is committed to improving education for all learners by publishing books and other professional development resources for those serving the field of PreK–12 education. By providing practical, hands-on materials, Corwin Press continues to carry out the promise of its motto: **"Helping Educators Do Their Work Better."**